# Introduction to Our New SEG

The Science Coordination Group was set up with the aim of producing specialised revision material for National Curriculum Science. Following popular demand we have taken our very successful Revision Guides for GCSE double science and from them produced a number of syllabus-specific versions for the SEG and NEAB double science syllabuses.

All of our Revision Guides exhibit several crucial features which set them apart from the rest:

## 1) Careful and Complete Explanations

Unlike other revision guides, we do not restrict ourselves to a brief outline of the bare essentials. Instead we work hard to give complete, concise and carefully written details on each topic.

## 2) Deliberate Use of Humour and Colourful Language

We consider the humour to be an essential part of our Revision Guides. It is there to keep the reader interested and entertained, and we are certain that it greatly assists their learning.
(It is not however expected to win us any awards...)

## 3) Carefully Matched to the SEG Modular Syllabus, and more...

We have taken great care to ensure that this book follows the exact detail of the SEG modular syllabus.
Once again however we feel that merely illustrating the syllabus is an inadequate approach. We have therefore done rather more than simply list the basic syllabus details and add pictures. Instead we have endeavoured to include all the relevant explanation which appears to us to be necessary. The result is a full 112 pages giving a clear explanation of the whole syllabus content. We hope you will appreciate the amount of time and care which has gone into this.

> **Higher** This book is suitable for both Higher and Foundation Tier candidates.
> The material which is required only for Higher Tier is clearly indicated in blue boxes like this. **Higher**
> In addition, the Higher Tier questions in the Revision Summaries are printed in blue.

### And Keep Learning the Basic Facts...

Throughout these books there is constant emphasis on the inescapable need to *__keep learning the basic facts__*. This simple message is hammered home without compromise and without remorse, and whilst this traditionally brutal philosophy may not be quite in line with some other approaches to education, we still rather like it. But only because it works.

# Contents

## Common Material for Modules 3, 5, 7 & 9

Solids, liquids and gases .................... Solids, Liquids and Gases .................... 1
" " " " .................... Changes of State .................... 2
Elements, compounds and mixtures .................... Elements, Compounds & Mixtures .................... 3
" " " " .................... Separation Techniques .................... 4
Chemical change .................... Nine Types of Chemical Change .................... 5
Elements, compounds and mixtures .................... Metals .................... 6
" " " " .................... Non-Metals .................... 7
Chemical equations .................... Chemical Equations .................... 8

## Module One — Maintenance of Life

(1.1) Life processes and cells .................... Life Processes .................... 9
(1.2) Blood and nutrition .................... Digestion .................... 10
(1.3) The nervous system .................... Neurones, Reflexes and The Eye .................... 12
" " " .................... The Nervous System .................... 13
(1.2) Blood and nutrition .................... The Circulatory System .................... 14
(1.4) Hormones .................... Hormones .................... 15
(1.5) Homeostasis .................... Homeostasis .................... 16
" .................... Kidneys .................... 17
Revision Summary for Module One .................... 20

## Module Two — Maintenance of the Species

(2.2) Growth .................... Genes, Chromosomes and DNA .................... 21
" .................... Genetics: Too Many Fancy Words .................... 22
(2.1) Reproduction and inheritance .................... Asexual Reproduction .................... 23
" " " .................... Meiosis & Sexual Reproduction .................... 24
" " " .................... Girl or Boy? — X and Y Chromosomes .................... 25
" " " .................... Monohybrid Crosses .................... 26
" " " .................... The Work of Mendel .................... 28
" " " .................... Selective Breeding .................... 29
" " " .................... Genetic Diseases .................... 30
(2.4) Variation and evolution .................... Mutations .................... 31
" " " .................... Variation in Plants and Animals .................... 32
(2.3) Adaptation and competition .................... Population Sizes .................... 33
" " " .................... Adapt and Survive .................... 34
(2.4) Variation and evolution .................... What Fossils Tell Us .................... 35
" " " .................... Evolution By Natural Selection .................... 36
" " " .................... Two Theories Of Evolution .................... 37
(2.5) Humans and the environment .................... The Greenhouse Effect .................... 38
" " " " .................... Environmental Damage .................... 39
" " " " .................... Fertilisers and Land Clearing .................... 40
" " " " .................... Managed Ecosystems .................... 41
(2.6) Health .................... Drugs .................... 42
Revision Summary for Module Two .................... 43

## Module Three — Structure and Changes

(3.1) Atomic structure .................... Atoms .................... 44
" " .................... Electron Shells .................... 45
(3.2) The periodic table .................... The Periodic Table .................... 46
" " " .................... Group O — The Noble Gases .................... 47
" " " .................... Group I — The Alkali Metals .................... 48
" " " .................... Reactions of the Alkali Metals .................... 49
" " " .................... Group VII — The Halogens .................... 50
" " " .................... Reactions of the Halogens .................... 51

(SEG Syllabus Section)

(3.3) The reactivity series ..............................  The Reactivity Series of Metals ....................... 52
    "    "    " ..............................  Reactivity of Metals ......................................... 53
    "    "    " ..............................  Metal Displacement Reactions ........................ 54
    "    "    " ..............................  Corrosion of Metals ......................................... 55
(3.4) Acids and bases ....................................  Acids and Alkalis ............................................. 56
    "    "    " ..............................  Acids with Metals and Oxides ........................ 57
    "    "    " ..............................  Acids with Carbonates and Ammonia ............... 58
(3.5) Rates of reaction ...................................  Rates of Reaction ............................................. 59
    "    "    " ..............................  Collision Theory .............................................. 60
    "    "    " ..............................  Rate of Reaction Experiments ........................ 61
(3.6) Useful products from oil .......................  Crude Oil .......................................................... 62
    "    "    "    " ..............................  Using Hydrocarbons ....................................... 63
    "    "    "    " ..............................  Alkanes and Alkenes ...................................... 64
    "    "    "    " ..............................  Cracking Hydrocarbons ................................. 65
    "    "    "    " ..............................  Polymers .......................................................... 66
                                  Revision Summary for Module Three ............... 67

## *Module Four*

### *Force and Transfers*

(4.1) Electrical circuits and mains electricity ..  Circuits ............................................................. 68
    "    "    "    "    " ..  Series Circuits ................................................. 70
    "    "    "    "    " ..  Parallel Circuits .............................................. 71
    "    "    "    "    " ..  Electricity in the Home .................................. 72
(4.2) Electromagnetic induction .....................  Electromagnetic Induction ............................. 74
(4.3) Speed and velocity ................................  Speed and Velocity ........................................ 76
(4.4) Force and motion .................................  Mass, Weight and Gravity .............................. 77
    "    "    " ..............................  Terminal Velocity ........................................... 78
    "    "    " ..............................  Turning Forces ................................................ 79
    "    "    " ..............................  Hooke's Law ................................................... 80
(4.5) Waves & the electromagnetic spectrum ...  Waves — Basic Principles ............................. 81
    "    "    "    "    " ...  Microwaves and Infrared ................................ 82
    "    "    "    "    " ...  Visible, UV, X-rays, g -Rays ......................... 83
(4.6) Light .......................................................  Reflection ........................................................ 84
                                  Revision Summary for Module Four ................ 86

## *Module Five*

### *Energy Sources*

(5.1) Energy resources ...................................  Sources of Power ............................................ 87
    "    " ..............................  Power from Renewables ................................ 88
(5.2) Energy transfer in reactions ..................  Energy Transfer in Reactions .......................... 89
(5.3) Other energy transfers ..........................  Types of Energy Transfer ............................... 90
    "    "    " ..............................  Heat Transfer .................................................. 91
    "    "    " ..............................  Conduction and Convection ........................... 92
    "    "    " ..............................  Heat Radiation ................................................ 93
    "    "    " ..............................  Applications of Heat Transfer ........................ 94
    "    "    " ..............................  Efficiency of Machines .................................. 95
    "    "    " ..............................  Energy Conservation ...................................... 96
(5.4) Radioactivity .........................................  Radioactivity ................................................... 97
    " ..............................  Half-life ........................................................... 98
    " ..............................  Background Radiation .................................... 99
    " ..............................  Uses of Radioactive Materials ........................ 100
(5.5) The solar system and the Universe .........  The Solar System ............................................ 101
    "    "    "    "    "    " .........  Orbiting Bodies ............................................... 102
    "    "    "    "    "    " .........  Days and Seasons ........................................... 103
    "    "    "    "    "    " .........  Satellites and the Universe .............................. 104
                                  Revision Summary for Module Five ................ 105
                                  Index ................................................................ 106

(SEG Syllabus Section)

Published by Coordination Group Publications
Typesetting and Layout by The Science Coordination Group
Illustrations by: Sandy Gardner e-mail: zimkit@aol.com

Consultant Editor: Paddy Gannon BSc MA

Text, design, layout and illustrations © Richard Parsons 1999. All rights reserved.
With thanks to CorelDRAW for providing one or two jolly bits of clipart.

Printed by Hindson Print, Newcastle upon Tyne.

# COMMON MATERIAL FOR MODULES 3, 5, 7 & 9

## Solids, Liquids and Gases

*Solids, Liquids, and Gases*

These are known as the *three states of matter*. Make sure you know everything there is to know.

### Solids have Strong Forces of Attraction

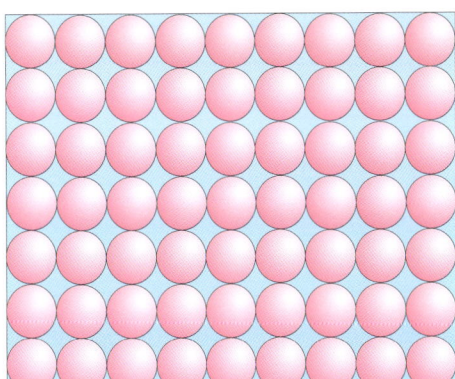

1) There are *strong forces* of *attraction* between molecules.
2) The molecules are held in *fixed positions* in a very regular lattice arrangement.
3) They *don't* move from their positions, so all solids keep a definite *shape* and *volume*, and don't flow like liquids.
4) They *vibrate* about their positions. The *hotter* the solid becomes, the *more* they *vibrate*. This causes solids to *expand* slightly when heated.
5) Solids *can't be compressed* because the molecules are already packed *very* closely together.
6) Solids are generally *very* dense.

### Liquids have Moderate Forces of Attraction

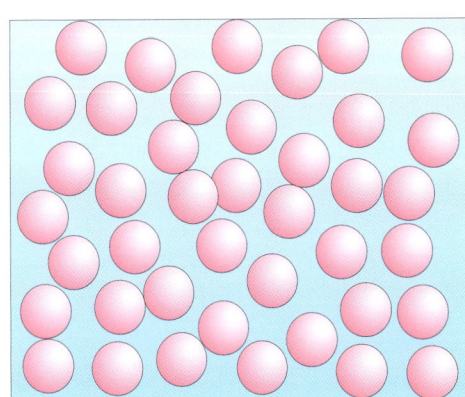

1) There is *some* force of *attraction* between the molecules.
2) The molecules are *free* to move past each other, but they do tend to *stick* together.
3) Liquids *don't* keep a *definite shape* and will flow to fill the bottom of a container. But they do keep the *same* volume.
4) The molecules are *constantly* moving in *random* motion. The *hotter* the liquid becomes, the *faster* they move. This causes liquids to *expand* slightly when heated.
5) Liquids *can't* be compressed because the molecules are already packed *closely* together.
6) Liquids are *quite dense*, but not as dense as solids.

### Gases have No Forces of Attraction

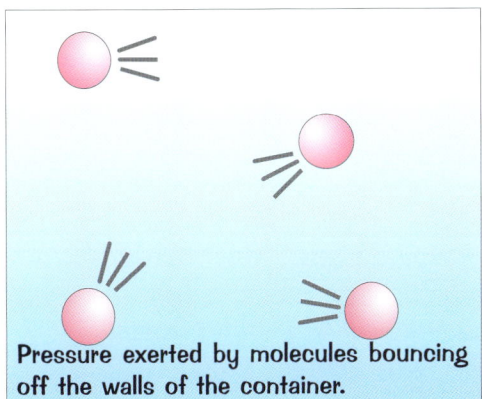

Pressure exerted by molecules bouncing off the walls of the container.

1) There is *no* force of *attraction* between the molecules.
2) The molecules are free to move. They travel in *straight lines* and only interact with each other when they *collide*.
3) Gases *don't* keep a *definite* shape or volume and will always *expand* to fill any container. Gases exert a *pressure* on the walls of the container, because the particles are constantly banging into them.
4) The molecules are *constantly* moving in *random* motion. The *hotter* the gas becomes, the *faster* they move. When *heated*, a gas will either *expand* or its *pressure* will *increase*.
5) *Gases* can be *compressed* easily because there's a lot of *free space* between the molecules.
6) Gases all have very low *densities*.

### Don't get yourself in a state about this lot, just learn it...

This is pretty basic stuff, but people still lose marks in the Exam because they don't make sure to learn all the little details really thoroughly. And there's only one way to do that: *COVER THE PAGE UP AND SCRIBBLE IT ALL DOWN FROM MEMORY*. That soon shows what you really know — and that's what you've got to do for every page. Do it now for this one, *AND KEEP TRYING UNTIL YOU CAN*.

COMMON MATERIAL FOR MODULES 3, 5, 7 & 9 — SEG SYLLABUS

# Changes of State

**Solids, Liquids, and Gases**

CHANGES OF STATE always involve HEAT ENERGY going either IN or OUT.

## Melting — the rigid lattice breaks down

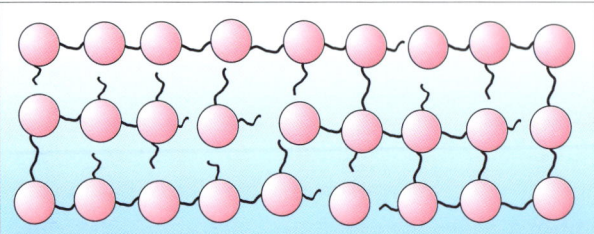

1) When a SOLID is heated, the heat energy goes to the molecules.
2) It makes them vibrate more and more.
3) Eventually the strong forces between the molecules (that hold them in the rigid lattice) are overcome, and the molecules start to move around. The solid has now MELTED.

## Evaporation — the fastest molecules escape

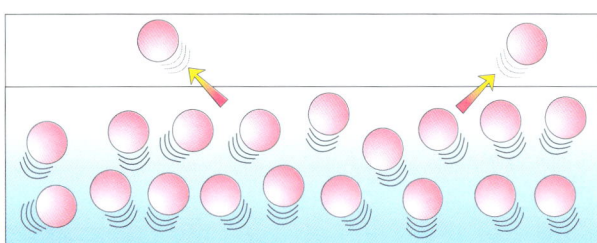

1) When a LIQUID is heated, the heat energy goes to the molecules, which makes them move faster.
2) Some molecules move faster than others.
3) Fast-moving molecules at the surface will overcome the forces of attraction from the other molecules and escape. This is EVAPORATION.

## Boiling — most molecules are fast enough to escape

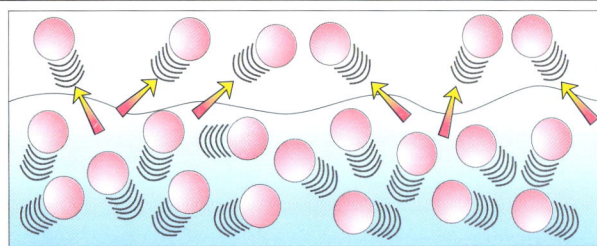

1) When the liquid gets hot enough, virtually all the molecules have enough speed and energy to overcome the forces and escape each other.
2) At this point big bubbles of gas form inside the liquid as the molecules break away from each other. This is BOILING.

## Heating and Cooling Graphs Have Important Flat Spots

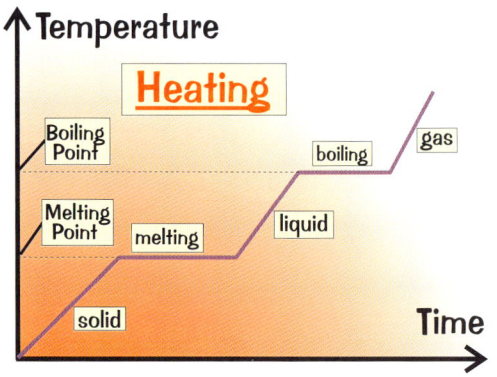
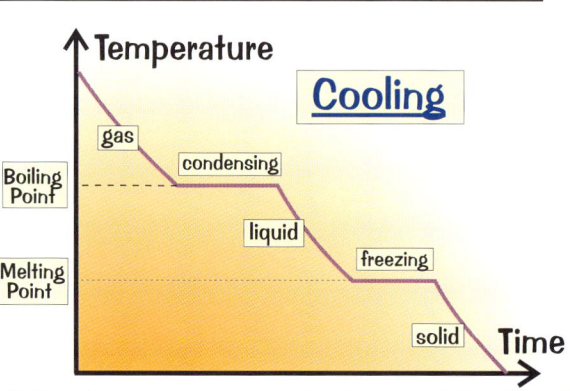

1) When a substance is MELTING or BOILING, all the heat energy supplied is used for breaking bonds rather than raising the temperature, hence the flat spots in the heating graph.
2) When a liquid is cooled, the graph for temperature will show a flat spot at the freezing point.
3) As the molecules fuse into a solid, HEAT IS GIVEN OUT as the bonds form, so the temperature won't go down until all the substance has turned to solid.

## Revision — don't get all steamed up about it...

There are five diagrams and a total of 11 numbered points on this page. They wouldn't be there if you didn't need to learn them. So learn them. Then cover the page and scribble them all down. You have to realise this is the only way to really learn stuff properly. And learn it you must.

# Elements, Compounds & Mixtures

*Elements, Mixtures & Compounds*

You'd better be sure you know the _subtle difference_ between these.

## Elements consist of one type of atom only

Quite a lot of everyday substances are _elements_:

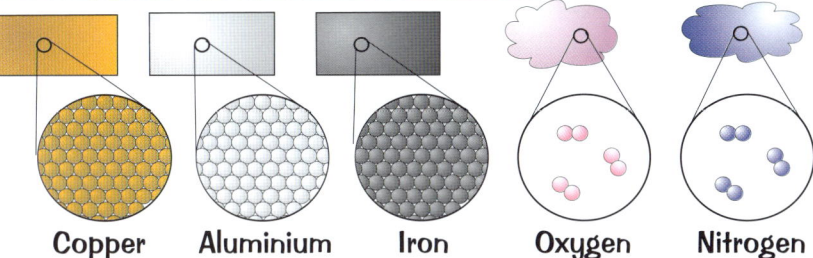

Copper  Aluminium  Iron  Oxygen  Nitrogen

## Compounds are chemically bonded

1) Carbon dioxide is a _compound_ formed from a _chemical reaction_ between carbon and oxygen.
2) It's _very difficult_ to _separate_ the two original elements out again.
3) The _properties_ of a compound are _totally different_ from the properties of the _original elements_.
4) If iron and sulphur react to form _iron sulphide_, the compound formed is a _grey solid lump_, and doesn't behave _anything like_ either iron or sulphur.

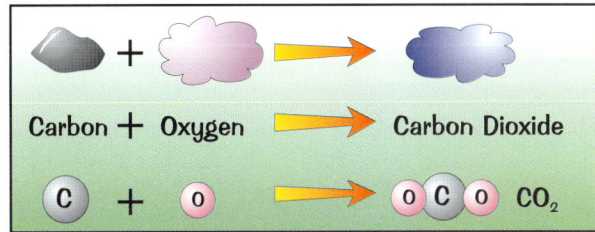

Carbon + Oxygen → Carbon Dioxide
C + O → O C O   $CO_2$

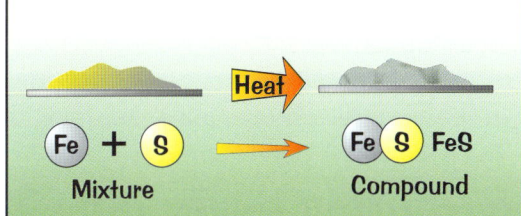

Fe + S → Fe S  FeS
Mixture    Compound

## Mixtures are easily separated

1) _Air_ is a _mixture_ of gases. The oxygen, nitrogen, argon and carbon dioxide can all be _separated_ out quite _easily_.
2) There is _no chemical bond_ between the different parts of a mixture.
3) The _properties_ of a mixture are like the properties of the _separate parts_.
4) A _mixture_ of _iron powder_ and _sulphur powder_ will show the properties of _both iron and sulphur_. It will contain grey magnetic bits of iron and bright yellow bits of sulphur.

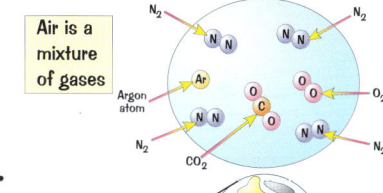

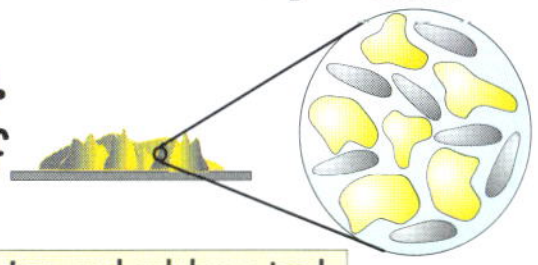

Iron and sulphur mixed together, but unreacted.

## Diffusion — Purple Potassium Manganate(VII) in water

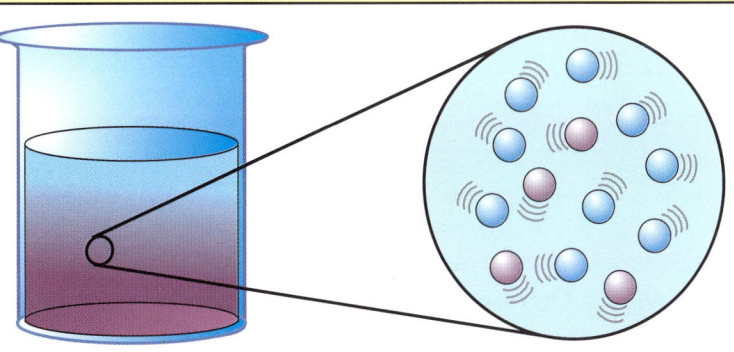

1) _As it dissolves into the water_, the molecules of the purple potassium manganate(VII) _gradually diffuse through the liquid_.
2) The constant _rapid random motion_ of all the molecules causes the purple colour to eventually _spread evenly_ through the whole liquid.

## Don't mix these up — it'll only compound your problems...

Elements, mixtures and compounds. To most people they sound like basically the same thing. _Ha!_ Not to GCSE Examiners they don't, pal. You make mighty sure you remember their different names and the differences between them. _Just more easy marks to be won or lost_.

*COMMON MATERIAL FOR MODULES 3, 5, 7 & 9*      **SEG SYLLABUS**

# Separation Techniques

## The Separation of Rock Salt — salt and sand

Rock salt is a MIXTURE of sand and salt, so it's easy to separate the salt from the sand.
LEARN THE STEPS of this method for separating the mixture of sand and salt:

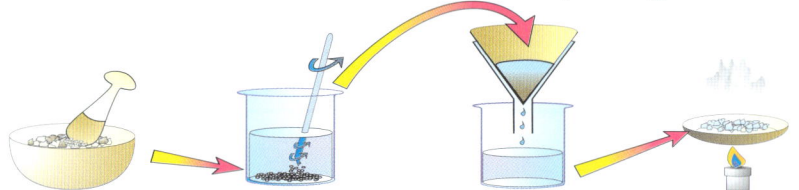

1) *Grind up* the rock salt with a *pestle and mortar*.
2) *Dissolve* in a beaker and *stir*.
3) *Filter* through *filter paper* in a *funnel*.
4) *Evaporate* in an evaporating dish.

The salt will form as crystals in the evaporating basin. This is called CRYSTALLISATION, oddly enough.
The sand and grit will be left on the filter paper. Easy peasy innit?

## Chromatography — for inks

The main use of chromatography is for separating out the dyes in a sample of ink.

1) *Drop spots of dye* onto a *baseline* marked on a square sheet of *filter paper*.
2) *Roll* the sheet up and put it in a *beaker* containing *shallow solvent*.
3) The solvent *seeps up the paper*, carrying the dyes with it.
4) Each different dye will *form a spot* in a different place.
5) You can *compare* an unknown ink to *known dyes* to see which of them it contains.
6) In the pictures shown, ink X contains dyes A and B but not C. Ink Y contains dyes B and C.

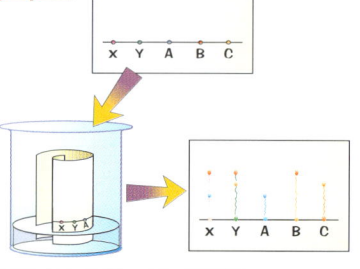

## Distillation — for obtaining pure water from all sorts

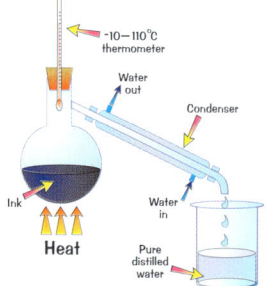

1) *Simple distillation* is used for *separating* a mixture of *a liquid and a solid*, such as *ink*.

2) It's also great for obtaining *pure water* from something like sea water or tap water.

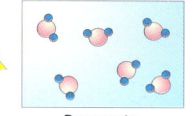

DISTILLED WATER IS VERY PURE WATER.
It has its uses (e.g. topping up batteries), but it tastes horrid.

## Fractional Distillation— for separating mixed liquids

1) *Fractional distillation* is used for separating a *mixture of liquids*.
2) *Different liquids* will boil off at *their own temperature*.
3) The *fractionating column* ensures that the "wrong" liquids *condense back down*, and only the liquid properly *boiling* at the temperature on the thermometer will make it to the top.
4) When each liquid has *boiled off*, the *temperature* reading *rises* until the *next fraction* starts to boil off.

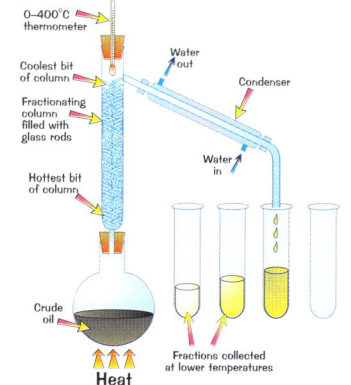

## Distillation — it's all moonshine to me but you've gotta learn it...

*Practise* learning the diagrams until you know them well enough to sketch them down from memory with scribbled labels. Also learn the numbered points and practise scribbling them down too.
*It surely isn't that difficult* to be able to reproduce all the main points from these two pages, is it...

SEG SYLLABUS                                    COMMON MATERIAL FOR MODULES 3, 5, 7 & 9

# Nine Types of Chemical Change

*Chemical Change*

A *chemical change* is a change where the products have *different chemical properties* from the reactants. That's what the syllabus says anyway. I reckon it's kinda obvious.
There are *nine* types of chemical change you should know about. It's well worth learning exactly what each of them is, *here and now*, rather than living the rest of your life in a confused haze.

### 1) THERMAL DECOMPOSITION — *breakdown on heating*

This is when a substance *breaks down* into simpler substances *when heated*, often with the help of a *catalyst*. It's different from a reaction because there's only *one substance* to start with.
Cracking of hydrocarbons is a good example of thermal decomposition.

### 2) NEUTRALISATION — *acid + alkali gives salt + water*

This is simply when an *acid* reacts with an *alkali* (or base) to form a *neutral* product, which is neither acid nor alkali (usually a *salt* solution). More on this later.

### 3) DISPLACEMENT — *one metal kicking another one out*

This is a reaction where a *more reactive* element reacts with a compound and *pushes out* a *less reactive* "rival" element. *Metals* are the most common example. Magnesium will react with iron sulphate to push the iron out and form magnesium sulphate.

### 4) PRECIPITATION — *solid forms in solution*

This is a reaction where two *solutions* react and a *solid* forms in the solution and *sinks*.
The solid is said to "*PRECIPITATE OUT*" and, confusingly, the solid is also called "*a precipitate*".

### 5) OXIDATION — *addition of oxygen*

*Oxidation* is the *addition of oxygen*. Iron becoming iron oxide is oxidation.
The more technical and general definition of oxidation is "*the LOSS of electrons*"

### 6) REDUCTION — *loss of oxygen*

*Reduction* is the *reverse of oxidation*, i.e. the *loss of oxygen*. Iron oxide is *reduced* to iron. The more technical and general definition is "*the GAIN of electrons*". Note that *reduction* is *gain* of electrons. That's the way to remember it — it's kinda the wrong way round.

### 7) EXOTHERMIC REACTIONS — *give out heat*

*Exothermic* reactions give *out energy*, usually as heat. "Exo-" as in "Exit", or "out".
Any time a *fuel burns* and *gives off heat* it's an *exothermic* reaction.

### 8) ENDOTHERMIC REACTIONS — *take in heat*

*Endothermic* reactions need heat putting *in* constantly to make them work. Heat is needed to *form* chemical bonds. The *products* of endothermic reactions are likely to be *more useful* than the *reactants*, otherwise we wouldn't bother putting all the energy in, e.g. turning *iron oxide* into *iron* is an endothermic process. We need a lot of heat from the coke to keep it happening.

### 9) REVERSIBLE REACTIONS — *they go both ways*

*Reversible* reactions are ones that will cheerfully go in *both* directions at the *same time*.
In other words, the *products* can easily turn back into the *original reactants*.

## Nine more fantastic chat-up lines just waiting to happen...

*A nice easy page to learn*. You should know a lot of this already.
Anyway, cover the page and expose each yellow box (*without* the other bit of the heading!) one by one and try to explain it to yourself before uncovering the text to check.

COMMON MATERIAL FOR MODULES 3, 5, 7 & 9          SEG SYLLABUS

# Metals

*Elements, Mixtures & Compounds*

All these elements are metals
Just look at 'em all
— there's loads of 'em!

## The Metallic Crystal Structure

1) All metals have the *same* basic *properties*.
2) Metals consist of a *giant structure*.

**Higher**
3) These are held together by the *metallic bonds* that exists in metals.
4) These bonds allow the *outer electron(s)* of each atom to move *freely*.
5) So you have a *regular arrangement* of metal ions in a "sea of electrons".
**Higher**

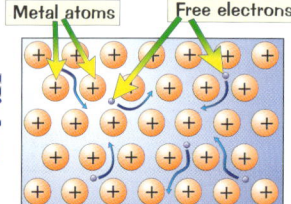

### 1) They all conduct electricity
This is entirely due to the *free electrons* which *carry* the current.

### 2) They're all good conductors of heat
Again this is entirely due to the *free electrons* which *carry the heat energy* through the metal.

### 3) Metals are strong, but also bendy and malleable
They are *strong* (hard to break), but they can be bent or hammered into a different shape.

### 4) They're all shiny (when freshly cut or polished)

### 5) They have high melting and boiling points
Which means you have to get them pretty *hot* to *melt them* (except good old mercury). e.g. copper 1100°C, tungsten 3377°C

### 6) They can be mixed together to form many useful alloys:
1) *Steel* is an *alloy* of *iron* and about *1% carbon*. Steel is much less *brittle* than iron.
2) *Bronze* is an *alloy* (mixture) of *copper and tin*. It's harder than copper but still easily shaped.
3) *Copper and nickel* (75%:25%) are used to make *cupro-nickel* which is hard enough for *coins*.

### 7) They are usually insoluble in water
Though lots of them will *react* with water.

## Metal Fatigue? — yeah, we've all had enough of this page now...
Phew.

*SEG Syllabus* — *Common Material for Modules 3, 5, 7 & 9*

# Non-Metals

Elements, Mixtures & Compounds

Only these squiddy few are non-metals

## Non-Metal elements are either dull, brittle solids or they're gases

Only about a *quarter* of the elements are *non-metals*. *Half* the non-metals are *gases* and half are *solids*, which tend to be brittle. *Bromine* is the only *liquid non-metal element*. (Mercury is the only other element which is liquid — at *room temperature*, that is)

### 1) Non-metals are poor conductors of heat

### 2) Non-metals don't conduct electricity at all

— except for *graphite* which conducts because of it has some *free electrons* between the *layers* of its crystal structure.

Ornamental glass sword

Ornamental glass sword

Don't try this either. Never mind why – just don't.

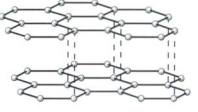

### 3) Non-metals usually bond in small molecules, e.g. O₂, N₂ etc.

### 4) But silicon and carbon form giant structures:

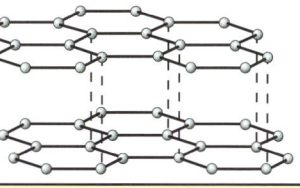
Graphite (pure carbon)

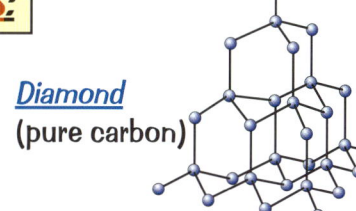
Diamond (pure carbon)

### 5) Non-metals tend to have low melting and boiling points

Which is no surprise — if half of them are gases at room temperature, they must boil easily.

## Non-metal Fatigue — I've just invented it, zzzzzzzz....

Metals and non-metals are really the only things that make Chemistry difficult. If it wasn't for them, the whole subject would be much more straightforward. *Learn and enjoy*.

*COMMON MATERIAL FOR MODULES 3, 5, 7 & 9*   *SEG SYLLABUS*

# Chemical Equations

**Equations**

*Equations* need a lot of *practice* if you're going to get them right. They can get *rather tricky* in no time, unless you *really* know the basics. Every time you do an equation you need to *practise* getting it right rather than skating over it.

## Make sure that you Know these Three Basics

1) Ammonia has the formula $NH_3$. This means that in any molecule of ammonia there will be: *three* atoms of hydrogen bonded to *one* atom of nitrogen. Simple.

2) A chemical reaction can be described by the process *reactants* → *products*.
   - e.g. methane *reacts* with oxygen to *produce* carbon dioxide and water
   - e.g. magnesium *reacts* with oxygen to *produce* magnesuim oxide.
   
   You have to know how to write these reactions in both words and symbols, as shown below.

3) You can always tell a *chemical change*. It's when the products have different *chemical properties* from the reactants.

## The Symbol Equation shows the atoms on both sides:

| Magnesium + Oxygen → Magnesium oxide | Methane + Oxygen → Water + Carbon Dioxide |
|---|---|
| $2\,Mg + O_2 \rightarrow 2\,MgO$ | $CH_4 + 2\,O_2 \rightarrow 2\,H_2O + CO_2$ |

## You need to know how to write out any Equation...

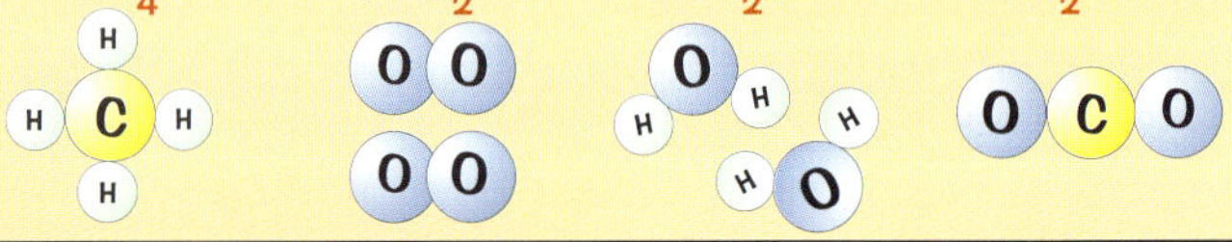

You *really* do need to know how to write out chemical equations. In fact you need to know how to write out equations for pretty well all the reactions in this book.

That might sound like an awful lot, but there aren't nearly as many as you think. Have a look. You also need to know the *formulae* for all the *ionic* and *covalent* compounds in here too. Lovely.

## State Symbols tell you what Physical State it's in

These are easy enough, *just make sure you know them*, especially aq (aqueous).

| (s) — Solid | (l) — Liquid | (g) — Gas | (aq) — Dissloved in water |
|---|---|---|---|

## Ionic Equations

If you can do the equations above, these are simple. It's just a way of writing some equations in a shorter way, that shows the *important* bits only. Here's an example:

If you're given: $CaCl_{2(aq)} + Na_2CO_{3(aq)} \rightarrow CaCO_{3(s)} + 2NaCl_{(aq)}$

Writing out the ions, you get: $Ca^{2+} + 2Cl^- + 2Na^+ + CO_3^{2-} \rightarrow CaCO_3 + 2Na^+ + 2Cl^-$

Then the *Ionic* equation is: $Ca^{2+}_{(aq)} + CO_3^{2-}_{(aq)} \rightarrow CaCO_{3(s)}$

You can see that all that's happened is the ions that are *in solution* (aqueous) at the beginning *and* at the end (i.e. that don't change) are left out. It's important that the equation still *balances*, and that the *total charge* on each side is the same.

## It's tricky — but don't get yourself in a state over it...

*Make sure* you know the formulae of *all* the ionic and covalent compounds you've seen so far. Plus, for practice, write symbol equations for the following equations and put the state symbols in too:

1) Iron(III) oxide + hydrogen → iron + water
2) Dilute hydrochloric acid + aluminium → aluminium chloride + hydrogen

SEG SYLLABUS — COMMON MATERIAL FOR MODULES 3, 5, 7 & 9

# MAINTENANCE OF LIFE

## Life Processes

*Life Processes and Cells*

### The Seven Life Processes which show you're Alive

There are seven things they call "LIFE PROCESSES" — things that _all plants and animals do_. You should learn all seven well enough to write them down _from memory_. Use the little jollyism "MRS NERG" to remind you of the first letter of each word.

| | |
|---|---|
| M — Movement | Being able to _move_. |
| R — Reproduction | Producing _offspring_. |
| S — Sensitivity | _Responding_ to the outside world. |
| N — Nutrition | Getting _food_ by feeding or photosynthesis. |
| E — Excretion | _Getting rid_ of waste products. |
| R — Respiration | Turning _food into energy_. |
| G — Growth | Getting to _adult size_. |

*(If you think about it, this list describes the entire life of a sheep — and a frighteningly large chunk of yours too.)*

### Similarities Between Plant and Animal Cells

**Animal Cell** — **Plant Cell**

You need to be able to draw both cells WITH ALL THE DETAILS for each...

1) **NUCLEUS** — the _genes_ which control what the cell _does_ are found here on _chromosomes_.

2) **CYTOPLASM** where _chemical reactions_ happen.

3) **CELL MEMBRANE** holds the cell together and _controls_ what goes _in and out_.

4) **MITOCHONDRIA** turn glucose and oxygen into _energy_.

*Higher:* The chemical reactions in the cytoplasm are _controlled_ by biological catalysts called _enzymes_.

*Higher — Higher*

### Levels of Organisation

They like asking this in Exams, so learn the sequence:

**A group of CELLS carrying out a particular function is called a TISSUE.**
**A group of TISSUES form an ORGAN.**
**A GROUP OF ORGANS working together form an ORGAN SYSTEM, or even A WHOLE ORGANISM.** (This can apply to plants as well as animals, of course.)

**A JOLLY EXAMPLE:**

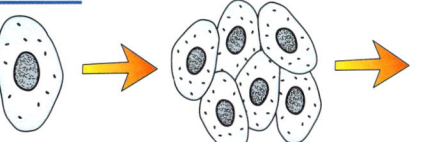

Liver CELLS... ...make up liver TISSUE...

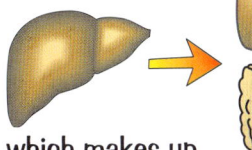

...which makes up the liver (an ORGAN)...

...and the liver and other organs make up the digestive system (an ORGAN SYSTEM).

### OK, let's see what you know...

When you think you've **LEARNED** everything on this page, _cover it up_ and do these:
1) What are the seven life processes, and what's the little jollyism for remembering them?
2) Draw an animal cell and a plant cell and put all the labels on them.
3) Give the full sequence from cells to organ systems and sketch the example given above.

*Module One — Maintenance of Life*

# Digestion

**Blood and Nutrition**

## Digestion is the Breakdown of Food into Small Particles

1) *Digestion* is how we obtain *nutrients* from the food we eat.
2) The digestive system *breaks down* large food molecules into *small particles*.
3) These particles can then be *absorbed into the bloodstream* and used by cells throughout the body.
   *Learn* this definition of digestion:

DIGESTION is the process of *breaking down food* into particles *small enough* to be *absorbed* into the blood.

## Ten Bits of Your Grisly Digestive System to Learn:

**Teeth**
For chomping and chewing your food.

**Tongue**

**Oesophagus**
Your gullet.

**Salivary glands**
These produce saliva which contains a digestive enzyme called AMYLASE.

**Stomach**
1) It PUMMELS FOOD with its muscular walls.
2) It produces HYDROCHLORIC ACID to *kill bacteria*.
3) It produces the PROTEASE enzyme.

**Liver**
Where BILE is produced.
Bile EMULSIFIES FATS into droplets and helps to *remove poisons*, such as alcohol, from the blood.
The liver also stores excess sugar as *glycogen*.

**Pancreas**
1) Produces INSULIN.
2) Produces LIPASE.

**Small intestine**
1) This is where the breakdown products of digestion are *absorbed into the blood*.
2) The inner surface is covered with *villi* (see below).

**Gall bladder**
Where *bile is stored*, before it's injected into the intestine.

**Large intestine**
Where *excess water is absorbed* from the food.

**Rectum**
Where the *faeces are stored* before they bid you a fond farewell through the anus.

## The Villi Provide a Really Really Big Surface Area

The inside of the *small intestine* is covered in *millions and millions* of these tiny little projections called VILLI.
They *increase* the *surface area* in a big way so that digested food is *absorbed* much more quickly into the *blood*. Notice they have:
   1) a *very thin* layer of cells
   2) a very good *blood supply* to assist *quick absorption*.
   3) a *moist surface*.

Villus diagram labels: A villus, Another villus, network of capillaries, circular muscle, longitudinal muscle, gland cells.

## So what have you LEARNED?

A real clever trick for learning lots of information is to get an overall image in your head of what each page looks like. It can really help you to remember all the little details. Try it with this page. *Learn* the diagrams, with all their little labels. Then *cover the page* and try and *picture the whole thing* in your head. Then try and *scribble it all down*. It takes practice but you *can* do it.

SEG Syllabus — Module One — Maintenance of Life

# Digestive System Extras

**Blood and Nutrition**

## Teeth are shaped differently to match their function

The *first step* in digesting food occurs in the mouth where the food is *bitten into smaller pieces* and then *ground up*. Humans have *four types of teeth*, each with a shape designed for their specific purpose.

Make sure you know the *four different types* of teeth:

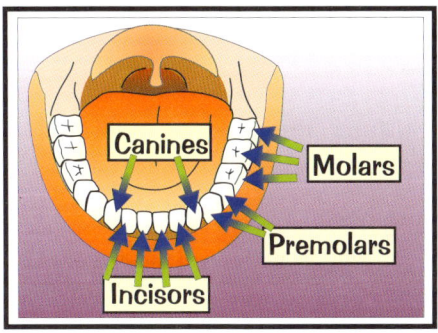
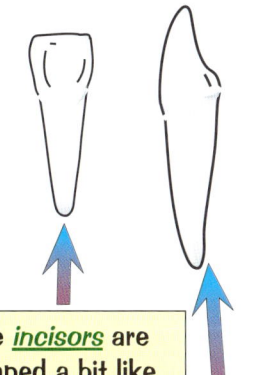
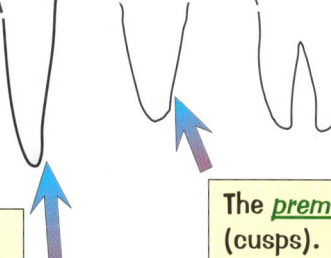

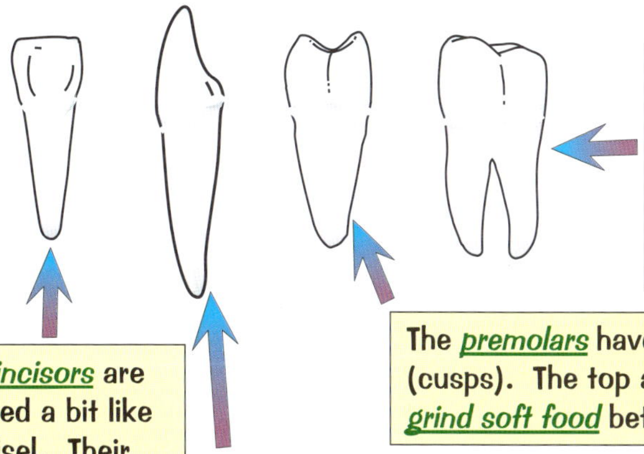

The *molars* have four cusps. The top and bottom teeth *grind hard food* between them.

The *incisors* are shaped a bit like a chisel. Their *sharp edge* allows them to *cut* food.

The *premolars* have two bumps (cusps). The top and bottom teeth *grind soft food* between them.

The *canines* are pointed and longer than the incisors. They can dig in and *tear* food.

## Enzymes break down Big Molecules into Small Ones

There are only THREE MAIN DIGESTIVE ENZYMES. Sadly they all have silly names that can be hard to learn and their "products of digestion" all have suitably silly names too. Ah well — that's Biology for you!
1) *Starch*, *proteins* and *fats* are *big molecules* which can't pass through cell walls into the blood.
2) *Sugars*, *amino acids* and *fatty acids/glycerol* are *much smaller molecules* which can pass easily into the blood.
3) *Enzymes* act as *catalysts* to break down the *big molecules* into the *smaller ones*.

### 1) Carbohydrase Converts Starch into Simple Sugars

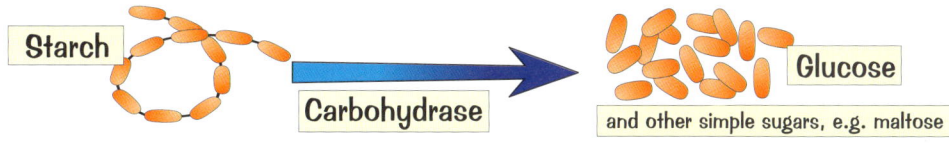

### 2) Protease Converts Proteins into Amino Acids

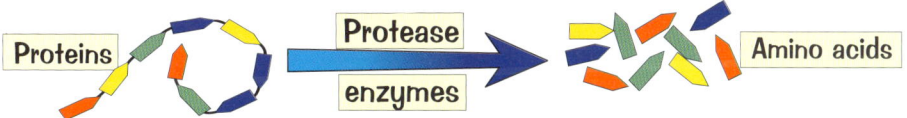

### 3) Lipase Converts Fats into Fatty Acids and Glycerol

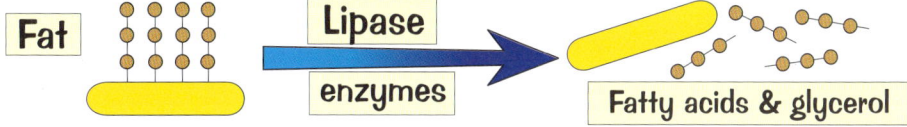

## Yes, you have to know all that stuff too...

OK it's a pretty dreary page of boring facts, but it all counts — you're expected to know *every bit* of information on this page. So, take a deep breath, *read it and learn it*, then *cover the page* and *scribble it all down*. Then try again, and again... until you can do it. Fun isn't it.

MODULE ONE — MAINTENANCE OF LIFE         SEG SYLLABUS

# The Nervous System

## Organisation of the Nervous System:

**SENSE ORGANS AND RECEPTORS:**
The FIVE SENSE ORGANS and the receptors which they contain:

**1) EYES** — Light receptors for sight.
(the eye also helps you BALANCE as you "see" your position relative to the outside world).

**2) EARS** — Sound and "balance" receptors.

**3) NOSE** — Taste and smell receptors. (Chemical stimuli).

**4) TONGUE** — Taste receptors: Bitter, salt, sweet and sour (Chemical stimuli).

**5) SKIN** — Touch, pressure and temperature receptors.

Receptors are groups of cells which are sensitive to a stimulus such as light or heat, etc.

**THE CENTRAL NERVOUS SYSTEM**
Consists of the brain and spinal cord only.

**SENSORY NEURONES**
The nerve fibres that carry signals from the receptors in the sense organs to the central nervous system.

**EFFECTOR NEURONES**
The nerve fibres that carry signals to the effector muscle or gland.

**EFFECTORS**
All your muscles and glands will respond to nervous impulses...

**SENSE ORGANS and RECEPTORS**
Don't get them mixed up:
The EYE is a SENSE ORGAN — it contains LIGHT RECEPTORS (retina).
The EAR is a SENSE ORGAN — it contains SOUND RECEPTORS.

RECEPTORS are cells which TRANSDUCE energy (e.g. light energy) into ELECTRICAL IMPULSES.

## The Central Nervous System and Effectors

1) THE CENTRAL NERVOUS SYSTEM is where all the sensory information is sent and where reflexes and actions are coordinated. It consists of THE BRAIN and SPINAL CORD only.
2) NEURONES (nerve cells) transmit electrical impulses very quickly around the body.
3) The EFFECTORS are muscles and glands which respond to the various stimuli according to the instructions sent from the central nervous system.

## The Three Types of Neurone are all Much the Same

The THREE TYPES of NEURONE are:

(They're all pretty much the same, they're just connected to different things, that's all.)

1) SENSORY neurone,
2) EFFECTOR neurone,
3) CONNECTOR neurone.

## A Typical Neurone:

Learn the names of all the bits:

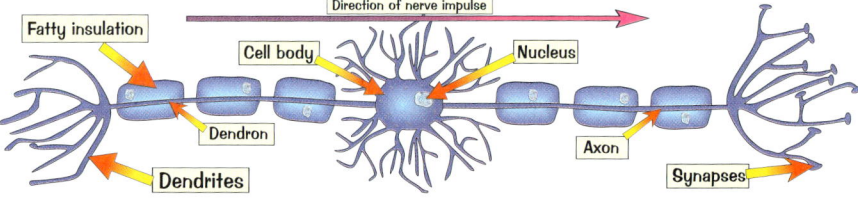

## This stuff is easy — I mean it's all just common senses...

There's quite a few names to learn here (as ever!). But there's no drivel. It's all worth marks in the Exam, so learn it all. Practise until you can cover the page and scribble down all the details from memory.

*SEG Syllabus* — *Module One — Maintenance of Life*

# Neurones, Reflexes and The Eye

**Nervous System**

## The Reflex Arc Allows Very Quick Responses

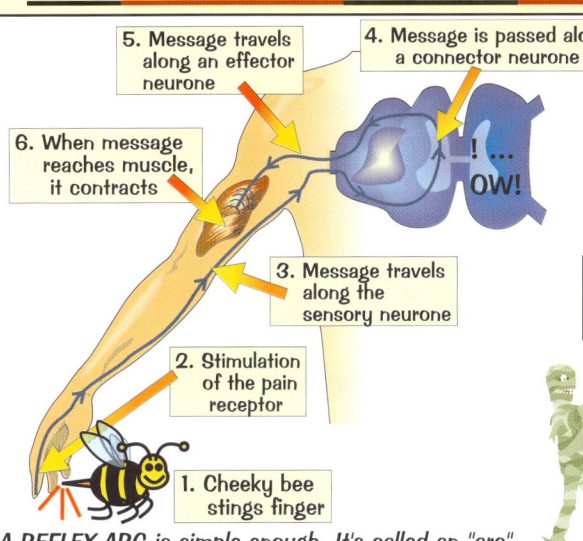

1. Cheeky bee stings finger
2. Stimulation of the pain receptor
3. Message travels along the sensory neurone
4. Message is passed along a connector neurone
5. Message travels along an effector neurone
6. When message reaches muscle, it contracts

A *REFLEX ARC* is simple enough. It's called an "arc" rather than a loop because the two ends don't connect.

1) The nervous system allows *very quick responses* because it uses *electrical impulses*.
2) *Reflex actions* are ones that you do *without thinking* so they are *even quicker*.
3) Reflex actions *save your body from injury*, e.g. pulling your hand off a hot object for you.

Make sure you also learn the **BLOCK DIAGRAM** of a Reflex Arc:

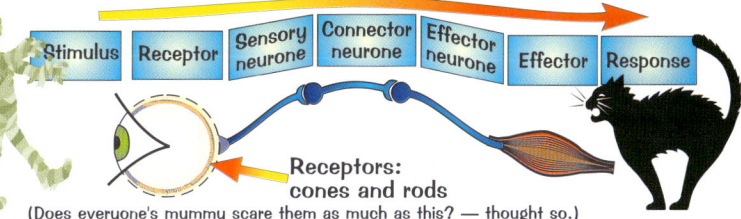

Stimulus → Receptor → Sensory neurone → Connector neurone → Effector neurone → Effector → Response

Receptors: cones and rods

(Does everyone's mummy scare them as much as this? — thought so.)

## Synapses Use Chemicals

1) The *connection* between *two neurones* is called a *synapse*.
2) The nerve signal is transferred by *chemicals* which *diffuse* across the gap.
3) These chemicals then set off a *new electrical signal* in the *next* neurone.

### A Synapse

Axon of sensory neurone — Nerve impulse — chemicals released — connector neurone

## Learn The Eye with all its labels:

1) The *pupil* is the *hole* in the middle of the *iris*, which the *light goes through*.
2) The *cornea* is the transparent layer where light first begins to be *focused*.
3) The *lens* makes the final adjustments to *focus* as its shape is changed by the *ciliary muscles*.
4) The *retina* is the *light sensitive* part and is covered in *light receptors*.
5) The *optic nerve* carries impulses from the *light receptors* in the retina to *the brain*.

Labels: iris, cornea, pupil, lens, ciliary muscle, retina, blind spot, optic nerve

## Adjusting for Light and Dark — the IRIS

**DIM LIGHT:**
1) The **RADIAL MUSCLES** contract.
2) The *iris opens out*, the *pupil* gets **BIGGER**.
3) This lets **MORE LIGHT** into the eye.

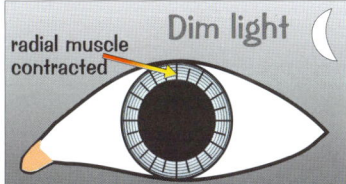

Dim light — radial muscle contracted

**BRIGHT LIGHT:**
1) The **CIRCULAR MUSCLES** contract.
2) The *iris closes up*, the *pupil* gets **SMALLER**.
3) **LESS LIGHT** gets into the eye.

Bright light — iris, circular muscle contracted, pupil

## Focusing on Objects

1) Light enters the eye and hits the *retina* for image formation.
2) *Parallel* light rays are *bent* by the *cornea* and *lens* so that they *focus* on the retina.

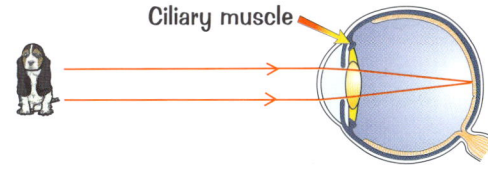

Ciliary muscle

## Let's see what you've learned then...

This is a pretty straightforward page of information. You need to make sure you know all the diagrams with all labels and the numbered points. Practise until you can *scribble* the whole lot down *from memory*.

*Module One — Maintenance of Life*  *SEG Syllabus*

# The Circulatory System

**Blood and Nutrition**

## The DOUBLE Circulatory System, actually

1) The **HEART** is actually **TWO PUMPS**. The **RIGHT SIDE** pumps deoxygenated blood to the **LUNGS** to **COLLECT OXYGEN**. Then the **LEFT SIDE** pumps this oxygenated blood **AROUND THE BODY**.

2) **ARTERIES** carry blood *away from the heart* at **HIGH PRESSURE**.

3) Normally, arteries carry **OXYGENATED BLOOD** and veins carry **DEOXYGENATED BLOOD**. The *pulmonary artery* and *pulmonary vein* are the *big exceptions* to this rule (see diagram).

4) The arteries eventually **SPLIT OFF** into thousands of tiny *capillaries* which take blood to *every cell* in the body.

5) The **VEINS** then collect the "*used*" *blood* and carry it *back to the heart* at *low pressure* to be pumped round again.

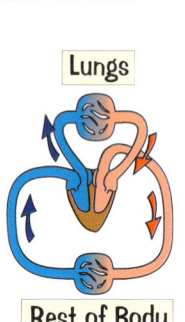
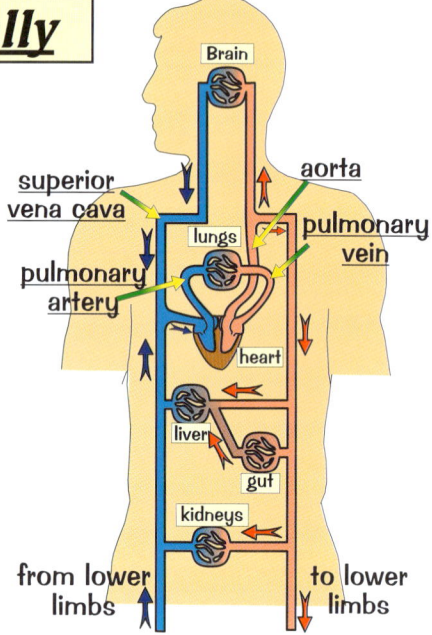

## The Components of Blood have different Functions

### Red Blood Cells

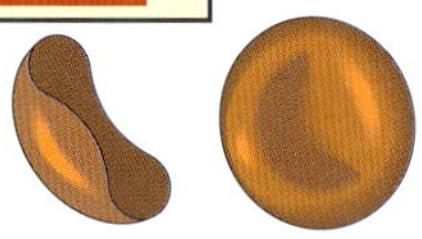

1) Their job is to **CARRY OXYGEN** to all the cells in the body.
2) They have a **FLYING DOUGHNUT SHAPE** to give **MAXIMUM SURFACE AREA** for *absorbing oxygen*.
3) They contain **HAEMOGLOBIN** which is very **RED**, and which contains a lot of **IRON**.
4) In the lungs, where the *oxygen concentration is high*, *haemoglobin absorbs oxygen* to become **OXYHAEMOGLOBIN**. In body tissues the reverse happens to *release oxygen to the cells*.
5) Red blood cells have **NO NUCLEUS** to *make more room for haemoglobin*.
6) In areas of *low oxygen concentration*, haemoglobin combines with *carbon dioxide*.

### White Blood Cells

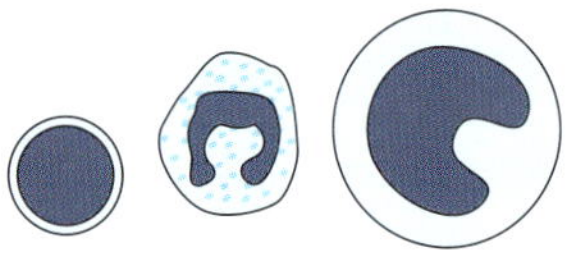

1) Their main role is **DEFENCE AGAINST DISEASE**.
2) They **GOBBLE UP UNWELCOME MICROBES**.
3) They produce **ANTIBODIES** to fight bacteria and **ANTITOXINS** to neutralise toxins produced by bacteria.

### Plasma
This is a pale straw-coloured liquid which **CARRIES JUST ABOUT EVERYTHING**:
1) **RED** and **WHITE BLOOD CELLS** and **PLATELETS**.
2) Digested food products like **GLUCOSE**, **AMINO ACIDS**, and **DISSOLVED MINERAL SALTS**.
3) **CARBON DIOXIDE**.    4) **UREA**.    5) **HORMONES**.
6) **ANTIBODIES** and **ANTITOXINS** produced by the white blood cells.

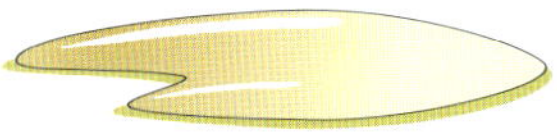

### Platelets

1) These are **SMALL FRAGMENTS OF CELLS**.
2) They have **NO NUCLEUS**.    3) They **HELP THE BLOOD TO CLOT** at a wound.
(So basically they float about waiting for accidents to happen!)

## Let's see what you know then...

At least this stuff on the circulatory system and blood is fairly interesting. Mind you, there are still plenty of picky little details you need to be clear about. And yes, you've guessed it, there's one surefire way to check just how clear you are — *read it, learn it, then cover the page and reproduce it*.

*SEG Syllabus*                                          *Module One — Maintenance of Life*

# Hormones

## Hormones are Chemical Messengers sent in the Blood

1) Hormones are *CHEMICALS* released *DIRECTLY INTO THE BLOODSTREAM*.
2) They are carried in *BLOOD PLASMA*, and so travel at *"THE SPEED OF BLOOD"*.
3) Hormones are produced by *ENDOCRINE GLANDS* (these glands *don't have ducts* unlike *exocrine glands* which *have ducts* to take their products to their targets.)
4) They *TRAVEL ALL OVER THE BODY* but only affect *PARTICULAR CELLS* in particular places.
5) The cells they affect are called *TARGET CELLS* which are in *TARGET ORGANS*.
6) They have *LONG-LASTING EFFECTS* on things that need *CONSTANT ADJUSTMENT*.

> **LEARN THIS DEFINITION**:
> *HORMONES* are substances *secreted by endocrine glands* directly into the *blood*. They are *carried by blood plasma* to other parts of the body where they *act upon a target organ*.

## Hormonal Control of ...

### ...Blood Sugar Levels

1) *THE PANCREAS* is an *endocrine gland* which *controls blood sugar levels*.
2) It makes *insulin*, a *hormone* which regulates how much *sugar* there is in your *blood*.
3) When blood sugar is *high*, like after eating *carbohydrates*, insulin is *released* by the pancreas.
4) *Insulin* travels in *the bloodstream* to the *liver* which is its *target organ*.
5) Insulin tells the liver to *store* sugar as *glycogen*, so the blood sugar level *returns to normal*.

### DIABETES — THE PANCREAS DOESN'T PRODUCE ENOUGH INSULIN.

1) The result is that a person's *blood sugar can rise to a level that can kill them*.
2) The problem can be controlled by *injecting insulin* into the bloodstream.
3) *Insulin is injected* before meals, especially ones *rich in carbohydrates*.
4) This makes the liver *remove the glucose* from the blood *as soon as it enters it*.
5) This *very effective treatment* stops blood sugar levels from getting too high.

### ...Sexual Development

**OVARIES — females only**

Produce *oestrogen* which promotes all *female secondary sexual characteristics* during puberty:
1) *Extra hair* in places.
2) Changes in body *proportions*.
3) *Egg* production.

**TESTES — males only**

Produce *testosterone* which promotes all *male secondary sexual characteristics* at puberty:
1) *Extra hair* in places.
2) Changes in body *proportions*.
3) *Sperm* production.

Women undergoing *fertility treatment* take a manufactured hormone to *stimulate egg production* in their ovaries.

## Learn all this stuff about hormones...

Make sure you know what hormones are and what they do. The definition of hormones is worth learning word for word. The points about hormonal control are best done with the good old *"mini-essay"* method. *Learn it*, *cover the page* and *scribble*. Then *try again*. And smile of course.

*MODULE ONE — MAINTENANCE OF LIFE*

# Homeostasis

**Homeostasis**

*Homeostasis* is a fancy word. It covers lot of things, so I guess it has to be. Homeostasis covers all the functions of your body which try to maintain a *"constant internal environment"*. Learn the definition:

## HOMEOSTASIS — the maintenance of a CONSTANT INTERNAL ENVIRONMENT

Talking about *"maintaining a constant internal environment"* (as you do), it'd be pretty tricky without skin wouldn't it.

### There are Three Main Things that Skin does for you:

1) It stops you DRYING UP (DEHYDRATING).
2) It keeps GERMS OUT.   3) It helps control your TEMPERATURE.

The first two are really pretty obvious. The skin is a waterproof, germproof, nearly-everything-that's-not-too-sharp-or-hot-or-moving-too-fast-proof layer that keeps the rest of the world out and so maintains your precious *"constant internal environment"* so all your little cells can carry on their daily business in warmth and comfort.

## The Skin has Three Tricks for Altering Body Temperature

### When you're TOO HOT:

1) HAIRS lie flat.
2) SWEAT is produced to cool you down.
3) The BLOOD SUPPLY to the skin opens up to release body heat. This is called *vasodilation*.

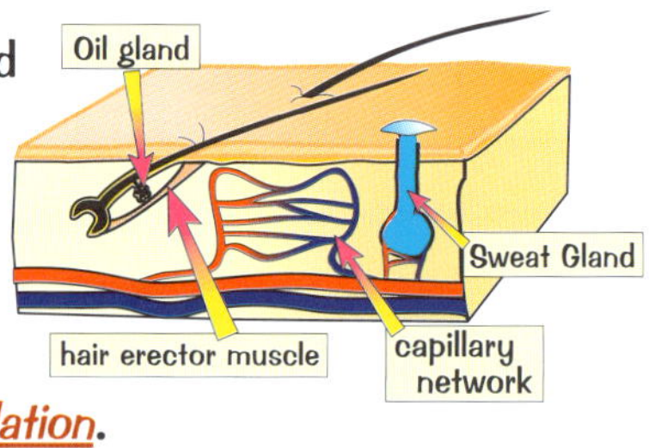

### When you're TOO COLD:

1) HAIRS stand on end to keep you warm.
2) NO SWEAT is produced.
3) The BLOOD SUPPLY to the skin CLOSES OFF. This is called *vasoconstriction*.

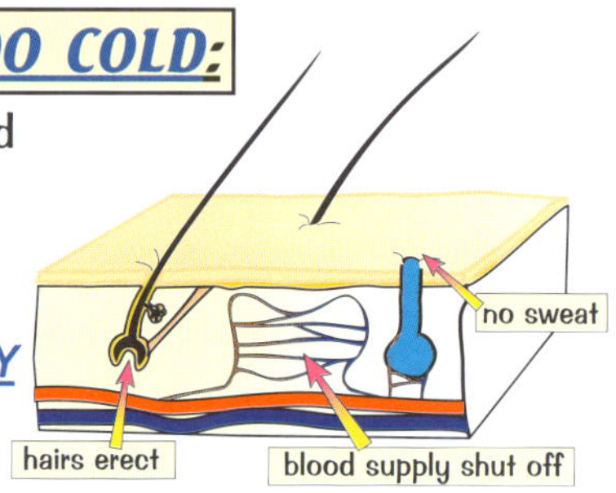

## Kidneys basically act as Filters to "Clean the Blood"

The kidneys perform *three main roles* in homeostasis:

### 1) Removal of Urea from the Blood

1) Proteins can't be *stored* by the body so *excess amino acids* are *broken down* by the *liver* into fats and carbohydrates and the waste product, *urea*.
2) Urea is *poisonous* and must be *removed* from the blood by the *kidneys* which FILTER it out into *urine*. Urea is also lost partly in *sweat*.

### 2) Adjustment of Ion Content in the Blood

1) *Ions*, such as sodium ($Na^+$) are taken into the body in *food*, and then absorbed into the blood.
2) If food contains *too much* of any ion then the excess is *removed* by the kidneys. For example, if a meal contains far too much $Na^+$, the kidneys will *remove the excess* from the blood.
3) Some ions are also lost in *sweat*, but the important thing to remember is that the *balance* is always maintained by the *kidneys*.

### 3) Adjustment of Water Content

Water is *taken into* the body as *food and drink* and is *lost* from the body in *four ways*:
1) in URINE   2) in FAECES   3) in SWEAT   4) in BREATH

Once again there's a need for the body to *constantly balance* the water coming in against the water going out. The *kidneys* maintain this balance by changing the amount of water they *reabsorb*.

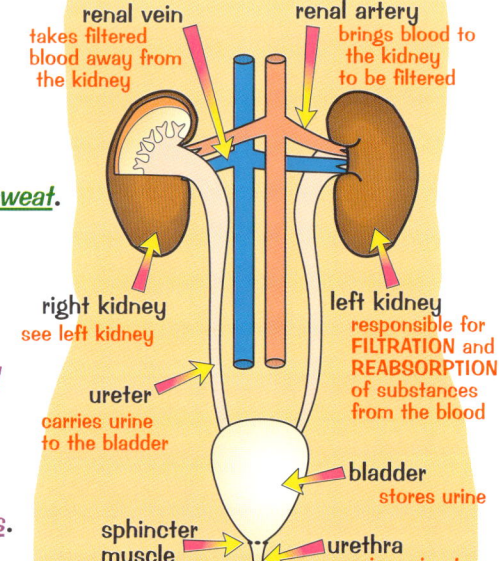

*SEG Syllabus*   *Module One — Maintenance of Life*

# Kidneys

## Homeostasis

## Three Stages of Filtration in the Kidneys

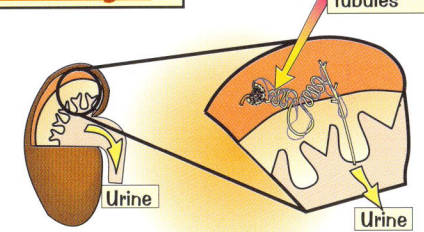

### 1) Ultrafiltration:

1) A _high pressure_ is built up which _squeezes water_, _urea_, _ions_ and _glucose_ out of the blood and into the _kidney tubule_.
2) However, _big molecules_ like _proteins_ are _not squeezed out_. They stay in the blood.

### 2) Reabsorption:

Useful substances are reabsorbed:
1) _All the sugar_ is reabsorbed. This involves the process of _active uptake_.
2) _Sufficient ions_ are reabsorbed. Excess ions are not. _Active uptake_ is needed.
3) _Sufficient water_ is reabsorbed, according to the level of the hormone _ADH_ (see below).

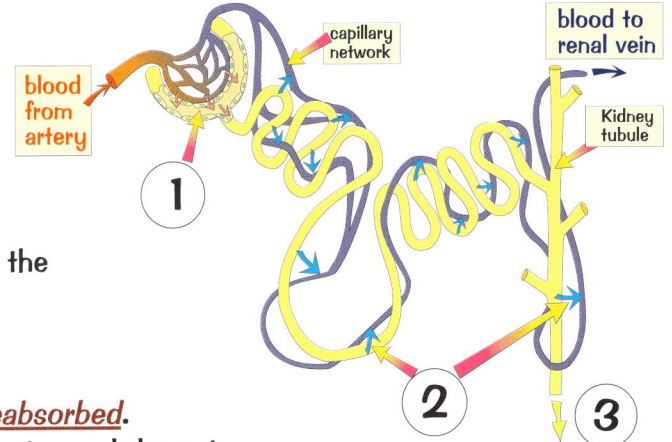

### 3) Release of Wastes:

1) All _urea_ and _excess ions and water_ are _not reabsorbed_.
2) These continue _out of the kidney_, into the ureter and down to the _bladder_ as _urine_.

## Kidney Failure: The Two Treatments

### 1) Dialysis by Kidney Machine

1) Blood is _taken from an arm_ and passed through a tube _bathed in a fluid_ a bit like _blood plasma_.
2) _Urea_ and other wastes then _diffuse out_ of the blood, which then _returns to the arm_.
3) This has to be done for _12-18 hours every week_.
4) The treatment is _expensive_.

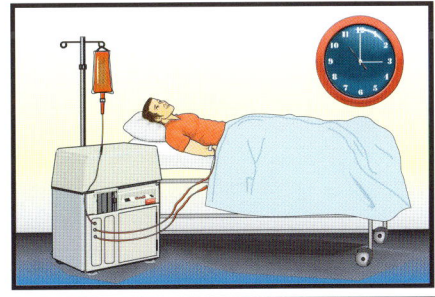

### 2) Kidney Transplant

1) A _healthy kidney_ from a person _recently dead_ or a _living relative_ is "plumbed in".
2) The _blood groups_ for the two people must be the _same_.
3) Ideally the _tissue types_ should also be the same — if so the _success rate_ is _80%_.
4) _Anti-rejection_ drugs and _antibiotics_ must be taken for the _rest of their life_.

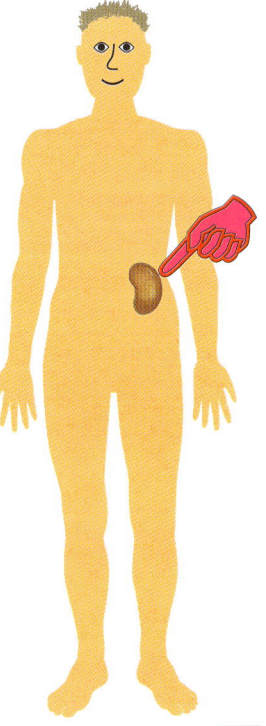

## Learn about homeostasis — and keep your cool...

This is all a bit technical. Homeostasis is really quite a complicated business. It's just a good job it does it automatically or we'd all be in real trouble. You still gotta _learn it_ for your Exam though. Learn the different headings, then _cover the page_, write them down, and then _scribble a mini-essay_ for each one. Then look back and see what you missed. _Then try again._

*MODULE ONE — MAINTENANCE OF LIFE*                    *SEG SYLLABUS*

# Negative Feedback

**Homeostasis**

*NEGATIVE FEEDBACK* mechanisms regulate bodily levels. When the level being monitored gets *TOO HIGH* or *TOO LOW*, a feedback mechanism is triggered which brings it *BACK TO NORMAL*.

The neat thing about negative feedback is that *the level itself triggers the response* necessary to bring it back to normal.

> **NEGATIVE FEEDBACK** is a *control mechanism* in which a substance *controls its own level* by triggering a response when it gets *too high* or *too low*. The response then brings the level *back to normal*.

Learn the *three examples* of *NEGATIVE FEEDBACK in action* on the next two pages:

## 1) Maintaining a Constant Water Level

The *water content* in the blood is regulated by *negative feedback*.

1) The *HYPOTHALAMUS* in the brain *monitors the water content of the blood*.
2) When the water level becomes *TOO HIGH* or *TOO LOW*, the hypothalamus sends a nerve impulse to the *PITUITARY GLAND*.
3) The pituitary gland releases a hormone, *ADH*, which acts on the kidneys.
4) The kidneys reabsorb *more water* or *less water* to bring the level *back to normal* as shown below:

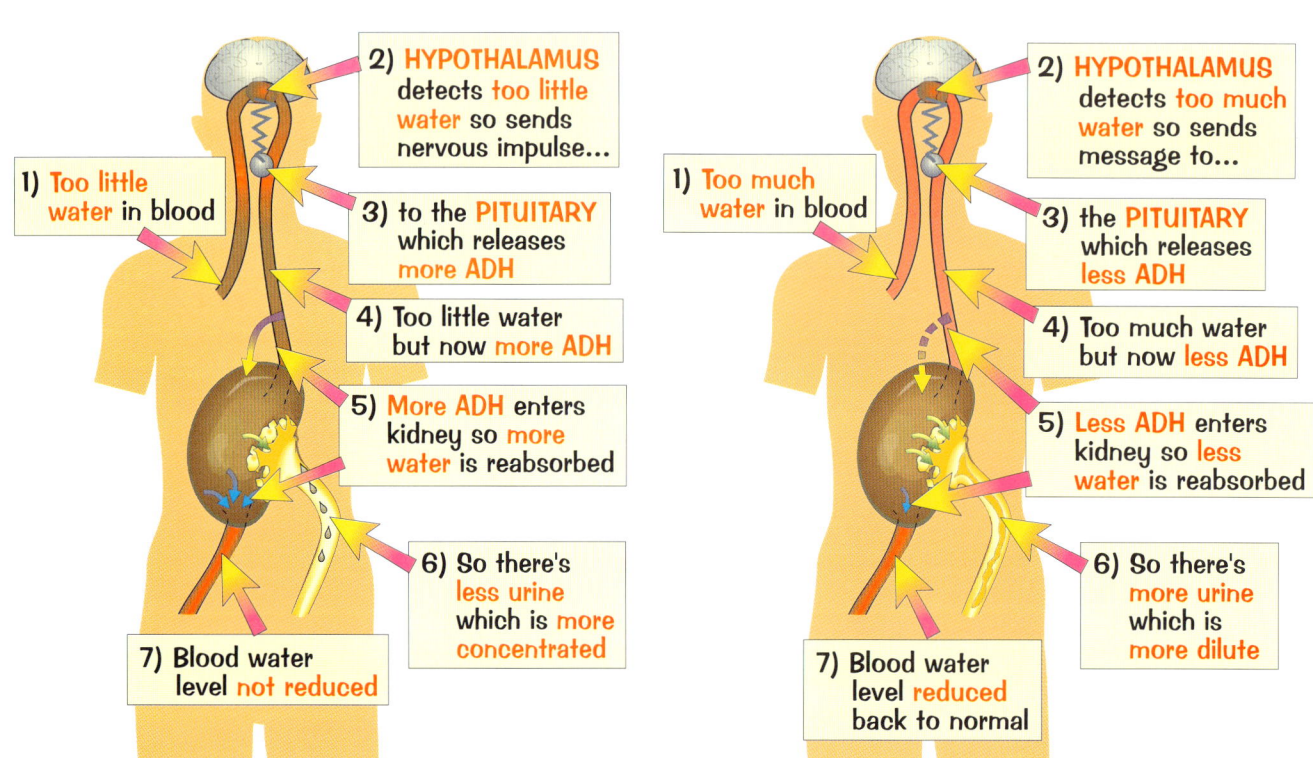

### Too Little Water in Blood

1) Too little water in blood
2) HYPOTHALAMUS detects too little water so sends nervous impulse...
3) to the PITUITARY which releases more ADH
4) Too little water but now more ADH
5) More ADH enters kidney so more water is reabsorbed
6) So there's less urine which is more concentrated
7) Blood water level not reduced

### Too Much Water in Blood

1) Too much water in blood
2) HYPOTHALAMUS detects too much water so sends message to...
3) the PITUITARY which releases less ADH
4) Too much water but now less ADH
5) Less ADH enters kidney so less water is reabsorbed
6) So there's more urine which is more dilute
7) Blood water level reduced back to normal

1) Remember, in *negative feedback*, the *level which is being regulated* triggers the response which brings it back to normal.
2) In this case the *change in water level* signals the hypothalamus to *start* the negative feedback mechanism.

# More Negative Feedback

**Homeostasis**

## 2) Maintaining Constant Body Temperature

The _hypothalamus_ also controls _body temperature_ in a _negative feedback response_ but this time it is the _body temperature_ which starts the response.

1) The hypothalamus detects _changes in body temperature_.
2) If the temperature varies from 37°C the hypothalamus sends a _nerve impulse to the skin_.
3) The _skin_ reacts to adjust the heat loss (see P. 16) and help bring body temperature _back to normal_ as shown below:

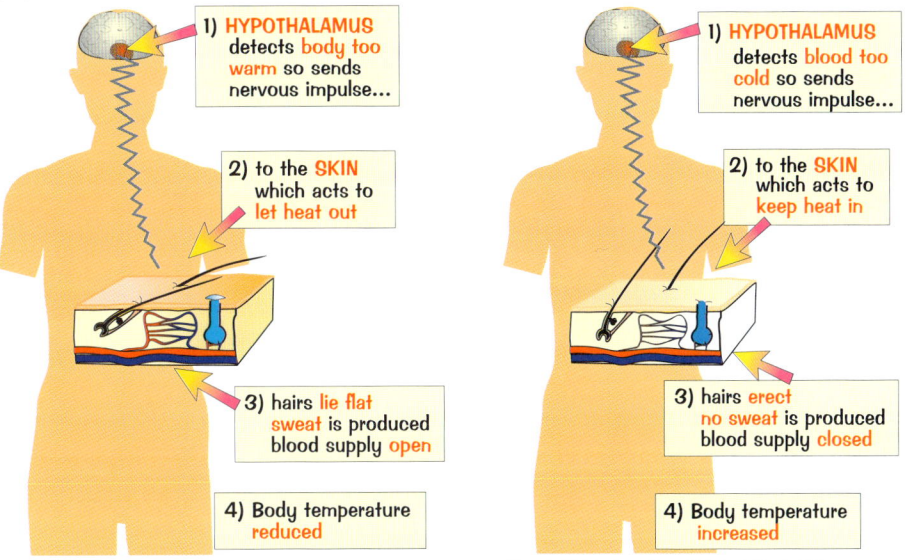

## 3) Maintaining a Constant Blood Sugar Level

Control of _blood sugar levels_ is by a _negative feedback_ mechanism involving the _pancreas_ and _insulin_ (see P. 15).

1) Blood sugar level is _controlled by the pancreas_.
2) If the level _varies from normal_ the pancreas changes the amount of _insulin_ it releases.
3) Insulin's target organ is the _liver_ which stores or releases _glucose_ as shown here:

### Blood glucose level TOO HIGH — insulin is ADDED

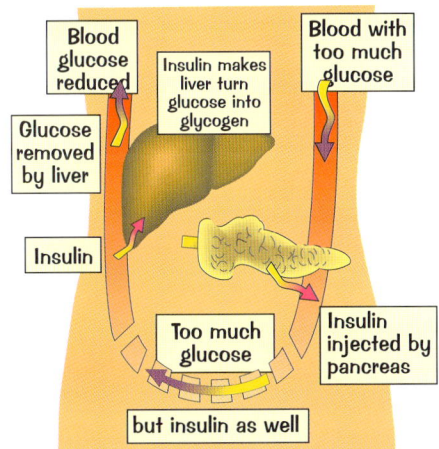

### Blood glucose level TOO LOW — insulin is NOT ADDED

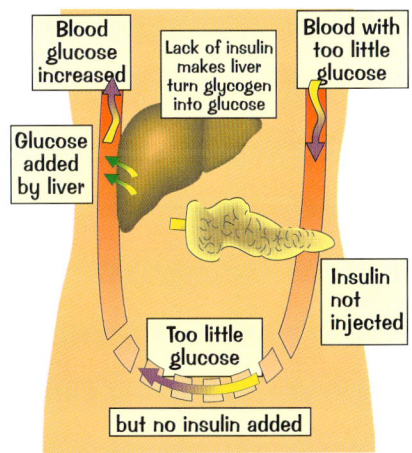

## Negative feedback — not just a bad school report...

This stuff on negative feedback can seem a bit confusing at first, but all these examples are based on the same principles. Make sure you understand the general idea and then learn each example till you can repeat all the details from memory. _Learn and scribble_... ☺

_Module One — Maintenance of Life_  **SEG Syllabus**

# Revision Summary for Module One

*Module One's got all sorts of grisly bits and bobs in it. And some of it can be really quite hard to understand too. But it's all worth points in the Exam, and what do points mean? Prizes! These questions are designed to test what you know. They're pretty tough I grant you, but they really are the best way of revising. Keep trying these questions any time you feel like it, and for any you can't do, look back in Module One and learn the answer to it for next time.*

1) What use is Mrs Nerg?
2) Sketch an animal cell and a plant cell showing the features they have in common.
3) Where is cell function controlled?
4) Where is energy produced in a cell?
5) What controls the chemical reactions which occur in cells?
6) What roles does the cell membrane have?
7) List the five levels of organisation in animals and plants.
8) Give an example of the levels of organisation in an animal (other than the digestive system).
9) Draw a diagram showing the levels of organisation in a plant.
10) Draw a diagram of the human circulatory system: heart, lungs, arteries, veins, etc.
11) Explain why it is a *double* circulatory system, and describe the pressure and oxygen content of the blood in each bit. What are the big words for saying if the blood has oxygen in or not?
12) Sketch a red blood cell and explain how its shape helps it carry out its function.
13) What is the role of white blood cells?
14) Sketch some blood plasma. List all the things that are carried in the plasma (around 10).
15) Sketch some platelets. What do they do all day?
16) Write the strict definition of digestion.
17) Sketch a diagram of the digestive system and label it with the functions of each part.
18) Sketch a villus, and say what it's for. Point out the three main features of villi.
19) What *two* things does bile do? Where is it produced? Where does it enter the system?
20) Draw a diagram of the four different types of teeth. Explain the shape of each tooth.
21) List the three main digestive enzymes, which molecules they act on, and which smaller molecules they produce.
22) Draw a diagram showing the main parts of the nervous system.
23) List the five sense organs and say what kind of receptors each one has.
24) What two things constitute the central nervous system? What are effectors?
25) Describe how a reflex arc works and why it's a good thing.
26) Explain how a synapse works.
27) Draw a full diagram of an eye with all labels and details.
28) Describe how the eye adjusts for light and dark.
29) Sketch a picture showing light being focused on the retina.
30) Give the proper definition of hormones. What is an endocrine gland?
31) Which hormone controls blood sugar levels and how is it used to treat diabetes?
32) Which hormones control sexual development and where are they produced?
33) What is the proper definition of homeostasis?
34) What are the three main things that the skin does for you?
35) What is the basic function of the kidneys?
36) What *three* particular things do kidneys deal with?
37) Sketch a kidney to show where a nephron is and then roughly draw an enlarged nephron.
38) Draw and label the main parts of a nephron describing its *three main processes*.
39) What are the two treatments for kidney failure? Give the pros and cons of both.
40) What is negative feedback? Describe the three examples given in the book.

**SEG Syllabus**

*Module One — Maintenance of Life*

# MAINTENANCE OF THE SPECIES

## Genes, Chromosomes and DNA — Growth

If you're going to get *anywhere* with this topic you definitely need to learn exactly what genes are and what they are for.
1) Genes are known as the *"units of inheritance"*.
2) This is because they determine which of your parents' *characteristics* you inherit.
3) Each *gene* controls *one* particular characteristic like hair colour or eye colour.

Each gene is made of a length of *chromosomal DNA*...

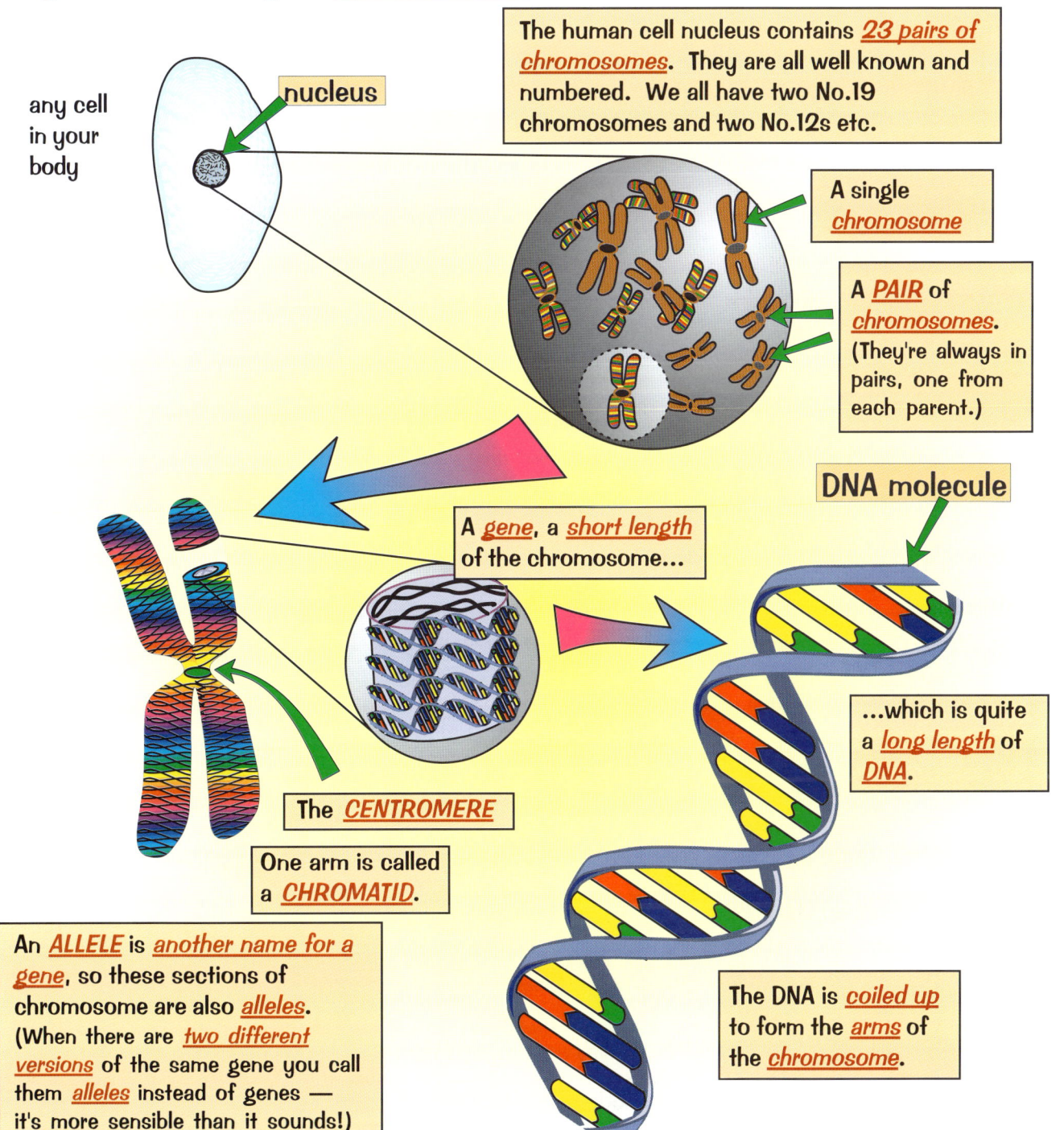

*any cell in your body* → **nucleus**

The human cell nucleus contains *23 pairs of chromosomes*. They are all well known and numbered. We all have two No.19 chromosomes and two No.12s etc.

A single *chromosome*

A *PAIR* of *chromosomes*. (They're always in pairs, one from each parent.)

A *gene*, a *short length* of the chromosome...

**DNA molecule**

...which is quite a *long length* of *DNA*.

The *CENTROMERE*

One arm is called a *CHROMATID*.

An *ALLELE* is *another name for a gene*, so these sections of chromosome are also *alleles*. (When there are *two different versions* of the same gene you call them *alleles* instead of genes — it's more sensible than it sounds!)

The DNA is *coiled up* to form the *arms* of the *chromosome*.

## Hard Learning? — don't blow it all out of proportion...

This is a real easy page to learn, don't you think. Why, you could learn the whole thing with both ears tied behind your head. *Cover the page* and *scribble down* all the diagrams and details.

Module Two — Maintenance Of The Species    SEG Syllabus

# Genetics: Too Many Fancy Words

**Growth**

When it comes to *big fancy words* then *Biology* is the subject where it's all happening. And *genetics* is the topic that *REALLY* walks away with all the prizes. It seems *hard to believe* that so many exceptionally cumbersome, excessively complicated and virtually unintelligible words can conceivably be necessary, or indeed be particularly desirable...

Here's a summary of all the fancy words used in *genetics* with an explanation of what they actually mean. *It really does make a big difference* if you *learn* these first. It's very difficult to understand *anything* in genetics if you don't actually know what half the words mean.

- **DNA** — is the *molecule* which contains *genes*. It's shaped like a *double helix* (a spiral).
- **Gene** — is a *section of DNA molecule*. It's also part of the *arm* of a chromosome.
- **Chromosomes** — are those funny *X-shaped* things that are found in the *cell nucleus*. The arms are made up of *very long coils of DNA*, so chromosomes also contain *genes*.
- **Chromatids** — are just the *separate arms* of the X-shaped *chromosomes*.
- **Centromere** — is just the bit in the *middle* of the chromosomes, where the arms *join*.
- **Allele** — is a *gene* too. When you have *two different versions* of the same gene you have to call them *alleles* instead of genes. (It *is* more sensible than it sounds.)
- **Dominant** — this refers to an *allele* or *gene*. The dominant allele is the one which will *determine* the characteristic which appears. *It dominates the recessive allele* on the other chromosome.
- **Recessive** — is the *allele* which does *not* usually affect how the organism turns out because it's *dominated* by the dominant allele (fairly obviously).
- **Homozygous** — is an individual with *two alleles the same* for that particular gene, e.g. **HH** or **hh**.
- **Heterozygous** — is an individual with *two alleles different* for that particular gene, e.g. **Hh**.
- **Genotype** — is simply a *description* of the *genes* you have, e.g. **Mm** or **RR**, that type of thing.
- **Phenotype** — is the description of your *physical attributes* due to the genes in question i.e. your *phenotype* describes the *physical result* (e.g. "Bald") of your *genotype*, (e.g. "bb").
- **Mitosis** — is the process of *cell division* where one cell splits into *two identical cells*.
- **Meiosis** — is the other process of *cell division* which *creates sperm or egg cells*. Meiosis only happens in the *ovaries* or the *testes*.
- **Diploid** — is the description of *cells* which have *all* 46 chromosomes i.e. *BOTH* sets of 23.
- **Haploid** — is the description of cells which only have *half* the chromosomes, i.e. 23.
- **Gamete** — is either a *sperm cell* or an *egg cell*. All *gametes* are *haploid* — they only have 23 chromosomes.
- **Zygote** — is the delightful name given to each newly-formed human life, just after the (equally delightfully-named) *gametes* *fuse together* at fertilisation.

*Higher Higher Higher*

*You'd think they could have come up with some slightly prettier names, as would befit this most awesome and wonderful moment, really. Your whole life, that great voyage of discovery and wonder, of emotion and reason, of conscience and consciousness, begins with that fateful and magical moment when...*
*..."two GAMETES fuse to form a ZYGOTE"...*        *Ahh, what poetry...*

## Too many fancy words, but you still gotta learn 'em...

Practise by covering up the right hand side of the page and scribbling down a description for each word. That's nice and easy. Just keep looking back and practising *till you can do them all*.

*SEG Syllabus*        MODULE TWO — MAINTENANCE OF THE SPECIES

# Asexual Reproduction

**Reproduction & Inheritance**

## Growth

1) *Growth* is how we get bigger. It happens at the level of the cell, beginning with an *increase in cell size*.
2) Cells then *divide*, creating more and more cells.
3) The next step is for them to *differentiate* (become different) in a process called *specialisation*.
4) All this means is that the *cells develop differently* so that they can carry out a *particular function*.
   For example — nerves develop long axons to carry impulses around the body.

You need to *learn* this definition:

> *Growth* is the process by which an organism *gets bigger*. It happens by cell *enlargement*, cell *division* and cell *specialisation* (*differentiation*).

## Mitosis: Ordinary Cell Division

*Higher Higher Higher*

"*MITOSIS* is when a cell reproduces itself *by splitting* to form *two identical offspring*."

The really riveting part of the whole process is how the chromosomes split inside the cell. Learn and enjoy...

1) All *growth* in plants and animals involves *cell division* as seen above.
2) The cell division which happens during growth is called *mitosis*.
3) When a cell *divides* and *multiplies* by the process of *mitosis*, the new cells are *genetically identical* to the original cell.

DNA all spread out in *long strings*.

DNA forms into chromosomes. Remember, the *double arms* are already *duplicates* of each other.

Chromosomes line up along centre and then *the cell fibres pull them apart*.

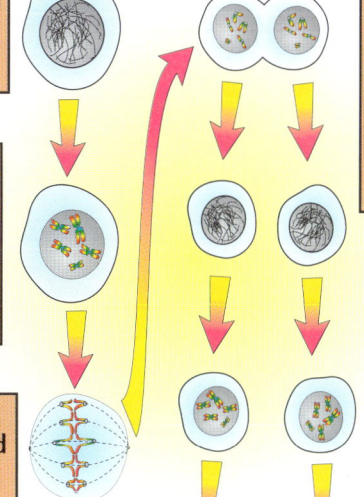

*Membranes form* around the two sets of chromosome threads. These become the *nuclei* of the two daughter cells.

The threads *unwind* into long strands of DNA and the whole process then starts over again.

## Asexual Reproduction

1) *Asexual reproduction* is a form of reproduction in which there is *only one parent*.
2) *Division* of the parent's cells produces the offspring which are *identical* to the parent.
3) This is because they have the *same genetic content* in their cells as the parent.

This is a *DEFINITION* of asexual reproduction for you to learn:

> In *ASEXUAL REPRODUCTION* there is only *ONE* parent. The offspring have *exactly the same genes* as the parent so are *genetically identical*.

## Many Plants Reproduce Asexually — all by themselves

This means they produce *exact genetic copies* of themselves *without involving another plant*. Here are three common ones:

1) STRAWBERRY PLANTS producing runners.

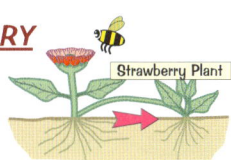

2) New POTATO PLANTS growing from tubers of old plant.

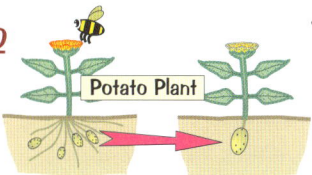

3) *Bulbs* such as *DAFFODILS* growing new bulbs off the side of them.

## Don't do a runner — it's easy to learn...

You need to *learn* the definition of *asexual reproduction*. *Cover the page* and *scribble down* the definition and the three plant examples — *don't waste time* with neatness — just find out if you've *learnt it all* yet.

*MODULE TWO — MAINTENANCE OF THE SPECIES*     *SEG SYLLABUS*

# Meiosis & Sexual Reproduction

**Reproduction & Inheritance**

You thought mitosis was exciting. Hah! You ain't seen nothing yet. Meiosis is the other type of cell division. It only happens in the reproductive organs (ovaries and testes).

> MEIOSIS produces "cells which have half the proper number of chromosomes".
> Such cells are also known as "haploid gametes".

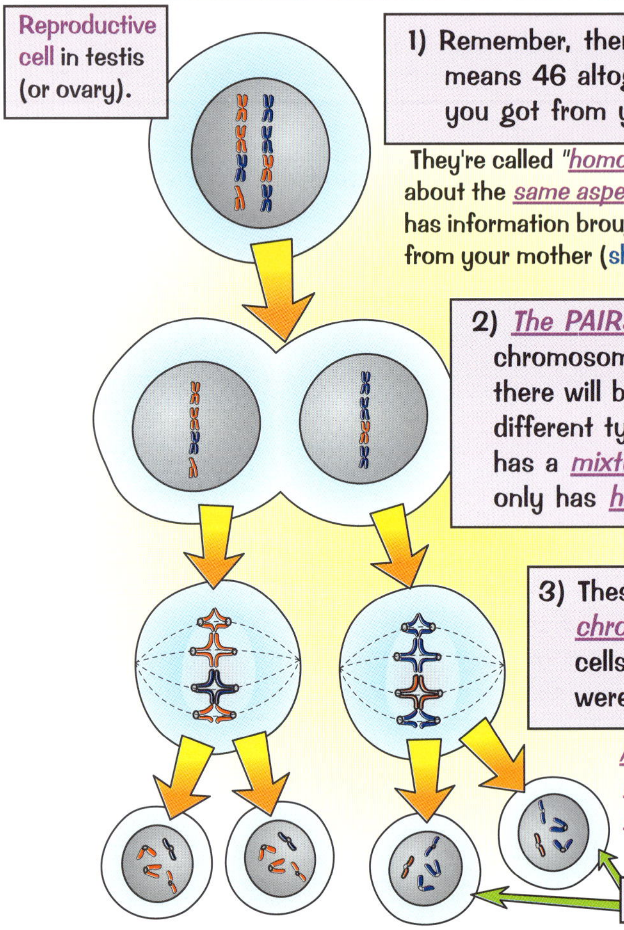

Reproductive cell in testis (or ovary).

1) Remember, there are 23 pairs of chromosomes at the start. That means 46 altogether, two of each type. In each pair, there is one you got from your father, and one you got from your mother.

They're called "homologous pairs" because both chromosomes have information about the same aspects of your body, e.g. hair colour, eye colour, etc., but one has information brought from your father (shown red) and one has information from your mother (shown blue). Note the little red y-chromosome.

2) The PAIRS now split up so that some of your father's chromosomes go with some of your mother's chromosomes, but there will be no pairs at all now. Just one of each of the 23 different types in each of the two new cells. Each cell therefore has a mixture of your mother's and father's characteristics, but only has half the full complement of chromosomes.

3) These cells now split mitosis-style, with the chromosomes themselves splitting to form two identical cells, called gametes. The twin-armed chromosomes were already duplicates, don't forget.

And that's meiosis done. Note the difference between the first stage where the pairs separate and the second stage where the chromosomes themselves split. It's tricky!

GAMETES i.e. sperm cells or (egg cells).

## Sexual Reproduction

1) Gametes are cells produced by males and females that combine during reproduction to create offspring.
2) The male gametes, sperm, are produced in the testes.
3) The female gametes, eggs, are produced in the ovaries.
4) Gametes are produced from the division of male and female reproductive cells as shown below:

## Fertilisation — The Meeting of Gametes

1) During sexual reproduction, a male sperm fuses with a female egg.
2) This meeting of the gametes is called fertilisation.
3) The fertilised egg then divides, soon becoming a veritable ball of cells.
4) Cells dividing and multiplying leads to the development of a fetus.

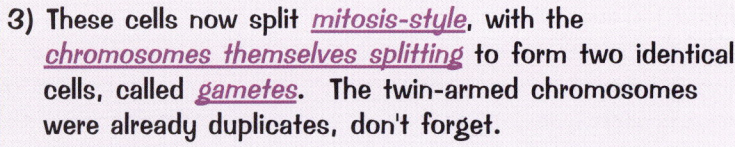

Fertilisation:

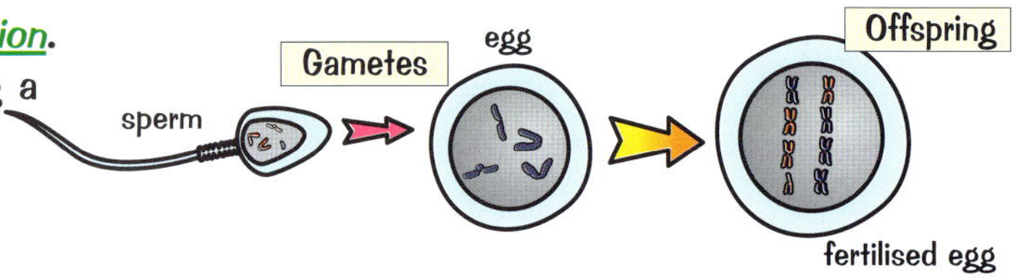

## Let's see how much you can reproduce then...

YOU KNOW THE DRILL. Learn the information, then turn over and scribble down what you can remember. You'll find there are always some bits that are harder to learn than others. That's why this method of revision is so perfect — it concentrates your effort just where it's needed.

SEG Syllabus — Module Two — Maintenance of the Species

# Girl or Boy? — X and Y Chromosomes

**Reproduction & Inheritance**

## There are 23 Pairs of Human Chromosomes

They are well known and numbered. In every _cell nucleus_ we have _two of each type_.
1) Normal body cells have 46 chromosomes, in _23 homologous pairs_ (as shown in the diagram below).
2) _One_ chromosome in _each pair_ is inherited from _each of our Parents_.
3) Remember, _"homologous"_ means that the two chromosomes in each pair are _equivalent_ to each other. In other words, the number 19 chromosomes from both your parents _pair off together_, as do the number 17s etc. What you _don't get_ is the number 12 chromosome from one parent pairing off with, say, the number 5 from the other.

The number of chromosomes _differs between species_. Not all species have 23 chromosomes like humans do. For example, dogs have 38 pairs of chromosomes and tomato plants have 12 pairs.

You'll notice the 23rd pair are labelled XY. They're the two chromosomes that _decide whether you turn out male or female_. They're called the X and Y chromosomes because they look like an X and a Y.

> **ALL MEN** have _an X_ and _a Y_ chromosome: **XY**
> The _Y chromosome is_ DOMINANT and causes _male characteristics_.
>
> **ALL WOMEN** have _two X chromosomes_: **XX**
> The **XX** combination allows _female characteristics_ to develop.

The diagram below shows the way the male XY chromosomes and female XX chromosomes _split up to form the gametes_ (eggs or sperms), and then _combine together at fertilisation_.
The criss cross lines show all the _possible_ ways the X and Y chromosomes _could_ combine.
Remember, _only one of these_ would actually happen for any offspring.
What the diagram shows us is the **RELATIVE PROBABILITY** of each type of zygote (offspring) occurring.

**PARENTS' PHENOTYPES:** (i.e. what physical features they have) — FEMALE XX, MALE XY
**PARENTS' GENOTYPES:** (i.e. what genes they have)
**GAMETES' GENOTYPES:** EGGS X X — SPERM X Y
**ZYGOTES' GENOTYPES:** XX XX XY XY
**ZYGOTES' PHENOTYPES:** FEMALE FEMALE MALE MALE

(You really do have to learn all these strange words, I'm afraid)

The lines look tricky but all you do is join each egg with each sperm, and do it _carefully_.

The other way of doing this is with a _checkerboard_ type diagram. If you don't understand how it works, ask "Teach" to explain it. The _pairs of letters_ in the middle show the _genotypes_ of the possible offspring.

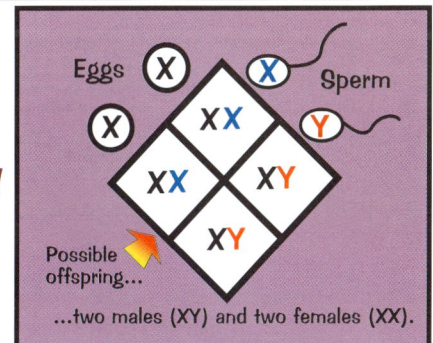
Possible offspring... ...two males (XY) and two females (XX).

Both diagrams show that there'll be the _same proportion_ of _male and female offspring_, because there are _two XX results_ and _two XY results_.

Don't forget that this _50:50 ratio_ is only a _probability_. If you had four kids they _could_ all be _boys_ — yes I know, terrifying isn't it.

## How can it take all that just to say it's a 50:50 chance...

Make sure you know all about X and Y chromosomes and who has what combination.
The diagrams are real important. Practise reproducing them until you can do it _effortlessly_.

MODULE TWO — MAINTENANCE OF THE SPECIES  SEG SYLLABUS

# Monohybrid Crosses: Terminology

**Reproduction & Inheritance**

"Hey man, like *monohybrid crosses*, yeah right... ...so like, *what does it mean*, man?"  Just this, pal:

Breeding *two plants* or *animals*, who have *one gene different*, to see what you *get*.

It's always best done with a diagram like either of these:

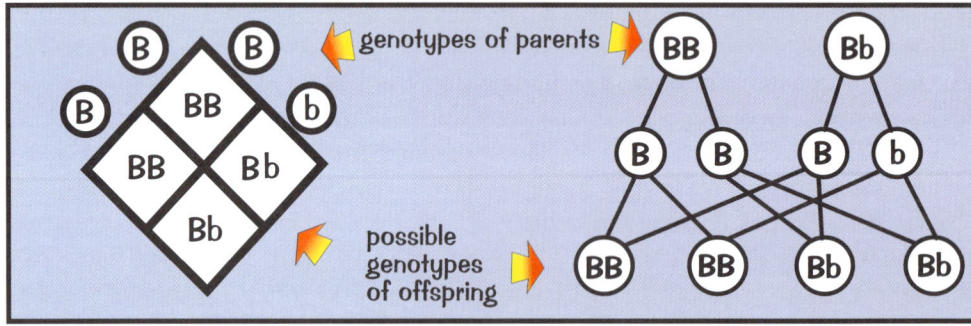

But first learn all these technical terms — it's real difficult to follow what's going on if you don't:

## 1) ALLELE

— this is just another name for a *GENE*. Remember how chromosomes come in *pairs*? This means that you have *two copies* of every gene. When the genes differ between the chromosomes they are called *alleles*. In the diagram above, *B* and *b* represent a gene for the *same characteristic*, e.g. hair colour, on a chromosome pair. But they are *different versions* of the gene, hence they are written with a big *B* and a little *b* and we call them *alleles*.

## 2) DOMINANT AND RECESSIVE

— self explanatory. A dominant allele *DOMINATES* a recessive allele. Let's say the gene for black hair, *B*, is *dominant* and the gene for blonde hair, *b*, is *recessive*. If you have both of these alleles your hair will be *black* because the *B* gene dominates the *b* gene.

## 3) GENOTYPE AND PHENOTYPE

— *genotype* is just what *"type o' genes"* you've got, e.g. BB, Bb, or bb. *PHENOTYPE* sounds a lot like genotype but, irritatingly, is nothing like it at all. Genotype is always a pair of letters like Bb, whilst *PHENOTYPE* is what *physical characteristics* result from the genotype, like "blue hair" or "big leaves" or "maleness".

## 4) "PARENTAL", "F1" AND "F2" GENERATIONS

— pretty obvious. The two *originals* that you cross are the *parental generation*, their *kids* are the *F1 generation* and the *"grandchildren"* are the *F2 generation*. Easy peasy.

## 5) HOMOZYGOUS AND HETEROZYGOUS

— *"Homo-"* means *"same kinda things"*, *"Hetero-"* means *"different kinda things"*. They stick *"-zygous"* on the end to show we're talking about *genes*, (rather than any other aspect of Biology), and also just to make it *sound more complicated*, I'm certain of it. So...

*"HOMOZYGOUS RECESSIVE"* is the descriptive shorthand (hah!) for this: bb
*"HOMOZYGOUS DOMINANT"* is the 'shorthand' for BB
*"HETEROZYGOUS"* is the 'shorthand' for Bb
*"A HOMOZYGOTE"* or *"A HETEROZYGOTE"* are how you refer to people with such genes.

Let's try out the brilliant descriptive "shorthand" shall we:

*"Alexander is homozygous recessive for the baldness gene"* is *so much easier* to say and understand than *"Alex is bb"*.    Hmm, well, that's Biology for you.

## Now it's time to homologate your intellectual stimuli...

You can't beat a fewdal big fancyfold wordsmiths to make things crystally clearasil, can you... Anyway, half the Exam marks are for knowing the fancy words *so just keep learning 'em!*

*SEG Syllabus*    *Module Two — Maintenance of the Species*

# Monohybrid Crosses: Hamsters

**Reproduction & Inheritance**

## Cross-Breeding Hamsters

It can be all too easy to find yourself cross-breeding hamsters, some with normal hair and a mild disposition and others with wild scratty hair and a leaning towards crazy acrobatics.

Let's say that the gene which causes the crazy nature is *recessive*, so we use a *small "h"* for it, whilst normal (boring) behaviour is due to a *dominant gene*, so we represent it with a *capital "H"*.
1) A *crazy hamster* must have the GENOTYPE: hh.
2) However, a NORMAL HAMSTER can have TWO POSSIBLE GENOTYPES: HH or Hh.
   This is pretty important — it's the basic difference between dominant and recessive genes:

> To display RECESSIVE CHARACTERISTICS you must have
> BOTH ALLELES RECESSIVE, hh, (i.e. be "homozygous recessive").
>
> But to display DOMINANT CHARACTERISTICS you can be EITHER
> HH ("homozygous dominant") or Hh ("heterozygous").

It's only that difference which makes monohybrid crosses even *remotely* interesting. If hh gave crazy hamsters, HH gave normal hamsters and Hh something in between, it'd all be pretty dull.

## An Almost Unbearably Exciting Example

Let's take a *thoroughbred crazy hamster*, genotype hh, with a *thoroughbred normal hamster*, genotype HH, and cross-breed them. You must learn this whole diagram thoroughly, till you can do it all yourself:

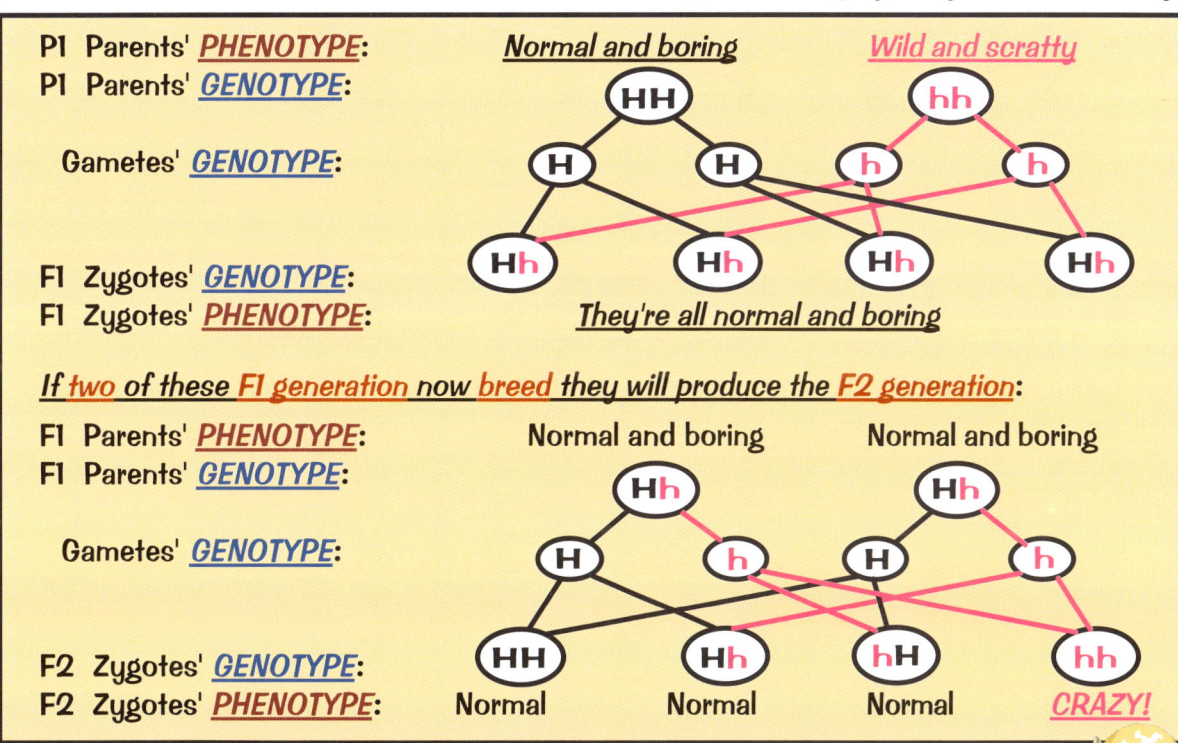

This gives a 3 : 1 RATIO of Normal to Crazy offspring in the F2 generation.
Remember that "results" like this are only PROBABILITIES. It doesn't mean it'll happen.
(Most likely, you'll end up trying to contain a mini-riot of nine lunatic baby hamsters.)

## See how those fancy words start to roll off the tongue...

The diagram and all its fancy words need to be second nature to you. So practise writing it out *from memory* until you get it all right. Because when you can do one — *you can do 'em all*.

MODULE TWO — MAINTENANCE OF THE SPECIES       SEG SYLLABUS

# The Work of Mendel

**Reproduction & Inheritance**

## Mendel's Pea Plant Experiments

Gregor Mendel was an Austrian monk who trained in mathematics and natural history at the University of Vienna. On his garden plot at the monastery, Mendel noted how characteristics in plants were passed on from one generation to the next. The results of his research became the foundation of modern genetics.

The diagrams show two _crosses for height_ in pea plants that Mendel carried out...

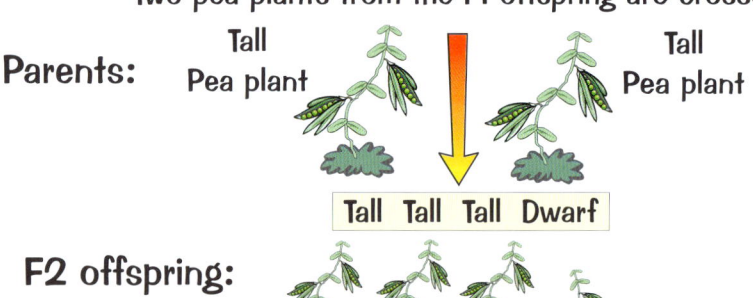

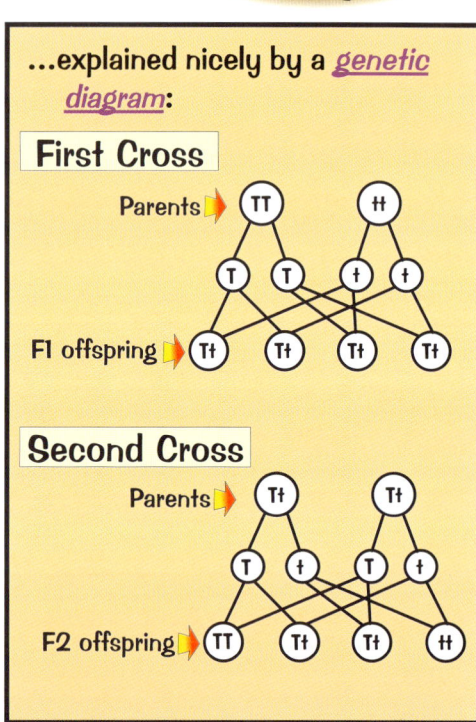

...explained nicely by a _genetic diagram_:

**First Cross**

Parents: TT, tt
F1 offspring: Tt Tt Tt Tt

**Second Cross**

Parents: Tt, Tt
F2 offspring: TT Tt Tt tt

Mendel had shown that the height characteristic in pea plants was determined by _"hereditary units"_ passed on from each parent. The ratios of tall and dwarf plants in the F1 and F2 offspring showed that the unit for tall plants, _T_, was _dominant_ over the unit for dwarf plants, _t_.

## Mendel's Conclusions

Mendel made these important conclusions about _heredity in plants_:

1) Characteristics in plants are determined by _"hereditary units"_.

2) Hereditary units are passed on from both parents, _one unit_ from _each parent_.

3) Hereditary units can be _dominant_ or _recessive_ — if an individual has both the dominant and the recessive unit for a characteristic, the dominant characteristic will be expressed.

From the benefit of modern science we know that the "hereditary units" are of course _genes_. In Mendel's time this technology was not as advanced and the significance of his work was not to be realised until after his death.

## Learn the facts then see what you know...

Mendel was a pretty clever chappy don't you think? Learn the details of the pea plant crosses he did and the genetic diagram. It's quite straightforward, once you get familiar with it. _Learn the whole page_, then _cover it up_ and _scribble it out_. They're bound to ask you about old rogues like Gregor.

SEG Syllabus — Module Two — Maintenance of the Species

# Selective Breeding

**Reproduction & Inheritance**

## Selective Breeding is Very Simple

SELECTIVE BREEDING is also called _artificial selection_, because humans artificially select the plants or animals that are going to breed and flourish, according to what _WE_ want from them.
This is the basic process involved in selective breeding:

1) From your existing stock select the ones which have the _BEST CHARACTERISTICS_.
2) _Breed them_ with each other.
3) Select the _best_ of the _OFFSPRING_, and combine them with the best that you already have and _breed again_.
4) Continue this process over _SEVERAL GENERATIONS_ to _develop_ the _desired traits_.

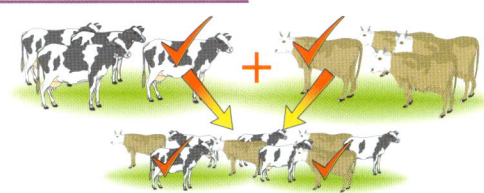

## Selective Breeding is Very Useful in Farming

Artificial Selection like this is used in _most areas of modern farming_, to great benefit:

**1) Better BEEF**
Selectively breeding _beef cattle_ to get the _best beef_ (taste, texture, appearance, etc.).

**2) Better MILK**
Selectively breeding _milking cows_ to increase _milk yield_ and _resistance to disease_.

**3) Better CHICKENS**
Selectively breeding _chickens_ to improve _egg size_ and _number_ of eggs per hen.

**4) Better WHEAT**
Selectively breeding _wheat_ to produce new varieties with better _yields_ and better _disease-resistance_ too.

**5) Better FLOWERS**
Selectively breeding _flowers_ to produce _bigger_ and _better_ and _more colourful ones_.

## Genetic Engineering is Ace — hopefully

This is a new science with exciting possibilities, but _dangers_ too. The basic idea is to move sections of _DNA_ (genes) from one organism to another so that it produces _useful biological products_. We presently use bacteria to produce _human insulin_ for diabetes sufferers and also to produce _human growth hormone_ for children who aren't growing properly.

### Genetic Engineering involves these Important Stages:

1) The useful gene is "_CUT_" from the DNA of say a human.
2) This is done using _ENZYMES_. Particular enzymes will cut out particular bits of DNA.
3) _ENZYMES_ are then used to _cut the DNA_ of a _bacterium_ and the human gene is then inserted.
4) Again this "_SPLICING_" of a new gene is controlled by certain _specific enzymes_.
5) The bacterium is now _CULTIVATED_ and soon there are _millions_ of similar bacteria all producing, say human insulin.
6) This can be done on an _INDUSTRIAL SCALE_ and the useful product can be _separated out_.
7) The same approach can also be used to _transfer useful genes into ANIMAL EMBRYOS_. Sheep for example can be developed which produce useful substances (i.e. drugs) in _their milk!_ This is a very easy way to produce drugs...

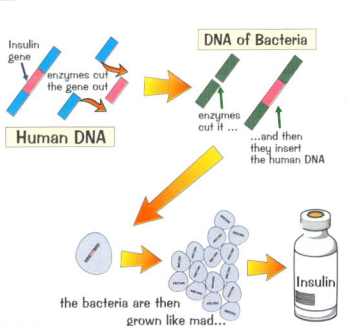

## Hmmph... Kids these days, they're all the same...

Once again, they could ask you about any of the details on this page. The only way to be sure you know it: _cover the page_ and write _mini-essays_ on both topics. Then see what you missed, and _try again_...

MODULE TWO — MAINTENANCE OF THE SPECIES — SEG SYLLABUS

# Genetic Diseases

**Reproduction & Inheritance**

## Cystic Fibrosis

1) CYSTIC FIBROSIS is a GENETIC DISEASE which affects about 1 in 1600 people in the UK.
2) It's caused by a defective gene which the person inherits from their parents. There's still no cure or effective treatment for this condition.
3) The result of the defective gene is that the body produces a lot of thick sticky mucous in the lungs, which has to be removed by massage.
4) Excess mucous also occurs in the pancreas, causing digestive problems.
5) Much more seriously though, THE BLOCKAGE OF THE AIR PASSAGES in the lungs causes a lot of CHEST INFECTIONS.
6) Physiotherapy and antibiotics clear them up but slowly the sufferer becomes more and more ill.

The genetics behind cystic fibrosis is actually very straightforward.
The gene which causes cystic fibrosis is a recessive gene, c, carried by about 1 person in 20.
If both parents are carriers there is a 1 in 4 chance of their child being a sufferer as shown here:

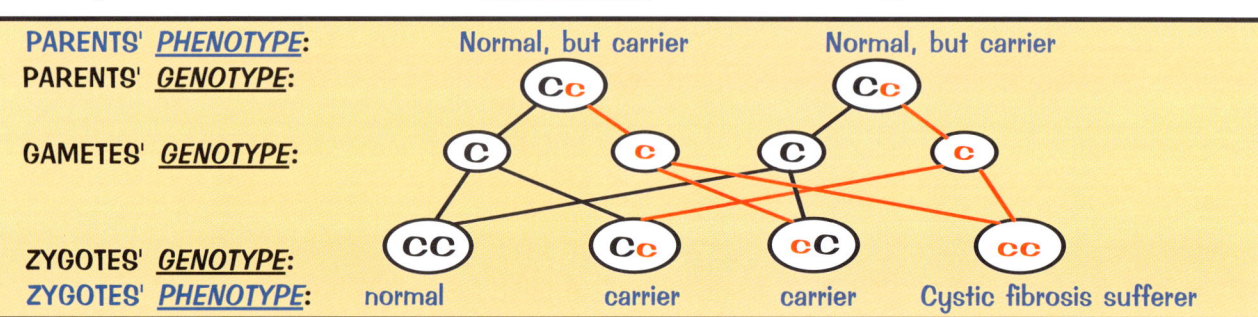

## Sickle Cell Anaemia

1) This disease causes the RED BLOOD CELLS to be shaped like SICKLES instead of the normal round shape.
2) They then get stuck in the capillaries which deprives body cells of oxygen.
3) It's an unpleasant, painful disease and sufferers die at an early age.
4) Yet even though sufferers often die before they can reproduce, the occurrence of sickle cell anaemia doesn't always die out as you'd expect it to, especially not in Africa.
5) This is because carriers of the recessive allele which causes it ARE MORE IMMUNE TO MALARIA. Hence, being a carrier increases their chance of survival in some parts of the world, even though some of their offspring are going to die young from sickle cell anaemia.

6) The genetics are identical to Cystic Fibrosis because both diseases are caused by a recessive allele. Hence if BOTH parents are carriers there's a 1 in 4 chance each child will develop it:

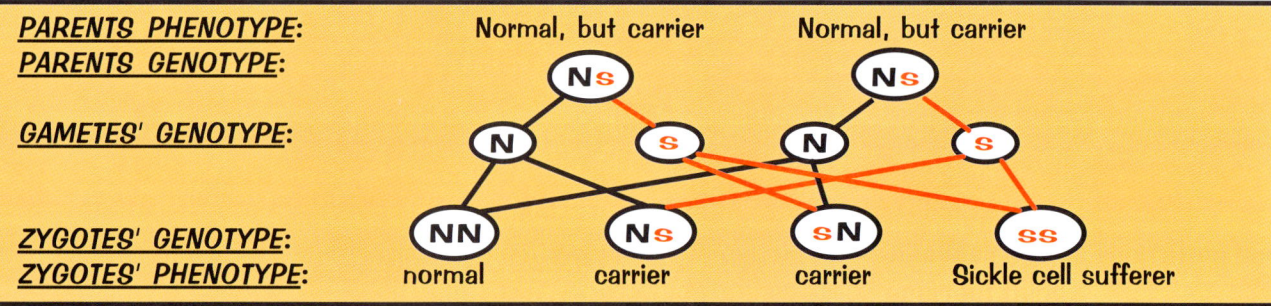

## Learn the facts then see what you know...

The symptoms should be relatively easy to learn. The genetic diagram is also quite straightforward, once you get familiar with it. Learn the whole page, then cover it up and scribble it out.

*SEG Syllabus* — *Module Two — Maintenance of the Species*

# Mutations

**Variation & Evolution**

*A MUTATION* occurs when an organism develops with some *strange new characteristic* that no other member of the species has had before. For example if someone was born with blue hair it would be caused by a mutation. Some mutations are beneficial, but *most are disastrous* (e.g. blue hair).

## Mutations are Caused by Faults in the DNA

There are *several ways* that mutations happen, but in the end they're all down to *faulty DNA*. Mutations *usually happen* when the DNA is *replicating itself* and something goes wrong. Because *DNA* is what *genes* are made of, and also what *chromosomes* are made of, then there are all these different *definitions* of what a mutation is:

1) A mutation is *faulty DNA*, or a change in the DNA.
2) A mutation is a *change to a gene* or several genes.
3) A mutation is a *change* in one or more *chromosomes*.
4) A mutation *starts in the nucleus* of one particular cell.
5) A mutation happens *when DNA isn't copied properly*.
6) A mutation is caused by *chemical changes* in a gene, or in the DNA, or in a chromosome.

## Radiation and Certain Chemicals cause Mutations

*Mutations occur 'naturally'*, probably caused by "natural" background radiation (from the Sun, and rocks etc.) or just the laws of chance that every now and then the DNA doesn't quite copy itself properly. However *the chance of mutation is increased* by exposing yourself:

1) to *nuclear radiation*, i.e. alpha, beta and gamma radiation. This is sometimes called *ionising radiation* because it creates ions (charged particles) as it passes through stuff.
2) to *X-rays* and *Ultraviolet light*, which are the *highest-frequency* parts of the *EM spectrum* (together with *gamma rays*).
3) to certain *chemicals* which are known to cause mutations. Such chemicals are called *mutagens*! If the mutations produce cancer then the chemicals are often called *carcinogens*. Cigarette smoke contains chemical mutagens (or carcinogens)... (I'm sayin' nowt — See P. 33).

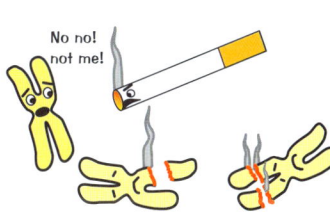

## Most Mutations are Harmful

1) If a mutation occurs in *reproductive cells*, then the young may *develop abnormally* or *die* at an early stage of their development.
2) If a mutation occurs in body cells, the mutant cells may start to *multiply* in an *uncontrolled* way and *invade* other parts of the body. This is what we know as *CANCER*.

## Some Mutations are Beneficial, giving us "EVOLUTION"

1) *Blue budgies* appeared suddenly as a mutation amongst yellow budgies. This is a good example of a *neutral effect*. It didn't harm its chances of survival and so it flourished (and at one stage, every grandma in Britain had one).
2) *Very occasionally*, a mutation will give the organism a survival *advantage* over its relatives. This is *natural selection* and *evolution* at work. A good example is a mutation in a bacteria that makes it *resistant to antibiotics*, so the mutant gene *lives on*, in the offspring, creating a *resistant "strain"* of bacteria (see P.27).

## Don't get your genes in a twist, this stuff's easy...

There are four sections with numbered points for each. *Memorise* the headings and learn the numbered points, then *cover the page* and *scribble down* everything you can remember. I know it makes your head hurt, but every time you try to remember the stuff, the more it sinks in. It'll all be worth it in the end.

*Module Two — Maintenance Of The Species*          *SEG Syllabus*

# Variation in Plants and Animals

**Variation & Evolution**

The word "*VARIATION*" sounds far too fancy for its own good.
All it means is how animals or plants of the same species *look or behave slightly different from each other*. You know, a bit *taller* or a bit *fatter* or a bit more *scary-to-look-at* etc. There are *two* causes of variation: *Genetic Variation* and *Environmental Variation*. Read on, and learn...

## 1) Genetic Variation

You'll know this already. *All animals* (including humans) are bound to be *slightly different* from each other because their *GENES* are slightly different. Genes are the code inside all your cells which determine how your body turns out. We all end up with a slightly different set of genes. The *exceptions* to that rule are *identical twins*, because their genes are *exactly the same*. But even identical twins are never *completely identical* — and that's because of the other factor:

## 2) Environmental Variation *is shown up by Twins*

If you're not sure what "*environment*" means, think of it as "*upbringing*" instead — it's pretty much the same thing — how and where you were "brought up".

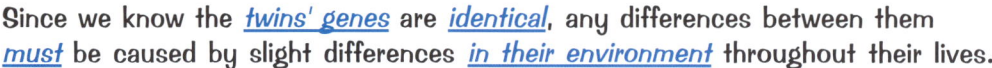

Since we know the *twins' genes* are *identical*, any differences between them *must* be caused by slight differences *in their environment* throughout their lives.

*Twins* give us a fairly good idea of how important the *two factors* (genes and environment) are, *compared to each other*, at least for animals — plants always show *much greater variation* due to differences in their environment than animals do, as explained below.

## Environmental *Variation in* Plants *is much* Greater

*PLANTS* are *strongly affected* by:
1) *Temperature*   2) *Sunlight*   3) *Moisture level*   4) *Soil composition*

For example, plants may grow *twice as big* or *twice as fast* due to *fairly modest* changes in environment such as the amount of *sunlight* or *rainfall* they're getting, or how *warm* it is or what the *soil* is like.

(A cat, on the other hand, born and bred in say, the North of Scotland, could be sent out to live in equatorial Africa and would show no significant changes — it would look the same, eat the same, and probably still puke up everywhere.)

## Continuous *and* Discontinuous *Variation:*

**CONTINUOUS VARIATION:** The feature can vary over a *continuous range of values*.

Continuous variation refers to things like *height* or *weight* or *skin colour*, where the thing can have *any value at all* (within reason).
For example, the weight of a dog could be *absolutely anything* between say 2kg and 60kg: 5.3kg, 24.2kg, 54.23kg, etc.

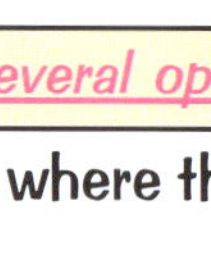

**DISCONTINUOUS VARIATION:** The feature can only take *one of several options*.

Discontinuous variation is things like *eye colour* or *blood group*, where there are just *a few definite options*, not a whole continuous range of possibles.
For example, eyes can only be *blue or brown or green or hazel*. They cannot be bluey-brown or kinda-greeney-bluey, or sorta-browney-bluey-kinda-hazeley, etc.

## Don't let Everything get to you — just learn the facts...

There are four sections on this paage. After you think you've learnt it all, *cover the page* and do a "*mini-essay*" on each of the four sections. Then *check back* and see what important points you missed. The coloured ink highlights the important bits — the rest is idle creative genius.

*SEG Syllabus*   *Module Two — Maintenance of the Species*

# Population Sizes

**Adaptation and Competition**

POPULATION SIZE just means how many of *one type of plant or animal* there is in a given ecosystem, and more importantly, *WHY ONLY THAT MANY*, why not more? The answer is that there are always *LIMITING FACTORS*, such as *too little food* or *too many other animals* eating the food as well, or *too many animals eating them*, etc... This can all start to get out of hand and sound really complicated. But it's *really very simple*, and you must keep telling yourself that!

## The Size of a Population Depends on Four Factors

1) The TOTAL AMOUNT OF FOOD, WATER AND SPACE.

2) The amount of COMPETITION there is (from other species) for the same food, water and space.

3) The NUMBER OF PREDATORS (or grazers) who may eat the animal (or plant) in question.

4) MIGRATION, i.e. some of the animals moving away to another place.

## The Distribution of Organisms Depends on Three Factors

The relative number of each type of organism in any habitat depends on three factors:

1) ADAPTATION — how well the animal has become *adapted to its environment*.

2) COMPETITION — how well the animal *competes with other species* for the same food.

3) PREDATION — how well the animal *avoids being eaten*.

In the Exam they could ask you about it from either viewpoint. Although these lists seem kind of hard to relate to, what they're saying is surely just common sense...

## In other words... organisms will thrive best if:

1) THERE'S PLENTY OF THE GOOD THINGS IN LIFE: food, water, space, shelter, light, etc.
2) THEY'RE BETTER THAN THE COMPETITION AT GETTING IT (better *adapted*)
3) THEY DON'T GET EATEN
4) THEY DON'T GET ILL

That's pretty much the long and the short of it, wouldn't you say? So learn those four things. Every species is different, of course, but those *FOUR* basic principles will always apply. In Exam questions *YOU* have to apply them to any new situation to work out what'll happen.

## Revision stress — don't let it eat you up...

It's a strange topic is population sizes. In a way it seems like common sense, but it all seems to get so messy. Anyway, *learn all the points on this page* and you'll be OK with it, I'd think.

MODULE TWO — MAINTENANCE OF THE SPECIES          SEG SYLLABUS

# Adapt and Survive

*Adaptation and Competition*

If you <u>learn the features</u> that make these animals and plants well adapted, you'll be able to apply them to any other similar creatures they might give you in the Exam.
Chances are you'll get a <u>camel</u>, <u>cactus</u> or <u>polar bear</u> anyway.

## The Polar Bear — Designed for Arctic Conditions

The <u>Polar bear</u> has all these features: (which <u>many other arctic creatures</u> have too, so think on...)
1) <u>Large size</u> and <u>compact shape</u> (i.e. rounded), including dinky little ears, to keep the <u>surface area</u> to a <u>minimum</u> (compared to the body weight) — this all <u>reduces heat loss</u>.
2) A thick layer of <u>blubber</u> for <u>insulation</u> and food storage.
3) <u>Thick hairy coat</u> for keeping the body heat in.
4) <u>Greasy fur</u> which <u>sheds water</u> after swimming to <u>prevent cooling</u> due to evaporation.
5) <u>White fur</u> to match the surroundings for <u>camouflage</u>.
6) <u>Strong swimmer</u> and <u>runner</u> to catch food in the water and on land.
7) <u>Big feet</u> to <u>spread the weight</u> on snow and ice.

## The Camel — Designed for Desert Conditions

The <u>camel</u> has all these features: (most of which are shared by <u>other desert creatures</u>...)
1) All <u>fat</u> is stored in the <u>hump</u>, there is <u>no layer of body fat</u>. This helps it to <u>lose</u> body heat.
2) <u>Large surface area</u>. The shape of a camel is anything but compact, which gives it more surface area to <u>lose body heat</u> to its surroundings.
3) It can <u>store</u> a lot of <u>water</u> without problem. Up to <u>20 gallons</u> at once.
4) Its <u>sandy colour</u> gives good <u>camouflage</u>.
5) <u>Large feet</u> to <u>spread load</u> on soft sand.
6) It <u>loses very little water</u>. There's little <u>urine</u> and very little <u>sweating</u>.
7) It can tolerate <u>big changes</u> in its own <u>body temperature</u> to remove the need for sweating.

## Plants are Adapted to their Environment

### 1) The Cactus — Designed for Desert Conditions

A cactus has all these features to help it <u>survive</u> in the desert:
1) It has a thick stem to <u>store</u> water.
2) <u>Spines</u> stop herbivores eating them.
3) It has a reduced <u>surface area</u> (no leaves) — to <u>reduce</u> water loss and heat gain.
4) Shallow but very <u>extensive</u> roots ensure water is absorbed quickly over a <u>large area</u>.
5) It has <u>few stomata</u> which only open at night so water loss is <u>reduced</u> during the day.

### 2) Adaptations help plants Compete for Space and Light

Plants have developed other features to <u>increase</u> their chance of <u>survival</u>.
1) Some plants can <u>climb</u> which means they can grow in more places and <u>make use of space</u> which would otherwise be inaccessible to them.
2) Development of <u>large leaves</u> and <u>root systems</u> means that plants can get even more of the things they need, like: <u>light</u>, <u>water</u>, <u>nutrients</u>, and <u>carbon dioxide</u>.

By and large the most important factors for plants are <u>space</u> and <u>light</u>. Remember these factors when describing <u>plant adaptations</u> which help them to survive.

## Creature features — learn and survive...

It's worth learning all these survival features well enough to be able to write them down <u>from memory</u>. There's a whole world full of animals and plants, all with different survival features, but explaining them eventually becomes kinda "common sense", because the same principles tend to apply to them all.

# What Fossils Tell Us

**Variation & Evolution**

## Evidence from Rock and Soil Strata

The fossils found in <u>rock layers</u> tell us <u>TWO THINGS</u>:

1) What the creatures and plants <u>LOOKED LIKE</u>.

2) <u>HOW LONG AGO THEY EXISTED</u>, by the type of rock they're in. Generally speaking, the <u>DEEPER</u> you find the fossil, the <u>OLDER</u> it will be, though of course rocks get pushed upwards and eroded, so very old rocks can become exposed. Fossils are usually <u>dated</u> by geologists who <u>ALREADY KNOW THE AGE OF THE ROCK</u>. The Grand Canyon in Arizona is about <u>1 mile deep</u>. It was formed by a river slowly cutting down through layers of rock. The rocks at the bottom are about <u>1,000,000,000 years old</u>, and the fossil record in the sides is pretty cool.

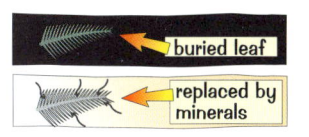

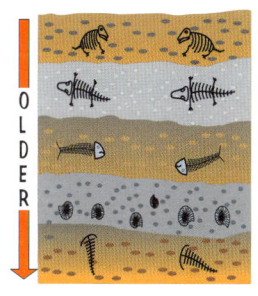

## Extinction is Pretty Bad News

When a species no longer has any living members it is said to be <u>EXTINCT</u>. <u>Selection against</u> a species causes extinction in one of <u>three ways</u>:

1) The species can't keep up with <u>changes</u> in the environment. Slow changes in the environment will gradually favour certain <u>new characteristics</u> amongst the members of the species. Over many generations those features will <u>proliferate</u> and the species <u>constantly adapts</u> to the changes in environment. But if the environment changes <u>too fast</u> the whole species may be <u>wiped out</u>.

2) A <u>new predator</u> or <u>disease</u> might appear which they have not been exposed to before. If they don't have the necessary <u>defences</u>, a particularly nasty bug or a new and effective predator could mean the end for a species.

3) A species can also be wiped out by <u>another organism</u> eating its food. If it <u>can't compete</u> with a new species for the food supply the species will die out by <u>starvation</u>.

## Evidence For Extinct Species

1) The <u>dinosaurs</u> became <u>EXTINCT</u> and it's only <u>FOSSILS</u> that tell us they ever existed at all.
2) Fossils provide <u>evidence</u> of their existence and have helped to give us a good idea of what these creatures were like.
3) A better record of an extinct species has been found for the <u>hairy mammoth</u>.
4) We know exactly what they were like from whole mammoths found <u>preserved in ice</u>.
5) Whole organisms preserved in this way provide a perfect <u>natural history record</u> of an extinct species.

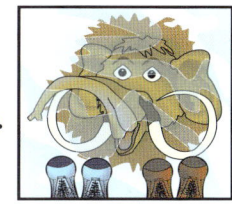

## The Theory of Evolution is Cool

1) This suggests that all the animals and plants on Earth gradually "<u>evolved</u>" over <u>millions of years</u>, rather than just suddenly popping into existence. Makes sense.
2) Life on Earth began as <u>simple organisms living in water</u> and gradually everything else evolved from there. And it only took about <u>3,000,000,000 years</u>.

## Fossils Provide Evidence for it

1) <u>Fossils</u> provide lots of <u>evidence</u> for evolution.
2) They show how today's species have <u>changed and developed</u> over <u>millions of years</u>.
3) There are quite a few "<u>missing links</u>" though because the fossil record is <u>incomplete</u>.
4) This is because <u>very very few</u> dead plants or animals actually turn into fossils. Most just <u>decay away</u>.

## Learn The Facts — before it's too late...

Another stupefyingly easy page to learn. Use the <u>mini-essay</u> method. Just make sure you <u>learn every fact</u>, that's all. Dinosaurs never did proper revision and look what happened to them. (Mind you they did last about 200 million years, which is about 199.9 million more than we have, so far...)

MODULE TWO — MAINTENANCE OF THE SPECIES · SEG SYLLABUS

# Evolution By Natural Selection

**Variation & Evolution**

## Species

You need to *learn* this definition:

A **SPECIES** is a group of organisms which can *interbreed* to produce *fertile* offspring.

1) *Organisms* belonging to the same species can *breed* and produce *fertile offspring*.
2) Organisms from the same species are usually *similar*, sharing many features.
3) However they aren't necessarily *identical* because within a species members *show variety*.

It is *important* to note that for this definition the offspring must be fertile and be able to interbreed. While a horse and a donkey *can reproduce*, it's clear they do not belong to the same species simply because the offspring are *infertile*.

## Natural Selection Increases the Chance of Survival

Gradual *evolution* of organisms over *millions of years* has happened by a process in which the *fittest survive*.

1) *Variety* within a species produces features which are an *advantage* for survival.
2) Members of a species with these adaptations are *more likely* to survive than those without.
3) These "fittest" individuals *breed* and pass their *genes* to their offspring.
4) The number of individuals within the population with the adaptation *gradually increases*.
5) Slowly the entire species changes, or *evolves*, to suit its surroundings.

*Learn* this definition:

**NATURAL SELECTION** is the process where offspring with features that *increase* their chance of survival then go on to *reproductive success*. These individuals pass their *genes* on to future generations causing the entire population to *evolve*.

## Mutations play a big part in Natural Selection

1) **MUTATIONS** introduce *variety* within a population.
2) A mutation which *helps* an individual to survive also gives it *increased* reproductive success.
3) This is important for the survival of a species in a *changing environment*.

*Learn* these two examples where a *mutation* has given a *survival advantage* to a population:

## 1) The Peppered Moth

A new variety of peppered moth has evolved because of a colour mutation.

1) Originally peppered moths were *light* in colour and survived predation by being *camouflaged* on trees.
2) *Dark* moths, the result of a *mutation*, were easy to see and so were caught by birds.
3) Soot from industry caused trees to become *darker* in colour.
4) *Light* coloured moths stood out against the sooty bark and were more likely to be preyed upon by birds.
5) The dark mutant moths *survived* and went on to breed and pass their *genes* onto their offspring
6) Gradually the entire population of moths became *dark* in colour in polluted areas.

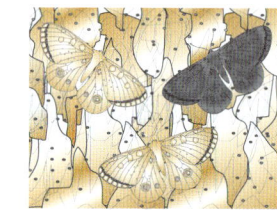

## 2) Penicillin-Resistant Bacteria

Bacterial *resistance* to antibiotics also happens because of a *mutation*.

1) Bacteria are normally *killed* by the antibiotic "*penicillin*".
2) A mutation makes some bacteria *resistant* to penicillin.
3) These bacteria will *survive* treatment with penicillin and go on to *multiply*.
4) A *new strain* of bacteria is created which will no longer be killed by treatment with penicillin.

## "Natural Selection" — sounds like Vegan Chocolates...

This page is split into four sections. *Memorise* the headings, then *cover the page* and *scribble down* all you can about each section. Keep trying until you can *remember* all the important points.

*SEG Syllabus*  MODULE TWO — MAINTENANCE OF THE SPECIES

# Two Theories Of Evolution

**Variation & Evolution**

## Darwin's Theory of Natural Selection is Ace

THIS THEORY IS COOL and provides a comprehensive explanation for all life on Earth. Mind you, it caused some trouble at the time, because for the first time ever, there was a highly plausible explanation for our own existence, without the need for a "Creator".
This was bad news for the religious authorities of the time, who tried to ridicule old Charlie's ideas. But, as they say, "THE TRUTH WILL OUT".

## Darwin made Four Important Observations...

1) All organisms produce MORE OFFSPRING than could possibly survive.
2) But in fact, population numbers tend to remain FAIRLY CONSTANT over long periods of time.
3) Organisms in a species show WIDE VARIATION due to different genes.
4) SOME of the variations are INHERITED AND PASSED ON to the next generation.

## ...and then made these Two Deductions:

1) Since most offspring don't survive, all organisms must have to STRUGGLE FOR SURVIVAL.
2) The ones who SURVIVE AND REPRODUCE will PASS ON THEIR GENES.

This is the famous "SURVIVAL OF THE FITTEST" statement. Organisms with slightly less survival-value will probably perish first, leaving the strongest and fittest to pass on their genes to the next generation.

## Lamarck's Theory of Evolution — talk about sticking your neck out

Darwin's theory of evolution is pretty obviously right. There was another theory which they seem to want you to know about by a chap called LAMARCK. His theory was that:

Animals EVOLVE FEATURES according to how much they USE THEM.

So giraffes, ever stretching to higher branches and straining their necks, passed on this fact to their offspring, who were then born with slightly longer necks. The theory isn't great and seems to be comprehensively disproved by experiments on mice who had their tails cut off for generation after generation and still grew tails just as long even though their forefathers never made any use of theirs.

## All Wild Creatures live in a very Harsh World indeed...

...which causes many to DIE YOUNG, due to PREDATORS, DISEASE and COMPETITION. But remember, this is an important element in the process of NATURAL SELECTION. There has to be a LARGE SURPLUS of offspring for nature to select the fittest from.
Life for any farm animal is a veritable dream compared to the "eat or be eaten" savage reality of the 'natural' world. Most wild animals are eventually either eaten alive or else they starve to death. Think about it — they've all gotta go somehow. Give them a nice cosy civilised farm any day, I say...

## Why the long face? — There isn't that much to learn...

Learn both theories of evolution. Memorise the headings, then cover the page and scribble down all you can about each section. Keep trying until you can remember all the important points.

MODULE TWO — MAINTENANCE OF THE SPECIES  SEG SYLLABUS

# The Greenhouse Effect

**Humans and The Environment**

## Carbon Dioxide and Methane Trap Heat from the Sun

1) The temperature of the Earth is a balance between the heat it gets from the Sun and the heat it radiates back out into space.
2) The atmosphere acts like an insulating layer and keeps some of the heat in.
3) This is exactly what happens in a greenhouse or a conservatory. The Sun shines into it and the glass keeps the heat in so it just gets hotter and hotter.
4) There are several different gases in the atmosphere which are very good at keeping the heat in. They are called "greenhouse gases", oddly enough. The main ones that we worry about are methane and carbon dioxide, because the levels of these are rising quite sharply.
5) The Greenhouse Effect is causing the Earth to warm up very slowly.

## The Greenhouse Effect may cause Flooding and Drought ....(!)

1) Changes in weather patterns and climate could cause problems of drought or flooding.
2) The melting of the polar ice-caps would raise sea-levels and could cause flooding to many low-lying coastal parts of the world including many major cities.

## Methane is Also a Problem

1) Methane gas is also contributing to the Greenhouse Effect.
2) It's produced naturally from various sources, such as natural marshland.
3) However, the two sources of methane which are on the increase are:
   a) Rice growing
   b) Cattle rearing — it's the cows "pumping" that's the problem, believe it or not.

## Pesticides Disturb Food Chains

1) Pesticides are sprayed onto most crops to kill the various insects that can damage the crops.
2) Unfortunately, they also kill lots of harmless insects such as bees and butterflies.
3) Destroying these insects is damaging because they are pollinators, essential for plant reproduction.
4) Their destruction can also cause a shortage of food for many insect-eating birds.
5) Pesticides tend to be poisonous and there's always the danger of the poison passing on to other animals (as well as humans) causing food chains to be disturbed.

This is well illustrated by the case of otters which were almost wiped out over much of crop dominated Southern England by DDT in the early 1960s. The diagram shows the food chain which ends with the otter. DDT is not excreted so it accumulates along the food chain and the otter ends up with all the DDT collected by all the other animals.

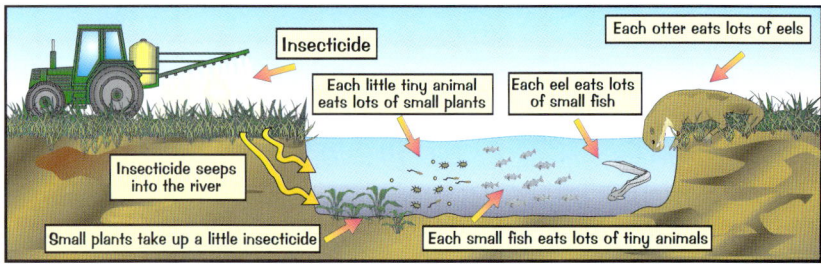

## Learn the facts first — then start building your ark...

I bet you never realised there were so many drivelly details on the Greenhouse Effect and Pesticides. Well there *are* and I'm afraid they could all come up in your Exam, so you just gotta learn them. Use the good old mini-essay method for each section, and scribble down what you know.

# Environmental Damage

**Humans and The Environment**

## Burning Fossil Fuels Causes Acid Rain

1) When fossil fuels are burned they release mostly carbon dioxide which is causing the Greenhouse Effect. They also release two other harmful gases:
   a) SULPHUR DIOXIDE   b) various NITROGEN OXIDES
2) When these mix with clouds they form acids. This then falls as acid rain.
3) Cars and power stations are the main causes of acid rain.

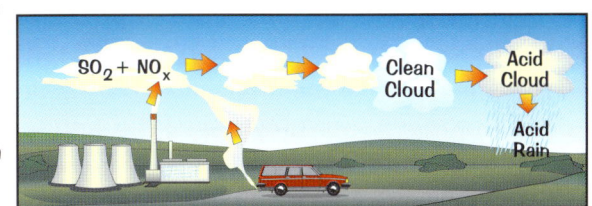

## Acid Rain Kills Fish, Trees and Statues

1) Acid rain causes lakes to become acidic which has a severe effect on their ecosystems.
2) The way this happens is that the acid causes aluminium salts to dissolve into the water. The resulting aluminium ions are poisonous to many fish and birds.
3) Acid rain kills trees.
4) Acid rain damages limestone buildings and ruins stone statues.

## DEFORESTATION — The Four Big Problems it Causes...

We have already pretty well deforested OUR COUNTRY.
Now many less developed countries are doing the same.
However, there are several serious environmental problems that can occur when they suddenly cut lots of trees down in these tropical climates:

1) DECREASE IN RAINFALL in that area because moisture is no longer evaporating into the air from the trees.
2) SERIOUS SOIL EROSION when it rains heavily because there are no roots to hold it all together.
3) SERIOUS FLOODING because the soil gets washed into the rivers, silts them up, and over they flow...
4) INCREASE IN $CO_2$ LEVELS in the atmosphere because the trees aren't there to remove it any more.

## CFCs Cause The Hole in The Ozone Layer

1) Ozone consists of molecules made of three oxygen atoms, $O_3$.
2) There is a layer of ozone high up in the atmosphere.
3) Ozone absorbs harmful UV rays from the sun.
4) CFC (chlorofluorocarbon) gases which are used in aerosols and fridges, react with ozone molecules and break them up.
5) This thinning of the ozone layer allows more harmful UV rays to reach the surface of the Earth.
6) This is making it dangerous to go out in the sun in many parts of the world due to the increased risk of skin cancer from the harmful UV rays.
7) CFCs are being replaced by other gases now, but the harmful effects of the CFCs already released may continue for centuries.

## So much to learn, so little time to learn it...

Lots of environmental problems. This stuff can certainly get a bit tedious. At first it can be quite interesting, but then having to make sure you've learnt all those drivelly little details is not.
Still, there's worse things in life than a bit of revision. So learn and enjoy. It's the only way.

MODULE TWO — MAINTENANCE OF THE SPECIES                    SEG SYLLABUS

# Fertilisers and Land Clearing

**Humans and The Environment**

## Fertilisers Damage Lakes and Rivers

1) *Fertilisers* which contain *nitrates* are essential to *modern farming*.
2) Without them *crops wouldn't grow* nearly so well, and *food yields* would be *well down*.
3) This is because the crops *take nitrates out of the soil* and these nitrates need to be *replaced*.
4) The *problems* start if some of the *rich fertiliser* finds its way into *rivers and streams*.
5) This happens *quite easily* if *too much fertiliser* is applied, *especially if it rains* soon afterwards.
6) As the picture shows, *too many nitrates* in the water cause a sequence of *"mega-growth"*, *"mega-death"* and *"mega-decay"* involving most of the *plant and animal life* in the water.

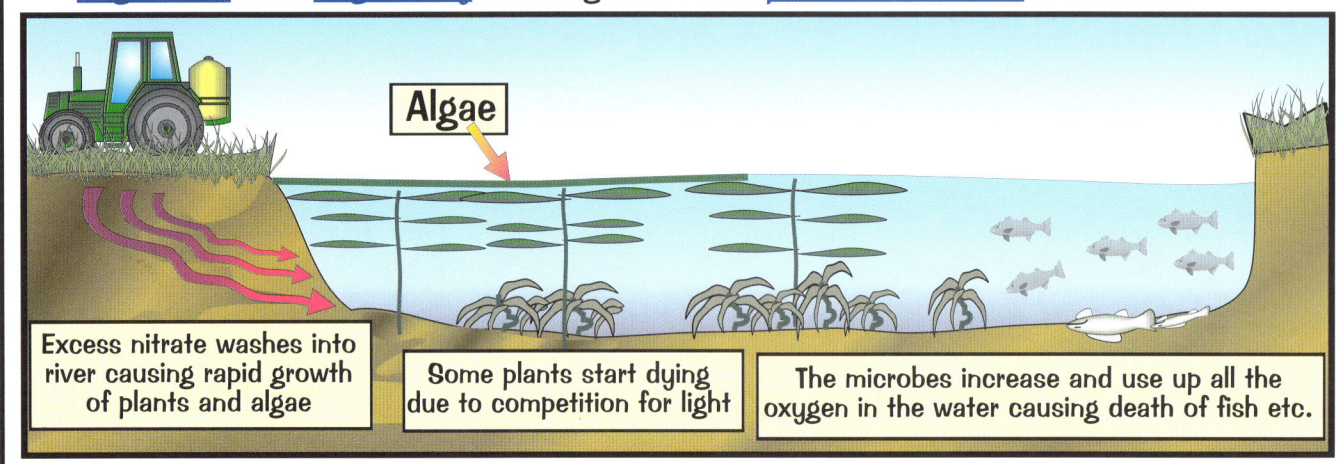

Excess nitrate washes into river causing rapid growth of plants and algae

Some plants start dying due to competition for light

The microbes increase and use up all the oxygen in the water causing death of fish etc.

**Higher**

7) This process of *fertilisers leaching* into lakes and rivers causing the build up of dead plant matter and eventually the suffocation of aquatic animals is called *EUTROPHICATION*. It basically means *"too much of a good thing"*. (*Raw sewage* pumped into rivers can cause the same problem.)

**Higher**

8) *Farmers* need to take *a lot more care* when spreading *artificial fertilisers*.

## Land Clearing can Destroy the Environment

1) A method of *increasing* food production is to *clear* more land to make *larger fields*.
2) This can have *devastating effects* on the environment.
3) Land clearing destroys the *natural habitat* of many *wild creatures* leaving them homeless.
4) Clearing land and the removal of hedges can lead to serious *soil erosion*.
5) Soil is *washed* and *blown* away when it is no longer protected from the wind and rain.
6) The most tragic result is the loss of meadowlands full of wild flowers, of natural woodlands and orchards of cherry trees, of rolling fields of grass and flowers, and tree-topped hills and leafy lanes — just *swept away* in a couple of decades, along with all the natural timeless beauty of rural England.

## There's nowt wrong wi' just spreadin' muck on it...

Make sure you learn how fertilisers can interfere with life in lakes and rivers. Learn all the consequences of land clearing for animals and the environment. You have to learn the details carefully. *Mini-essay* time again I'd say. *Cover the page and scribble*...

*SEG Syllabus* — *Module Two — Maintenance of the Species*

# Managed Ecosystems

**Humans and The Environment**

## Farming Produces a Lot of Food, Which is Great, but...

Modern methods of farming and agriculture give us the ability to produce *plenty of food* for everyone. But there's a hefty *price* to pay. One that we're already paying.
Modern Farming methods can *damage the world we live in*, making it *polluted*, *unattractive* and *bereft of wildlife*. As we have seen pesticides, fertilisers and land clearing can have serious consequences:

1) **REMOVAL OF HEDGES** to make huge great fields *destroys the natural habitat* of many *wild creatures*, and can lead to serious *soil erosion*.
2) Careless use of **FERTILISERS** pollutes *rivers* and *lakes*, making them *green, slimy and horrible*.
3) **PESTICIDES DISTURB FOOD CHAINS** and reduce many *insect*, *bird* and *mammal* populations.

It *is* possible to farm efficiently and still maintain a healthy and beautiful environment. *But maximum profit and efficiency will have to be compromised*, if we are to make our countryside more than just one big *industrial food factory*, and also to treat our fellow creatures (many of whom we will eventually *eat*) with some basic level of *decency and respect and humanity*.

## Organic Farming is still perfectly Viable

*Modern farming* produces a lot of *top quality food* and we all appreciate it on the supermarket shelves. However, you certainly could **NOT** describe modern farming as "*a carefully managed ecosystem*" and each *new modern farming technique* tends to create various "*unforeseen*" or "*unfore-cared-about*" consequences.

*Traditional farming methods* do still work (amazingly!), but they produce rather *less food per acre* and it's *a bit more expensive* too. The positive side to it is that the *whole ecosystem* stays *in balance*, the countryside *still looks pretty* and the *animals* get a *fair deal* too.

Now that Europe is *over-producing food* in a big way, it may be time to pay more attention to these things rather than "*maximum food yield at all costs*". It *is* possible to produce plenty of food and still maintain a *balanced ecosystem*. The **THREE MAIN THINGS** that can be done are:

1) Use of *organic fertilisers* (i.e. spreadin' muck on it — and there's nowt wrong wi' that).
2) *Reforestation* and "*set-aside*" land for meadows, to give *wild plants and animals* a chance.
3) *Biological control* of pests. Trying to control pests which damage crops with *other creatures* which eat them is a reasonable alternative to using *pesticides*, and although it's not always quite so effective, at least there are *no harmful food chain problems*.

*Higher Higher Higher*

## The Answers are Not Straightforward

When *making decisions* about the *environment* many considerations must be taken into account. *Historical*, *economic* and *social* questions must be addressed before changes can be made. Farming may be the *sole income* for some countries and it is not as simple as telling people to stop doing things which they have been doing for *thousands of years*.
It is a very complex issue, a lot like life in general really. (But that's what makes it interesting!)

### Learn It and Make a Real Difference...

Phew! Just look at all those words crammed onto one page. Geesh.... I mean blimey, it almost looks like a page from a normal science book. Almost. Anyway, there it all is, on the page, just waiting to be blended with the infinite void inside your head. *Learn and enjoy*... and *scribble*.

MODULE TWO — MAINTENANCE OF THE SPECIES          SEG SYLLABUS

# Drugs

**Health**

1) Drugs are substances which alter the way the body works. Some drugs are useful of course, for example pain killers or antibiotics such as penicillin. However there are many drugs which are *dangerous* if misused, and many of them are *addictive* or "habit-forming".
2) The loss of control and judgement caused by many drugs can easily lead to *death* from various other causes e.g. choking on vomit, falling down stairs, passing under vehicles, etc.

## Solvents

1) Solvents are found in a variety of "household" items e.g. glues, paints etc.
2) They are *dangerous* and have many *damaging effects* on your body and personality.
3) They cause hallucinations and adversely affect personality and behaviour.
4) They cause *damage* to the *lungs*, *brain* and *liver*.

## Alcohol

1) The main effect of alcohol is to reduce the activity of the nervous system. The positive aspect of this is that it makes us feel less inhibited, and there's no doubt that alcohol in moderation helps people to socialise and relax with each other.
2) However, if you let alcohol take over, *it can wreck your life*. And it does. It wrecks a lot of people's lives. You've got to control it.
3) Once alcohol starts to take over someone's life there are many *harmful effects*:
    a) Alcohol is basically *poisonous*. Too much drinking will cause *severe damage* to the *liver* and the *brain* leading to *liver disease* and a noticeable *drop* in brain function.
    b) Too much alcohol *impairs judgement* which can cause accidents, and it can also severely affect the person's work and home life.
    c) *Serious dependency on alcohol* can eventually lead to *loss of job*, *loss of income* and the start of a *severe downward spiral*.

## How Healthy Lungs Work

1) A *mucous membrane* and many *cilia* cover the inside surfaces of the air passages.
2) The membrane produces a sticky liquid called *mucous* which helps to keep conditions *moist and warm* inside the lungs.
3) Mucous also *traps dust particles and bacteria* which might be breathed in.
4) The action of the mucous membrane and cilia helps keep the lungs *clean and free of small particles*.

## Smoking Tobacco

Smoking is no good to anyone. It doesn't have any positive social aspects and is *without any doubt at all a very serious cause of ill health*.
Tobacco smoke does this inside your body:
1) It *coats* the *inside of your lungs* with tar so they become *hideously inefficient*.
2) It covers the cilia in *tar* preventing them from getting bacteria out of your lungs.
3) It causes *disease* of the *heart* and *blood vessels*, leading to *heart attacks* and *strokes*.
4) It causes *lung cancer*. Out of every *ten* lung cancer patients, *nine* of them smoke.
5) It causes *damage to foetuses*, depriving them of oxygen and causing a *low birth weight*.
6) It produces *carbon monoxide* which reduces the oxygen carrying capacity of the blood.
7) It causes *severe* loss of lung function leading to diseases like *emphysema* and *bronchitis*. People with severe bronchitis can't manage even a brisk walk, because their lungs can't get enough oxygen into the blood. It eventually *kills* over *20,000 people* in Britain every year.
8) But this is the best bit. The effect of the nicotine is *negligible* — other than to make you *addicted* to it. It doesn't make you high — just *dependent*. Great. Fantastic.

## Learn the Numbered Points for your Exam...

It's the disease aspects they concentrate on most in the Exams. Learn the rest for a nice life.

*SEG Syllabus* — *Module Two — Maintenance of the Species*

# Revision Summary for Module Two

*Gee, all that business about genes and chromosomes and the like — it's all pretty serious stuff, don't you think? It takes a real effort to get your head round it all. There's too many big fancy words, for one thing. But there you go — life's tough and you've just gotta face up to it.*
*Use these questions to find out what you know — and what you don't. Then look back and learn the bits you didn't know. Then try the questions again, and again...*

1) On P. 22 there are 18 fancy words to do with genetics. List them all — with explanations.
2) Draw a set of diagrams showing the relationship between: cell, nucleus, chromosomes, genes, DNA.
3) Write down the strict definition of growth.
4) Give a definition of mitosis. Draw a set of diagrams showing what happens in mitosis.
5) What is asexual reproduction? Give a proper definition for it.
6) What are the male and female gametes called? Where are they produced?
7) How many pairs of chromosomes are there in a normal human cell nucleus?
8) Where does meiosis take place? What kind of cells does meiosis produce?
9) Draw out the sequence of diagrams showing what happens during meiosis.
10) What happens to the chromosome numbers during meiosis and then during fertilisation?
11) What are X and Y chromosomes to do with? Who has what combination?
12) Draw a genetic inheritance diagram to show how these genes are passed on.
13) What is meant by monohybrid crosses? Give three examples of the genetics descriptive shorthand.
14) Starting with parental genotypes HH and hh, draw a full genetic inheritance diagram to show the eventual genotypes and phenotypes of the F1 and F2 generations (of hamsters).
15) Describe fully the pea plant crosses for height that Mendel did.
16) List the symptoms and treatment of cystic fibrosis. What causes this disease?
17) Draw a genetics diagram to show the probability of a child being a sufferer.
18) Give the cause and symptoms of sickle cell anaemia.
19) Draw a genetics diagram showing the probability of a child being a sufferer.
20) Why does sickle cell anaemia not die out?
21) Describe the process involved in selective breeding. List five uses for selective breeding in farming.
22) What is genetic engineering used for? Describe the process of making human insulin in bacteria.
23) Give an example of harmful, neutral and beneficial mutations. List the four main causes of mutations.
24) What are the *four* basic things which determine the size of a population of a species?
25) What conditions will allow a population to thrive?
26) List seven survival features of the polar bear and of the camel.
27) What adaptations do plants have to increase their chance of survival?
28) List five adaptations of the cactus which help it to survive in the desert.
29) What are the two types of variation? Describe their relative importance for plants and animals.
30) What is meant by continuous and discontinuous variation? Give two examples of each.
31) What are fossils? How are they formed? Explain how fossils rocks support the theory of evolution.
32) Name two extinct species. What is the evidence for their existence?
33) What is natural selection? Give two examples of mutations being involved in natural selection.
34) What were Darwin's four observations and two deductions? Is it a cosy life for wild animals?
35) Describe Lamarck's theory of evolution and give evidence against it.
36) Which gases cause acid rain? Where do these gases come from? What are the harmful effects?
37) Explain how the greenhouse effect happens. What dire consequences could there be?
38) List the four problems resulting from deforestation in tropical countries. Why do they do it?
39) What does CFC stand for? Where do CFCs come from? What damage do they do?
40) Explain in detail how pesticides enter the food chain. What happened with DDT in the '60s?
41) What happens when too much nitrate fertiliser is put onto fields? Give full details.
42) What is the big fancy name given to this problem? How can it be avoided?
43) What are the environmental consequences of land clearing? Why is it done?
44) What is the great bonus of modern farming methods? What are the drawbacks?
45) Explain the dangers of drinking alcohol. Explain why smoking is just *so cool — not*.
46) List in detail all eight major health problems that result from smoking.

*Module Two — Maintenance Of The Species*   *SEG Syllabus*

# STRUCTURES AND CHANGES

## Atoms — Atomic Structure

The structure of atoms is *real simple*. I mean, gee, there's nothing to them. In the past it was even easier. People thought that atoms were the *smallest things around*. But it's much more fun now we've changed all that and have protons, neutrons and electrons. Just learn and enjoy.

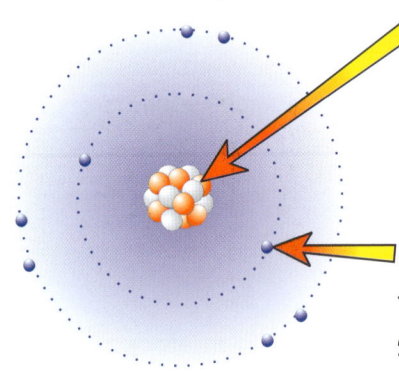

### The Nucleus
1) It's in the *middle* of the atom, and contains *protons* and *neutrons*.
2) It has a *positive charge* because of the protons.
3) Almost the *whole* mass of the atom is *concentrated* in the nucleus.
4) But size-wise it's *tiny* compared to the rest of the atom.

### The Electrons
1) Move *around* the nucleus.
2) They're *negatively charged*.
3) They're *tiny*, but they cover *a lot of space*.
4) The *volume* their orbits occupy determines how big the atom is.
5) They have virtually *no* mass.
6) They occupy *shells* around the nucleus.
7) These shells explain *the whole of Chemistry*.

Atoms are *real tiny*, don't forget. They're *too small to see*, even with a microscope.

## Number of Protons Equals Number of Electrons

1) Neutral atoms have *no charge* overall.
2) The *charge* on the electrons is the *same* size as the charge on the *protons* but *opposite*.
3) This means the *number* of *protons* always equals the *number* of *electrons* in a *neutral atom*.
4) If some electrons are *added or removed*, the atom becomes *charged* and is then an *ION*.
5) The number of neutrons isn't fixed but is usually just a bit *higher* than the number of protons.

## Know Your Particles

PROTONS are HEAVY and POSITIVELY CHARGED
NEUTRONS are HEAVY and NEUTRAL
ELECTRONS are *Tiny* and NEGATIVELY CHARGED

| PARTICLE | MASS | CHARGE |
|---|---|---|
| Proton | 1 | +1 |
| Neutron | 1 | 0 |
| Electron | 1/1840 | −1 |

## Atomic Number and Mass Number

**THE MASS NUMBER** — Total of Protons and Neutrons (sometimes referred to as A)

**THE ATOMIC NUMBER** — Number of Protons (sometimes called proton number, and referred to as Z)

$^{23}_{11}Na$

### POINTS TO NOTE
1) The *proton number* (or *atomic number*) tells you how many *protons* there are (oddly enough).
2) This *also* tells you how many *electrons* there are.
3) All atoms of the *same element* have the *same atomic number*.
4) Any atoms of two *different elements* will have *different atomic numbers*.
5) To get the number of *neutrons* — just *subtract* the *atomic number* from the *mass number*.
6) The *mass* number is always the *biggest* number. It tells you the relative mass of the atom.

## Basic Atom facts — they don't take up much space...

This stuff on atoms should be permanently engraved in the minds of everyone.
I don't understand how people can get through the day without knowing this stuff, really I don't.
**LEARN IT NOW**, and watch as the Universe unfolds and reveals its timeless mysteries to you...

# Electron Shells

**Atomic Structure**

The fact that electrons occupy "shells" around the nucleus is what causes the whole of chemistry. Remember that, and watch how it applies to each bit of it. It's ace.

## Electron Shell Rules:

1) Electrons always occupy *SHELLS* (sometimes called *ENERGY LEVELS*).
2) The *LOWEST* energy levels are *ALWAYS FILLED FIRST*.
3) Only *a certain number* of electrons are allowed in each shell:
   *1st shell:* 2    *2nd Shell:* 8    *3rd Shell:* 8
   (You don't need to know the numbers for the other shells)
4) Atoms are much *HAPPIER* when they have *FULL electron shells*.
5) In most atoms the *OUTER SHELL* is *NOT FULL* and this makes the atom want to *REACT*.
6) We always write the shell numbers with dots between them. So argon, with it's three full shells, is 2.8.8

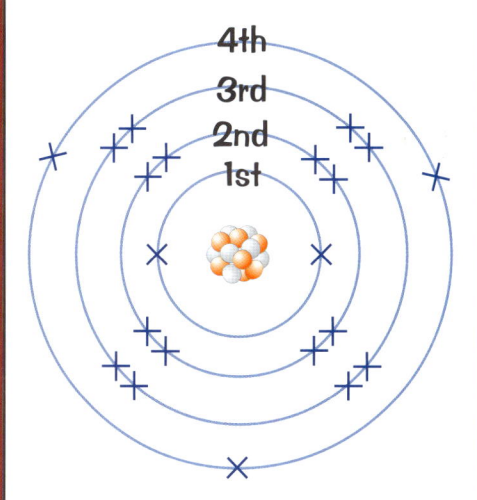

4th shell still filling

## Dot and Cross diagrams

A '*Dot and Cross*' diagram is a picture of the shells of two or more atoms, usually shown reacting. The *electrons* from one are drawn as *crosses*, and on the other are drawn as *dots*. Simple, huh? Here's an example:

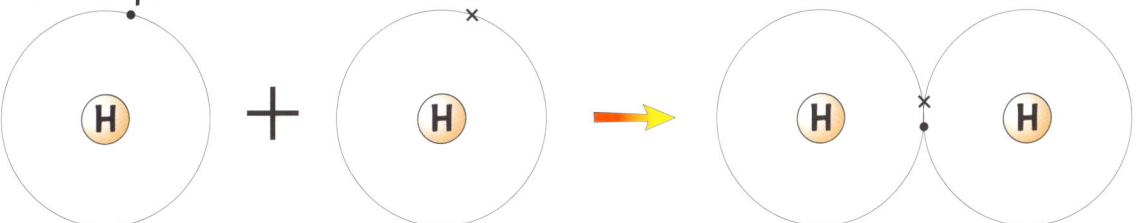

H + H → H H

## Working out Electron Configurations

You need to know the *electron configurations* for the first *20* elements. But they're not hard to work out. For a quick example, take nitrogen. *Follow the steps...*

1) The periodic table (see the inside front cover) tells us Nitrogen has *seven* protons... so it must have *seven* electrons.
2) Follow the "*Electron Shell Rules*" above. The *first* shell can only take 2 electrons and the *second* shell can take a *maximum* of 8 electrons.
3) So the electron configuration for nitrogen *must* be *2.5*. Easy peasy.
4) Now *you* try it for chlorine.

*Answer...* To calculate the electron configuration of chlorine, *follow the rules*. It's got 17 protons, so it *must* have 17 electrons. The first shell must have *2* electrons, the second shell must have *8*, and so there are *7* left for the third shell. It's as easy as *2.8.7*.

## Electrons rule...

There's some *really important stuff* on this page and you *really do* need to *learn all of it*. Once you have, it'll make all of the rest of the stuff in this book an awful lot *easier*. Practise calculating *electron configurations* and drawing *electron shell* diagrams.

MODULE THREE — STRUCTURE AND CHANGES                    SEG SYLLABUS

# The Periodic Table

## A Brief History of the Periodic Table

The early Chemists were keen to try to find patterns in the elements. The more elements they had that were identified, the easier it became to find patterns, of course.

A chap called Newlands had the first good stab at it, in 1863. He noticed that every eighth element had similar properties and so he listed some of the known elements in rows of seven.

In 1869, Dmitri Mendeleev arranged about 50 known elements into a table. Like Newlands, he put them in order of atomic mass (they didn't know about atomic number then), but his smart idea was to leave gaps to keep elements with similar properties in the same columns. Later on elements were discovered that fitted into the gaps — great news for Mendeleev. The old rogue.

## The Periodic Table is Ace

1) The modern Periodic Table shows the elements in order of proton number.
2) The Periodic Table is laid out so that elements with similar properties form columns.
3) These vertical columns are called Groups and Roman numerals are often used for them.
4) For example the Group II elements are Be, Mg, Ca, Sr, Ba and Ra.
   They're all metals which form 2+ ions and they have many other similar properties.
5) The rows are called periods. Each new period represents another full shell of electrons.

## The Elements of a Group Have the Same Outer Electrons

1) The elements in each Group all have the same number of electrons in their outer shell.
2) That's why they have similar properties. And that's why we arrange them in this way.
3) You absolutely must get that into your head if you want to understand any Chemistry.

The properties of the elements are decided entirely by how many electrons they have.
Atomic number is therefore very significant because it is equal to how many electrons each atom has.
But it's the number of electrons in the outer shell which is the really important thing.

## I can't see what all the fuss is — it all seems quite elementary...

Make sure you learn the whole periodic table including every name, symbol and number.
No, only kidding! Just learn the numbered points and scribble them down, mini-essay style.

SEG Syllabus — MODULE THREE — STRUCTURE AND CHANGES

# Group 0 — The Noble Gases

*Periodic Table*

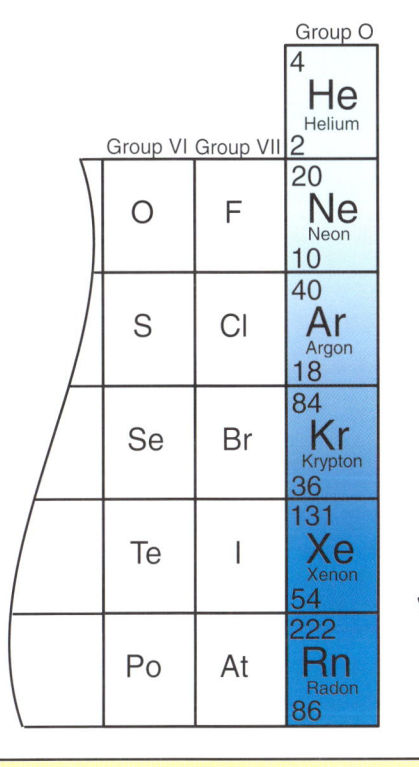

## As you go down the Group:

### 1) The density increases
because the atomic mass increases.

### 2) The boiling point increases
Helium boils at –269°C (that's cold!)
Xenon boils at –108°C (that's still cold)

## They all have full outer shells
— That's why they're so inert

## HELIUM, NEON AND ARGON ARE NOBLE GASES

There's also krypton, xenon and radon, which you may get asked about.
They're also sometimes called the inert gases. Inert means "doesn't react".

## THEY'RE ALL COLOURLESS, MONATOMIC GASES

Most gases are made up of molecules, but these only exist as individual atoms, because they won't form bonds with anything.

## THE NOBLE GASES DON'T REACT AT ALL

Helium, neon and argon don't form any kind of chemical bonds with anything. They always exist as separate atoms. They won't even join up in pairs.

## HELIUM IS USED IN AIRSHIPS AND PARTY BALLOONS

Helium is ideal: it has very low density and won't set on fire (like hydrogen does).

## NEON IS USED IN ELECTRICAL DISCHARGE TUBES

When a current is passed through neon it gives out a bright light.

## ARGON IS USED IN FILAMENT LAMPS (LIGHT BULBS)

It provides an inert atmosphere which stops the very hot filament from burning away.

## ALL THREE ARE USED IN LASERS TOO

There's the famous little red helium-neon laser and the more powerful argon laser.

## They don't react — that's Noble De-use to us Chemists...

Well they don't react so there's obviously not much to learn about these. Nevertheless, there's likely to be several questions on them so make sure you learn everything on this page.

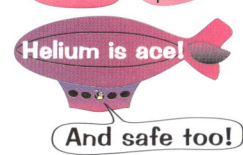

*MODULE THREE — STRUCTURE AND CHANGES*

*SEG SYLLABUS*

# Group I — The Alkali Metals

## Learn These Trends:

As you go **DOWN** Group I, the Alkali Metals become:

1) **Bigger atoms**
   ...because there's one extra full shell of electrons for each row you go down.

2) **Higher density**
   because the atoms have more mass.

3) **More Reactive**
   ...because the outer electron is more easily lost, because it's further from the nucleus.

4) Even **Softer** to cut
5) **Lower melting point**
6) **Lower boiling point**

| Group I | Group II |
|---|---|
| 7 Li Lithium 3 | Be |
| 23 Na Sodium 11 | Mg |
| 39 K Potassium 19 | Ca |
| 85.5 Rb Rubidium 37 | Sr |
| 133 Cs Caesium 55 | Ba |
| 223 Fr Francium 87 | Ra |

These **Group II** metals are quite similar to Group I, except that they have two electrons in the outer shell and form 2+ ions. They are less reactive.

### 1) The Alkali metals are very Reactive
They have to be *stored in oil* and handled with *forceps* (they burn the skin).

### 2) They are: Lithium, Sodium, Potassium and a couple more
Know those three names real well. They may also mention rubidium and caesium.

### 3) The Alkali Metals all have ONE outer electron
This makes them very *reactive* and gives them all similar properties.

### 4) The Alkali Metals all form 1⁺ ions
They are *keen to lose* their one outer electron to from a *1⁺ ion*:

### 5) The Alkali metals always form Ionic Compounds
They are so keen to lose the outer electron there's *no way* they'd consider *sharing*, so covalent bonding is *out of the question*.

### 6) The Alkali metals are soft — they cut with a knife
Lithium is the hardest, but still easy to cut with a scalpel.
They're *shiny* when freshly cut, but *soon go dull* as they react with the air.

### 7) The Alkali metals melt and boil easily (for metals)
Lithium melts at 180°C, caesium at 29°C. Lithium boils at 1330°C, caesium at 670°C.

### 8) The Alkali metals have low density (they float)
Lithium, sodium and potassium are all *less dense than water*. The others "*float*" anyway, on bubbles of the hydrogen gas they give off when they react with water.

## Learn about Alkali Metals — or get your fingers burnt...
Phew, now we're getting into the seriously dreary facts section. This takes a bit of learning this stuff does, especially those trends in behaviour as you go down the group. *Enjoy*.

# Reactions of the Alkali Metals

*Periodic Table*

## Reaction with Cold Water produces Hydrogen Gas

1) When *lithium*, *sodium* or *potassium* are put in *water*, they react very *vigorously*.
2) They *move* around the surface, *fizzing* furiously.
3) They produce *hydrogen*. Potassium gets hot enough to *ignite* it. A lighted splint will *indicate* hydrogen by producing the notorious "*squeaky pop*" as the $H_2$ ignites.
4) Sodium and potassium *melt* in the heat of the reaction.
5) They form a *hydroxide* in solution, i.e. *aqueous $OH^-$ ions*.

$$2Na_{(s)} + 2H_2O_{(l)} \rightarrow 2NaOH_{(aq)} + H_{2(g)}$$
$$2K_{(s)} + 2H_2O_{(l)} \rightarrow 2KOH_{(aq)} + H_{2(g)}$$

The solution becomes *alkaline*, which changes the colour of the pH indicator to *purple*.

## Reaction with Chlorine etc. to produce Neutral Salts

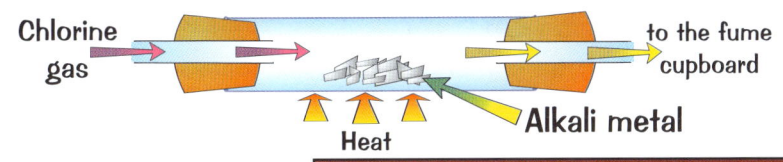

*Lithium*, *sodium* and *potassium* all react *very vigorously* with *chlorine* when *heated*. They produce chloride salts.

Learn these easy equations:

$$2Na_{(s)} + Cl_{2(g)} \rightarrow 2NaCl_{(s)} \quad \text{(sodium chloride)}$$
$$2K_{(s)} + Cl_{2(g)} \rightarrow 2KCl_{(s)} \quad \text{(potassium chloride)}$$

*Fluorine*, *bromine* and *iodine* produce similar salts. They all cheerfully *dissolve* in water.

## Alkali Metals burn in Air to produce Oxides

They all *burn in air* with *pretty coloured flames*:

*Lithium*: $\quad 4Li_{(s)} + O_{2(g)} \rightarrow 2Li_2O_{(s)} \quad$ (lithium oxide) — *Bright red* flame

*Sodium*: $\quad 4Na_{(s)} + O_{2(g)} \rightarrow 2Na_2O_{(s)} \quad$ (sodium oxide) — *Bright orange* flame

*Potassium*: $\quad 4K_{(s)} + O_{2(g)} \rightarrow 2K_2O_{(s)} \quad$ (potassium oxide) — *Bright lilac* flame

## Alkali Metal Oxides and Hydroxides are Alkaline

This means that they'll react with *acids* to form *neutral salts*, like this:

$$NaOH + HCl \rightarrow H_2O + NaCl \text{ (salt)}$$
$$Na_2O + 2HCl \rightarrow H_2O + 2NaCl \text{ (salt)}$$

## All Alkali Compounds look like 'Salt' and Dissolve with Glee

1) All alkali metal compounds are *ionic*, so they form *crystals* which *dissolve* easily.
2) They're all very *stable* because the alkali metals are so *reactive*.
3) Because they always form *ionic* compounds with *giant ionic lattices* the compounds *all* look pretty much like the regular '*salt*' you put in your chip butties.

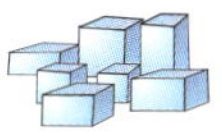

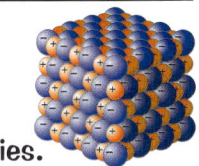

## The Notorious Squeaky Pop? — weren't they a Rock Band...

This stuff's pretty grisly isn't it. Still, if you keep covering the page and repeating bits back to yourself, or scribbling bits down, then little by little *it does go in*. Little by little. *Nicely*.

MODULE THREE — STRUCTURE AND CHANGES · SEG SYLLABUS

# Group VII — The Halogens

*Periodic Table*

## Learn These Trends:

As you go DOWN Group VII, the HALOGENS become:

1) **Bigger atoms**
   ...because there's one extra full shell of electrons for each row you go down.

2) **Less reactive**
   ..because there's less inclination to gain the extra electron to fill the outer shell when it's further out from the nucleus.

3) **Darker in colour**

4) **They go from gas to solid**
   Fluorine and chlorine are gases, bromine is a liquid, and iodine is a solid.

5) **Higher melting point**

6) **Higher boiling point**

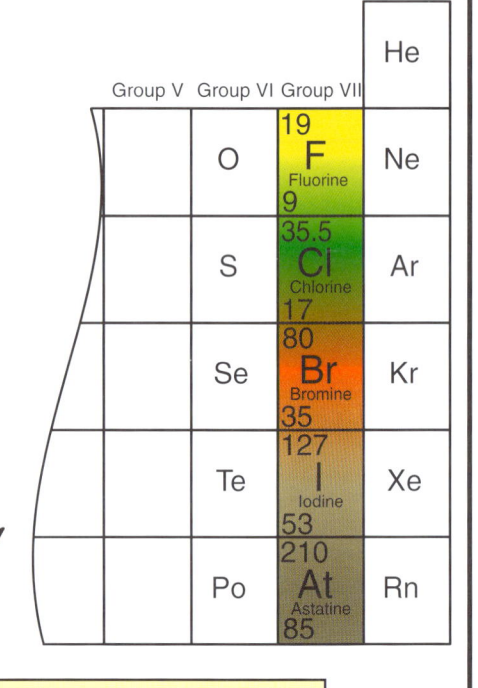

| Group V | Group VI | Group VII | Group 0 |
|---|---|---|---|
|  |  |  | He |
| O | 19 F Fluorine 9 | Ne |
| S | 35.5 Cl Chlorine 17 | Ar |
| Se | 80 Br Bromine 35 | Kr |
| Te | 127 I Iodine 53 | Xe |
| Po | 210 At Astatine 85 | Rn |

## 1) The Halogens are all non-metals with coloured vapours

Fluorine is a very reactive, poisonous yellow gas.
Chlorine is a fairly reactive poisonous dense green gas.
Bromine is a dense, poisonous, red-brown volatile liquid.
Iodine is a dark grey crystalline solid or a purple vapour.

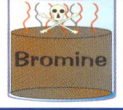

## 2) They all form molecules which are pairs of atoms:

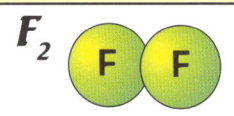

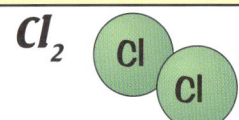

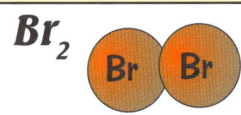

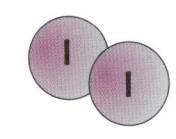

$F_2$   $Cl_2$   $Br_2$   $I_2$

## 3) The Halogens do both ionic and covalent bonding

The Halogens all form ions with a 1⁻ charge:   $F^-$  $Cl^-$  $Br^-$  $I^-$ as in $Na^+Cl^-$ or $Fe^{3+}Br_3^-$
They form covalent bonds with themselves and in various molecular compounds like these:

Carbon tetrachloride: ($CCl_4$)

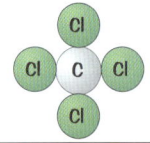

Hydrogen chloride: (HCl)

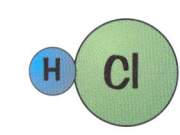

## 4) The Halogens are poisonous — always use a fume cupboard

What else can I say?  Use a fume cupboard, or else...

## I've never liked Halogens — they give me a bad head...

Well, I think Halogens are just slightly less grim than the Alkali metals.  At least they change colour and go from gases to liquid to solid.  *Learn the boring facts anyway.*   And smile ☺.

*SEG Syllabus*                    MODULE THREE — STRUCTURE AND CHANGES

# Reactions of the Halogens

*Periodic Table*

## 1) The Halogens react with metals to form salts

They react with most metals including *iron* and *aluminium*, to form *salts* (or "*metal halides*").

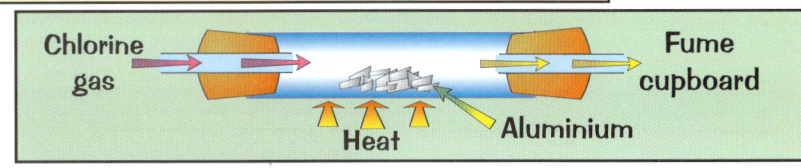

### Equations:

$$2Al_{(s)} + 3Cl_{2(g)} \rightarrow 2AlCl_{3(s)} \quad \text{(Aluminium chloride)}$$

$$2Fe_{(s)} + 3Br_{2(g)} \rightarrow 2FeBr_{3(s)} \quad \text{(Iron(III) bromide)}$$

### Chloride, Bromide and Iodide salts are sorted using Silver Nitrate

Metal halide salts like the ones above are *ionic* so they usually *dissolve*.
However, the *SILVER* halide salts are *not* soluble and this gives a good *test* for the *three* halides:

1) Adding *silver nitrate* to a *chloride* produces a *white* precipitate (of *silver chloride*).
2) Adding *silver nitrate* to a *bromide* produces a *creamy-coloured* precipitate (of *silver bromide*).
3) Adding *silver nitrate* to an *iodide* produces a *yellow* precipitate (of *silver iodide*).

## 2) More reactive Halogens will displace less reactive ones

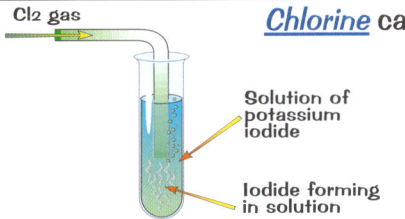

*Chlorine* can displace *bromine* and *iodine* from a solution of *bromide* or *iodide*.
*Bromine* will also displace *iodine* because of the *trend* in *reactivity*.

$$Cl_{2(g)} + 2KI_{(aq)} \rightarrow I_{2(aq)} + 2KCl_{(aq)}$$
$$Cl_{2(g)} + 2KBr_{(aq)} \rightarrow Br_{2(aq)} + 2KCl_{(aq)}$$

## 3) Hydrogen Chloride gas dissolves to form HCl acid

1) *Hydrogen chloride* is a *diatomic* molecule, (a two atom molecule) held together by a *covalent* bond.
2) It has a *simple molecular* structure.
3) It is a *dense, colourless gas* with a choking smell.
4) Gaseous hydrogen chloride is important in the manufacture of *polymers*.
5) It *dissolves* in water, which is very unusual for a covalent substance, to form the well-known strong acid, *hydrochloric acid*.
6) The *proper* method for dissolving hydrogen chloride in water is to use an *inverted funnel* as shown:
7) HCl gas *reacts with water* to produce *$H^+$ ions*, which is what makes it *acidic*:

$$HCl_{(g)} \xrightarrow{water} H^+_{(aq)} + Cl^-_{(aq)}$$

### Hydrogen Bromide and Hydrogen Iodide do the same

Just like hydrogen chloride, these two *gases* will also *dissolve easily* to form *strong acids*:

$$HBr_{(g)} \rightarrow H^+_{(aq)} + Br^-_{(aq)} \qquad HI_{(g)} \rightarrow H^+_{(aq)} + I^-_{(aq)}$$

## Salts and Acids — what an unsavoury combination...

More exciting reactions to delight and entertain you through the shove and shuffle of your otherwise dreary teenage years. Think of all the poor third-world children who never get to learn about chloride salts and hydrogen bromide — you're very lucky. *Learn and enjoy*...

MODULE THREE — STRUCTURE AND CHANGES · SEG SYLLABUS

# The Reactivity Series of Metals

## You must learn about this Reactivity Series

You really should know which are the more reactive metals and which are the less reactive ones.

**THE REACTIVITY SERIES**

| Reactivity | Metal | Symbol |
|---|---|---|
| Very Reactive | POTASSIUM | K |
| | SODIUM | Na |
| | CALCIUM | Ca |
| Fairly Reactive | MAGNESIUM | Mg |
| | ALUMINIUM | Al |
| | (CARBON) | |
| | ZINC | Zn |
| | IRON | Fe |
| Not very Reactive | LEAD | Pb |
| | (HYDROGEN) | |
| | COPPER | Cu |
| Not at all Reactive | SILVER | Ag |
| | GOLD | Au |
| | PLATINUM | Pt |

Metals *above carbon* must be extracted from their ores by *electrolysis*.

Metals *below carbon* can be extracted from their ore by *reduction* with *coke or charcoal*.

Metals *below hydrogen* don't react with *water* or *acid*. They don't easily *tarnish* or *corrode*.

This *reactivity series* was determined by doing experiments to see how *strongly* metals *react*. The *standard reactions* to determine reactivity are with:
1) *oxygen* (i.e. in air)  2) *water*  and  3) *dilute hydrochloric* or *sulphuric acid*.

These are *important* so make sure you know about all three in reasonable detail, as follows:

## Reacting Metals in Air

1) *Most metals* will lose their *bright surface* over a period of time (they "tarnish").
2) The *dull* finish they get is due to a layer of *oxide* that forms.
3) *Heating them* makes it easier to see how *reactive* they are, compared to each other.
4) The equation is *real simple*:

**Metal + Oxygen → Metal Oxide**

## Reaction with Air

| Metals | Reaction |
|---|---|
| POTASSIUM, SODIUM, CALCIUM, MAGNESIUM | Burn very easily with a bright flame |
| ALUMINIUM, ZINC, IRON, LEAD, COPPER | React slowly with air when heated |
| SILVER, GOLD | No reaction |

Examples:  1) $2Fe + O_2 \rightarrow 2FeO$    2) $4Na + O_2 \rightarrow 2Na_2O$

## How to get a good reaction — just smile ... ☺

Believe it or not they could easily give you a question asking what happens when copper is heated in air, and when calcium is heated in air. That means *all these details need learning*.

*SEG Syllabus* — MODULE THREE — STRUCTURE AND CHANGES

# Reactivity of Metals

**Reactivity Series**

## Reacting Metals With *Water*

1) If a _metal_ reacts with _water_ it will always release _hydrogen_.
2) The _more reactive_ metals react with _cold water_ to form _hydroxides_:

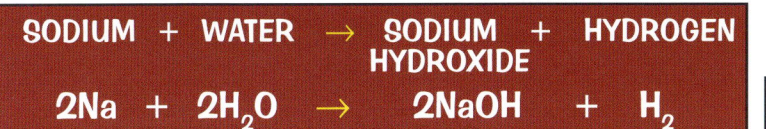

SODIUM + WATER → SODIUM HYDROXIDE + HYDROGEN
$2Na + 2H_2O → 2NaOH + H_2$

3) The _less reactive_ metals don't react quickly with water but _will_ react with _steam_ to form _oxides_:

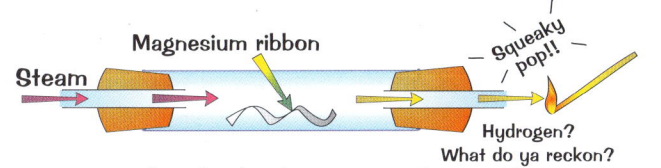

You can _test_ for the hydrogen gas by putting a _lighted splint_ into the gas. If it is hydrogen, you will hear a _squeaky pop_.

ZINC + WATER → ZINC OXIDE + HYDROGEN
$Zn + H_2O → ZnO + H_2$

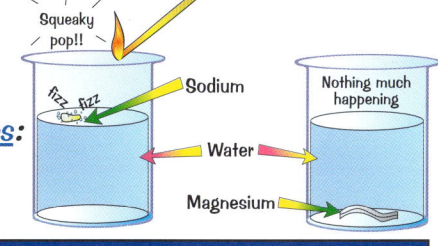

### Reaction with Water

| POTASSIUM, SODIUM, CALCIUM | React with cold water |
| MAGNESIUM, ALUMINIUM, ZINC | React with steam |
| IRON | Reacts reversibly with steam |
| LEAD, COPPER, SILVER, GOLD | No reaction with water or steam |

## Reacting Metals With *Dilute Acid*

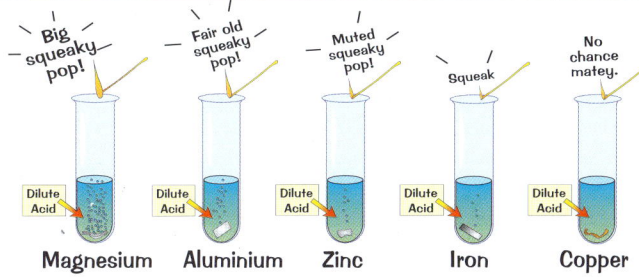

Magnesium — Big squeaky pop!
Aluminium — Fair old squeaky pop!
Zinc — Muted squeaky pop!
Iron — Squeak
Copper — No chance matey.

1) Metals _above_ hydrogen in the reactivity series react with _acids_. Those _below_ hydrogen _won't_.
2) The reaction becomes _slower_ as you go _down the series_ — as you'd _expect_.
3) The equation is real simple:

METAL + ACID → SALT + HYDROGEN
$Mg + 2HCl → MgCl_2 + H_2$
$Mg + H_2SO_4 → MgSO_4 + H_2$

### Reaction with Dilute Acid

| POTASSIUM, SODIUM, CALCIUM | Violent reaction with dilute acids |
| MAGNESIUM, ALUMINIUM, ZINC, IRON | React fairly well with dilute acids |
| LEAD, COPPER, SILVER, GOLD | No reaction with dilute acids |

## These reactions with water and acids are "Competition Reactions"

1) If the metal is _more reactive_ than _hydrogen_ it pushes the hydrogen _out_, hence the _bubbles_.
2) If the metal is _less reactive_ than hydrogen, then it _won't_ be able to displace it and _nothing will happen_.

## All this just to say "some metals react more than others"...

I must say there's quite a lot of tricky details in these two pages. It's tempting to say that they can't possibly expect you to know them all. But then you look at the Exam questions and there they are, asking you precisely these kind of tricky details. Tough toffee, pal. _Learn and enjoy_.

MODULE THREE — STRUCTURE AND CHANGES         SEG SYLLABUS

# Metal Displacement Reactions

**Reactivity Series**

There's only one _golden rule_ here:

> A **MORE** reactive metal will **displace**
> a **LESS** reactive metal from a compound

1) You know all about the reactivity series — some metals react _more strongly_ than _others_.
2) So if you put a _reactive_ metal like magnesium in a chemical solution you'd expect it to react.
3) If the chemical solution is a _dissolved metal compound_, then the reactive metal that you add will _replace_ the _less_ reactive metal in the compound.
4) The metal that's _"kicked out"_ will then appear as _fresh metal_ somewhere in the solution.
5) But if the metal added is _less reactive_ than the one in solution, then _no reaction_ will take place.
6) So if someone comes up to you in the street and asks what would happen if you mixed _magnesium_ with _iron oxide_ in a solution, you'd know that the magnesium would steal the oxygen from the iron, giving you _magnesium oxide_, and _iron_.

## The (Virtually) World Famous Iron Nail in Copper Sulphate demo

**A _MORE_ REACTIVE METAL WILL _DISPLACE_ A _LESS_ REACTIVE METAL:**

1) Put an _iron_ nail in a solution of _copper(II) sulphate_ and you'll see _two_ things happen:

   a) The iron nail will become coated with _copper_.
   b) The _blue_ solution will turn _colourless_.

2) This is because the iron is _more_ reactive than the copper and _displaces_ it from the solution.
3) This produces _fresh copper metal_ on the nail and a _colourless_ solution of _iron sulphate_.

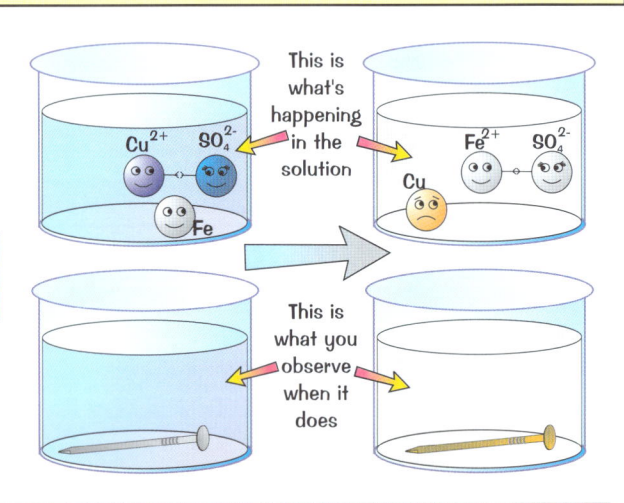

**YOU'LL ALWAYS SEE A _DEPOSIT OF METAL_ AND POSSIBLY A _COLOUR CHANGE_:**

The equation is very, very easy:

> iron + copper sulphate → iron sulphate + copper
> Fe + $CuSO_4$ → $FeSO_4$ + Cu

## There are lots of different examples, but they're all the same...

Just remember the _golden rule_ at the top of the page, and you can't go wrong.
The equations are always _simple_. The only tricky bit comes if the metals aren't both _2+ ions_ like in this one:

> zinc + silver nitrate → zinc nitrate + silver
> Zn + $2AgNO_3$ → $Zn(NO_3)_2$ + 2Ag

But remember, if the metal added is _less_ reactive, nothing will happen.
For example if you add _iron_ to _magnesium sulphate_ there'll be **NO REACTION**.

---

## Even atoms squabble — and I thought it was only school kids...

This is simple enough. Just make sure you learn all the little details. Then cover the page and scribble down a _mini-essay_ of the main points. Then see what you missed. _Then try again._

_SEG Syllabus_    MODULE THREE — STRUCTURE AND CHANGES

# Corrosion of Metals

**Reactivity Series**

*Reactive metals* will form *oxides* quite *quickly* when *exposed to the air*.
*Most metals* form quite decent *hard oxides* that form a good *protective layer*.
　The most *important* example of that is *aluminium*. It rapidly forms *aluminium oxide* which is a *very tough coating*, and barely visible. This *appears* to make aluminium very *unreactive*, even in the lab. But *scrub off the oxide* and stick it in *acid* and then you'll see how *reactive* aluminium *really is*.

　But *iron*, woe of woes, does *no such thing*. No, iron has to form the most appalling *red flaky oxide* imaginable — the metal we use the *most* just had to be the one that turns to *horrible useless rust*. When God invented all the elements I bet he had a good old cackle to himself over that one.

## The Rusting of Iron requires both Air and Water

The *classic experiment* on rust is to put *iron nails* in various test tubes to see *how quickly* they rust.

The *rusting is quickest* where there is most *air and water* reaching the iron nail.
If *either* air or water is *totally absent* there'll be *no rusting at all*.

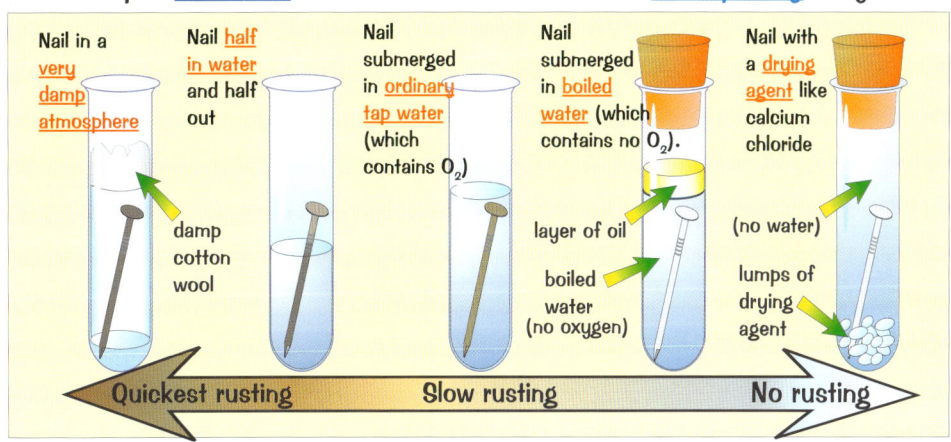

- Nail in a *very damp atmosphere* — damp cotton wool
- Nail *half in water* and half out
- Nail submerged in *ordinary tap water* (which contains $O_2$)
- Nail submerged in *boiled water* (which contains no $O_2$) — layer of oil, boiled water (no oxygen)
- Nail with a *drying agent* like calcium chloride — (no water), lumps of drying agent

Quickest rusting ← Slow rusting → No rusting

## More Reactive Metals Corrode faster

OK, so iron rusts *quickly*. But lead doesn't corrode very much. Yet a magnesium statue would be gone before you could say 'Coordination Group makes the best revision guides in the world'.
In fact the more *reactive* a metal is, the *faster* it corrodes.
It's not surprising — reactivity is just how easily a metal reacts, and corrosion is a reaction.

## Rust is prevented by paint, oil or galvanising

1) *Painting* is OK but where the *paint surface* gets *damaged*, rust will get a grip and *spread*.
2) A coating of *oil or grease* is better on bits of *moving machinery* or on tools.
   However the oil has to be *constantly re-applied* because it soon wears or washes off.

## Galvanising gives great protection even when damaged

1) *Galvanising* is the *best solution* to rust prevention but it's more expensive.
   Galvanising is a process that *bonds a layer of zinc metal* onto the surface of the *steel*.
   The zinc soon *reacts* with the air to form *zinc oxide* which gives a good *protective layer*.
2) The *big advantage* with galvanisation is that even if the zinc coating gets *scratched* or *damaged*, the exposed steel will *still not rust*! The zinc will react *instead* of the iron.
3) This is known as *sacrificial protection*. A *more* reactive metal in good contact with a *less* reactive metal will always *react first*, thereby *protecting* the less reactive metal from corrosion.
4) *Iron boats* often have a lump of *magnesium* bolted to their hulls which works in the same way. The *magnesium* turns to *magnesium oxide* rather than the iron turning to *rust*. Easy peasy.

## Rust! Yeah, very funny, ho ho ho — but what about my little MGB...

At last! A page that has some relevance to everyday life. Who said you never learn anything useful at school. Not too much to learn here either. Try a couple of *mini-essays* and make sure you can draw all those pretty test tubes too. *Then check back and see what you missed*.

MODULE THREE — STRUCTURE AND CHANGES　　　SEG SYLLABUS

# Acids and Alkalis

*Acids & Bases*

## The pH Scale and Universal Indicator

pH is a *measure* of the *acidity* or *alkalinity* of an aqueous solution.

pH  1  2  3  4  5  6  7  8  9  10  11  12  13  14

← **ACIDS** — **NEUTRAL** — **ALKALIS** →

- car battery acid, stomach acid
- vinegar, lemon juice
- acid rain, normal rain
- tap water, milk
- pancreatic juice, washing up liquid
- soap powder
- ammonia

## An Indicator is just a Dye that changes colour

The dye changes *colour* depending on whether it's in an *acid* or in an *alkali*.
*Universal indicator* is a very useful combination of dyes which give the colours shown above.

## The pH scale goes from 1 to 14

1) The *strongest acid* has *pH 1*.   The *strongest alkali* has *pH 14*.
2) If something is *neutral* it has *pH 7* (e.g. pure water).
3) Anything less than 7 is *acid*. Anything more than 7 is *alkaline*. (An alkali can also be called a base.)

## Neutralisation

This is the equation for *any* neutralisation reaction. Make sure you learn it:

**Acid + alkali → salt + water**

## Acids have H⁺ ions    Alkalis have OH⁻ ions

The *strict definitions* of acids and alkalis are:

> *ACIDS* are substances which form $H^+_{(aq)}$ *ions* when added to *water*.
> *ALKALIS* are substances which form $OH^-_{(aq)}$ *ions* when added to *water*.

Neutralisation can also be seen *in terms of ions* like this, so learn it too:

$$H^+_{(aq)} + OH^-_{(aq)} \rightarrow H_2O_{(l)}$$

*(Higher)*

## Three "Real life" Examples of Neutralisation:

1) *Indigestion* is caused by too much *hydrochloric acid* in the stomach.
   Indigestion tablets contain *alkalis* such as *magnesium oxide*, which *neutralise* the excess HCl.
2) *Fields* with *acidic soils* can be improved no end by adding *lime*.
   The lime added to fields is *calcium hydroxide* $Ca(OH)_2$ which is of course an *alkali*.
3) *Lakes* affected by *acid rain* can also be *neutralised* by adding *lime*. This saves the fish.

## Hey man, like "acid", yeah — eeuuucch...

Try and enjoy this page on acids and alkalis, because it gets *really* tedious from now on. These are very basic facts and possibly quite interesting. *Cover the page and scribble them down.*

*SEG Syllabus*    MODULE THREE — STRUCTURE AND CHANGES

# Acids with Metals and Oxides

*Acids & Bases*

## Acid + Metal → Salt + Hydrogen

That's written big 'cos it's kinda worth remembering. Here's the *typical experiment*:

1) The *more reactive* the metal, the *faster* it will go.
2) *Copper* does *not* react with dilute acids *at all* — because it's *less reactive than hydrogen*.
3) The *speed of reaction* is indicated by the *rate* at which the *bubbles of hydrogen* are given off.
4) The *hydrogen* is confirmed by the *burning splint test* giving the notorious "*squeaky pop*".
5) The *type of salt* produced depends on which *metal* is used, and which *acid* is used:

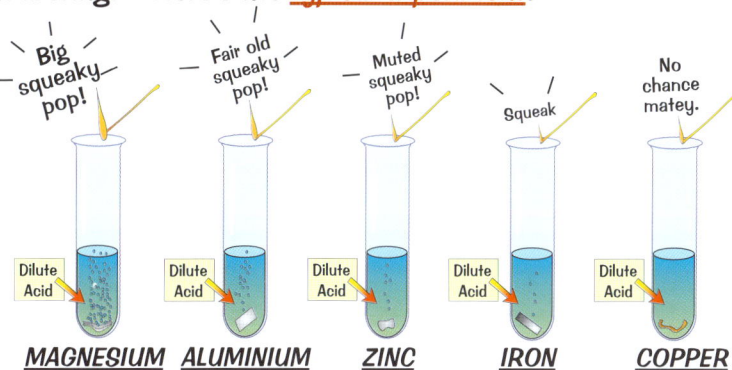

Big squeaky pop! — MAGNESIUM
Fair old squeaky pop! — ALUMINIUM
Muted squeaky pop! — ZINC
Squeak — IRON
No chance matey. — COPPER

### Hydrochloric acid will always produce chloride salts:

$2HCl + Mg \rightarrow MgCl_2 + H_2$ (Magnesium chloride)
$6HCl + 2Al \rightarrow 2AlCl_3 + 3H_2$ (Aluminium chloride)
$2HCl + Zn \rightarrow ZnCl_2 + H_2$ (Zinc chloride)

### Sulphuric acid will always produce sulphate salts:

$H_2SO_4 + Mg \rightarrow MgSO_4 + H_2$ (Magnesium sulphate)
$3H_2SO_4 + 2Al \rightarrow Al_2(SO_4)_3 + 3H_2$ (Aluminium sulphate)
$H_2SO_4 + Zn \rightarrow ZnSO_4 + H_2$ (Zinc sulphate)

## Metal Oxides and Metal Hydroxides are Alkalis

1) Some *metal oxides* and *metal hydroxides* dissolve in *water* to produce *alkaline* solutions.
2) In other words, metal oxides and metal hydroxides are generally *alkalis*.
3) This means they'll *react with acids* to form a *salt* and *water*.
4) Even those that won't dissolve in water will still react with acid.

## The Combination of Metal and Acid decides the Salt

This isn't exactly exciting but it's pretty easy, so try and get the hang of it:

| | | | | | |
|---|---|---|---|---|---|
| Hydrochloric acid | + | Copper oxide | → | Copper chloride | + water |
| Sulphuric acid | + | Zinc oxide | → | Zinc sulphate | + water |
| Nitric acid | + | Magnesium oxide | → | Magnesium nitrate | + water |

The symbol equations are all pretty much the same. Here's two of them:

$H_2SO_4 + ZnO \rightarrow ZnSO_4 + H_2O$
$HNO_3 + KOH \rightarrow KNO_3 + H_2O$

## Revision of Acids and Metals — easy as squeaky pop...

Actually, this stuff isn't too bad I don't think. I mean it's *fairly* interesting. Not quite in the same league as the Spice Girls, I grant you, but for Chemistry it's not bad at all. At least there's bubbles and flames and noise and that kinda thing. Anyway, *learn it, scribble it down, etc*...

MODULE THREE — STRUCTURE AND CHANGES    SEG SYLLABUS

# Acids with Carbonates and Ammonia

*Acids & Bases*

More gripping reactions involving acids. At least there's some bubbles involved here.

## Acid + Carbonate → Salt + Water + Carbon dioxide

hydrochloric acid + sodium carbonate → sodium chloride + water + carbon dioxide
$2HCl + Na_2CO_3 → 2NaCl + H_2O + CO_2$

sulphuric acid + sodium carbonate → sodium sulphate + water + carbon dioxide
$H_2SO_4 + Na_2CO_3 → Na_2SO_4 + H_2O + CO_2$

*Higher Higher Higher*

## Acid + Hydrogencarbonate → Salt + Water + Carbon dioxide

hydrochloric acid + sodium hydrogencarbonate → sodium chloride + water + carbon dioxide
$HCl + NaHCO_3 → NaCl + H_2O + CO_2$

sulphuric acid + sodium hydrogencarbonate → sodium sulphate + water + carbon dioxide
$H_2SO_4 + 2NaHCO_3 → Na_2SO_4 + 2H_2O + 2CO_2$

1) *Definitely* learn the fact that *carbonates* (and for you higher people *hydrogencarbonates*) give off *carbon dioxide*.
2) If you also *practise* writing the above equations out *from memory*, it'll do you no harm at all.

## Dilute Acid + Ammonia → Ammonium salt

Learn that, then learn these three equations till you can write them out yourself, *from memory*:

Hydrochloric acid + Ammonia → Ammonium chloride
$HCl_{(aq)} + NH_{3\,(aq)} → NH_4Cl_{(aq)}$

Sulphuric acid + Ammonia → Ammonium sulphate
$H_2SO_{4\,(aq)} + 2NH_{3\,(aq)} → (NH_4)_2SO_{4\,(aq)}$

Nitric acid + Ammonia → Ammonium nitrate
$HNO_{3\,(aq)} + NH_{3\,(aq)} → NH_4NO_{3\,(aq)}$

This last reaction with nitric acid produces the famous *ammonium nitrate* fertiliser, much appreciated for its *double dose* of essential nitrogen.

## Still Awake, eh? — learning this page should finish you off...

Phew, the last page on acids, thank goodness. *Learn* the last of these dreary facts and try to *scribble it down*. (If there's an Acid Appreciation Action Group, they're sure gonna be after me.)

*SEG Syllabus* — *Module Three — Structure and Changes*

# Rates of Reaction

*Reaction Rates*

## Reactions can go at all sorts of different rates

1) One of the <u>slowest</u> is the <u>rusting</u> of iron (it's not slow enough though — what about my little MGB).
2) A <u>moderate speed</u> reaction is a <u>metal</u> (like magnesium) reacting with <u>acid</u> to produce a <u>gentle stream of bubbles</u>.
3) A <u>really fast</u> reaction is an <u>explosion</u>, where it's all over in a <u>fraction of a second</u>.

## Three ways to Measure the Speed of a Reaction

The <u>speed of reaction</u> can be observed <u>either</u> by how quickly the <u>reactants are used up</u> or how quickly the <u>products are forming</u>. It's usually a lot easier to measure <u>products forming</u>. There are <u>three different ways</u> that the speed of a reaction can be <u>measured</u>:

### 1) Precipitation

This is when the <u>product</u> of the reaction is a <u>precipitate</u> which <u>clouds the solution</u>. Observe a <u>marker</u> through the solution and measure <u>how long it takes</u> for it to <u>disappear</u>.

### 2) Change in mass (usually gas given off)

Any reaction that <u>produces a gas</u> can be carried out on a <u>mass balance</u> and as the gas is released the mass <u>disappearing</u> is easily measured.

### 3) The volume of gas given off

This involves the use of a <u>gas syringe</u> to measure the volume of gas given off. But that's about all there is to it.

## The Rate of a Reaction Depends on Four Things:

1) <u>TEMPERATURE</u>
2) <u>CONCENTRATION</u> — (or <u>PRESSURE</u> for gases)
3) <u>CATALYST</u>
4) <u>SIZE OF PARTICLES</u> — (or <u>SURFACE AREA</u>)

**LEARN THEM!**

## Typical Graphs for Rate of Reaction

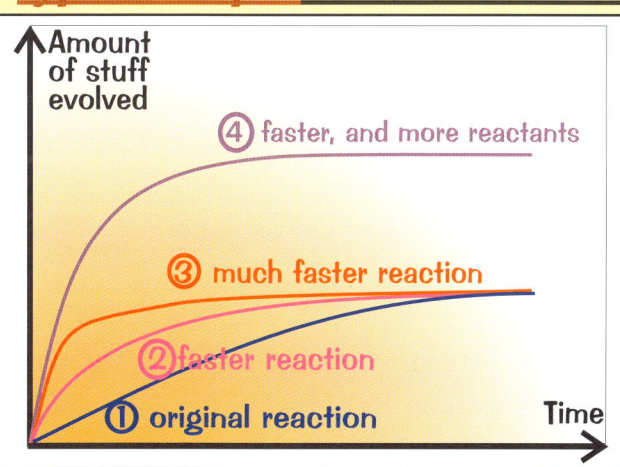

- ④ faster, and more reactants
- ③ much faster reaction
- ② faster reaction
- ① original reaction

(Amount of stuff evolved vs Time)

1) <u>Graph 1</u> represents the original <u>fairly slow</u> reaction.
2) <u>Graphs 2 and 3</u> represent the reaction taking place <u>quicker</u> but with the <u>same initial amounts</u>.
3) The <u>increased rate</u> could be due to <u>any</u> of these:
   a) increase in <u>temperature</u>
   b) increase in <u>concentration</u> (or pressure)
   c) <u>catalyst</u> added
   d) solid reactant crushed up into <u>smaller bits</u>.
4) <u>Graph 4</u> produces <u>more product</u> as well as going <u>quicker</u>. This can <u>only</u> happen if <u>more reactant(s)</u> are added at the start.

## How to get a fast, furious reaction — crack a wee joke...

There's all sorts of bits and bobs of information on this page. To learn it all, you've got to learn to split it up into separate sections and do them one at a time. Practise by <u>covering the page</u> and seeing how much you can <u>scribble down</u> for each section. <u>Then try again, and again...</u>

*MODULE THREE — STRUCTURE AND CHANGES*          *SEG SYLLABUS*

# Collision Theory

**Reaction Rates**

*Reaction rates* are explained perfectly by *Collision Theory*. It's really simple. It just says that *the rate of a reaction* simply depends on *how often* and *how hard* the reacting particles *collide* with each other. The basic idea is that particles have to *collide* in order to *react*, and they have to collide *hard enough* as well.

## More Collisions increase the Rate of Reaction

All *four* methods of increasing the *rate of reactions* can be *explained* in terms of increasing the *number of collisions* between the reacting particles;

### 1) TEMPERATURE increases the number of collisions

When the *temperature is increased* the particles all *move quicker*. If they're moving quicker, they're going to have *more collisions*.

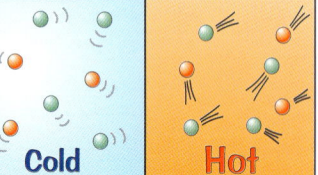

### 2) CONCENTRATION (or PRESSURE) increases the number of collisions

If the solution is made more *concentrated* it means there are more particles of *reactant* knocking about *between the water molecules* which makes collisions between the *important* particles *more likely*. In a *gas*, increasing the *pressure* means the molecules are *more squashed up* together so there are going to be *more collisions*.

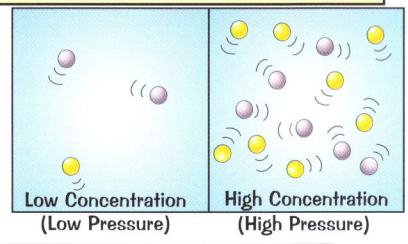

### 3) SIZE OF SOLID PARTICLES (or SURFACE AREA) increases collisions

If one of the reactants is a *solid* then *breaking it up* into *smaller* pieces will *increase its surface area*. This means the particles around it in the solution will have *more area to work on* so there'll be *more useful collisions*.

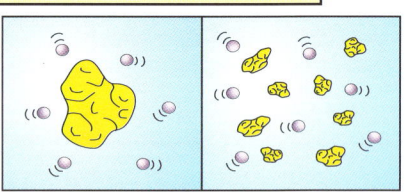

### 4) A CATALYST increases the number of collisions

A *catalyst* is a substance that *speeds up* the rate of a reaction without being used up itself. They work by giving the *reacting particles* a *surface* to *stick to* where they can *bump* into each other. This obviously increases the *number of collisions* too.

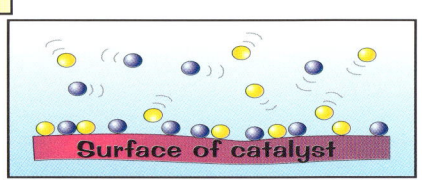

## Faster Collisions increase the Rate of Reaction

*Higher temperature* also increases the *energy* of the collisions, because it makes all the particles *move faster*.

### Faster collisions are ONLY caused by increasing the temperature

Reactions *only happen* if the particles collide with *enough energy*. At a *higher temperature* there will be *more particles* colliding with *enough energy* to make the reaction happen. This *initial energy* is known as the *activation energy*, and it's needed to *break the initial bonds*.

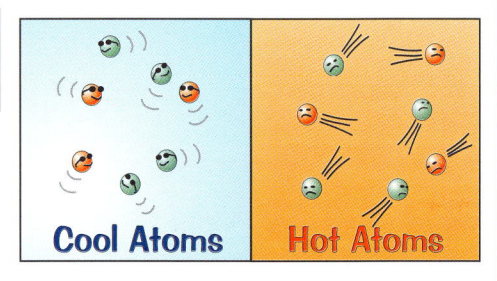

## Collision Theory — I reckon it's always women drivers...

This is quite easy I think. Isn't it all kind of obvious — at least once you've been told it, anyway. The more often particles collide and the harder they hit, the greater the reaction rate. There's a few extra picky details of course (isn't there always!), *but you've only got to LEARN them...*

*SEG Syllabus* — *MODULE THREE — STRUCTURE AND CHANGES*

# Rate of Reaction Experiments

*Reaction Rates*

*REMEMBER:* *Any reaction* can be used to investigate *any* of the four factors that affect the *rate*. (Except if there's no solid, you can't check the effect of the size of the particles of a solid — obviously.)

## 1) Reaction of Hydrochloric Acid and Marble Chips

This experiment is often used to demonstrate the effect of *breaking* the solid up into *small bits*.
1) Measure the *volume* of gas evolved with a *gas syringe* and take readings at *regular intervals*.
2) Make a *table of readings* and plot them as a *graph*.
3) *Repeat* the experiment with *exactly the same* volume of *acid*, and *exactly the same* mass of *marble* chips, but with the marble *more crunched up*.
4) Then *repeat* with the same mass of *powdered chalk* instead of marble chips.

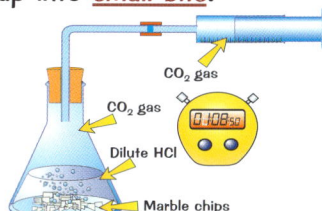

### This graph shows the effect of using finer particles of solid

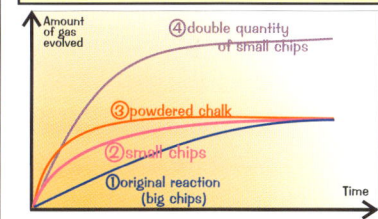

1) The increase in *surface area* causes *more collisions* so the rate of reaction is *faster*.
2) *Line 4* shows the reaction if a *greater mass* of small marble chips is added.
3) The *extra surface area* gives a *quicker reaction* and there is also *more gas evolved* overall.

## 2) Sodium Thiosulphate and HCl produce a Cloudy Precipitate

1) These two chemicals are both *clear solutions*.
2) They react together to form a *yellow precipitate* of *sulphur*.
3) The experiment involves watching a black mark *disappear* through the *cloudy sulphur* and *timing* how long it takes to go, *repeating* for solutions at different *temperatures*.
4) The *depth* of liquid must be kept the *same* each time, of course.
5) The results will of course show that the *higher* the temperature the *quicker* the reaction and therefore the *less time* it takes for the mark to *disappear*. These are typical results:

| Temperature | 20°C | 25°C | 30°C | 35°C | 40°C |
|---|---|---|---|---|---|
| Time taken for mark to disappear | 193s | 151s | 112s | 87s | 52s |

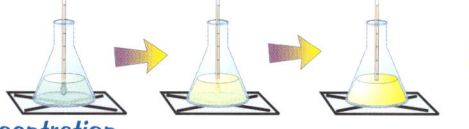

This reaction can *also* be used to test the effects of *concentration*.
One sad thing about this reaction is it *doesn't* give a set of graphs. Well *I* think it's sad. All you get is a set of *readings* of how long it took till the mark disappeared for each temperature. Boring.

## 3) The Decomposition of Hydrogen Peroxide

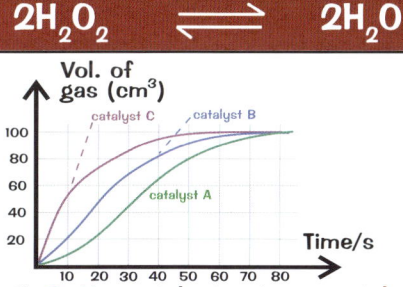

$$2H_2O_2 \rightleftharpoons 2H_2O + O_2$$

1) This is normally quite *slow* but a sprinkle of *manganese(IV) oxide catalyst* speeds it up no end.
2) *Oxygen gas* is given off which provides an *ideal way* to measure the rate of reaction using the good ol' *gas syringe* method.

You can check that the gas is oxygen with the old *glowing splint* test. Oxygen will *relight* a splint that's just been blown out. Neat, huh?

1) *Better* catalysts give a *quicker reaction* which is shown by a *steeper graph* which levels off quickly.
2) This reaction can also be used to measure the effects of *temperature*, or of *concentration* of the $H_2O_2$ solution. The graphs will look just the same.

## Top rate reactions — learn and enjoy...

There's always so much happening with reaction rates. Is it products or reactants we're looking at? Are we measuring gas, or mass, or cloudiness? Is it the effect of temp. or conc. or catalyst or surface area we're investigating? There's so much going on, *but you'll just have to sort it all out and learn it*.

MODULE THREE — STRUCTURE AND CHANGES

SEG Syllabus

# Crude Oil

**Useful Products from Oil**

## Fossil Fuels were formed from dead plants and animals

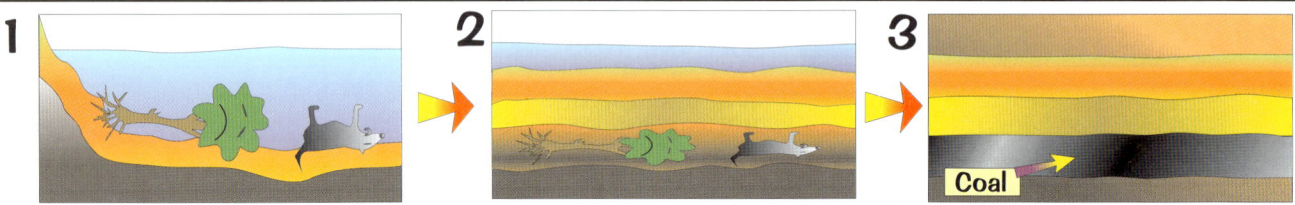

*Millions of years of heat and pressure*

1) Millions of years ago plants and animals _died_ and were _immediately_ covered by _sediment_.
2) This _stopped_ them decaying.
3) Further layers of sediment buried the plant and animal remains _deeper_ and _deeper_.
4) After _millions_ of years of _pressure and heat_ (90°C to 120°C), in an environment with no air, these remains turned into _COAL_, _OIL_ and _NATURAL GAS_.
5) _Coal_ comes mainly from _dead plants_, like trees, falling into swamps.
6) _Oil_ and _gas_ occur _together_ and were formed from _both plants_ and _animals_ being buried.
7) These three are limited, _non-renewable_ resources. More fossil fuels are being made, but very, very slowly. We're gonna run out sometime.
8) Some care has to be taken whilst extracting and transporting oil, — an oil spill can have some _pretty serious consequences_ to the environment. Oil slicks on the sea can stick the feathers of sea-birds together, so they can't fly. This can mean they _die_.

## Crude Oil is Split into Separate Hydrocarbons (fuels)

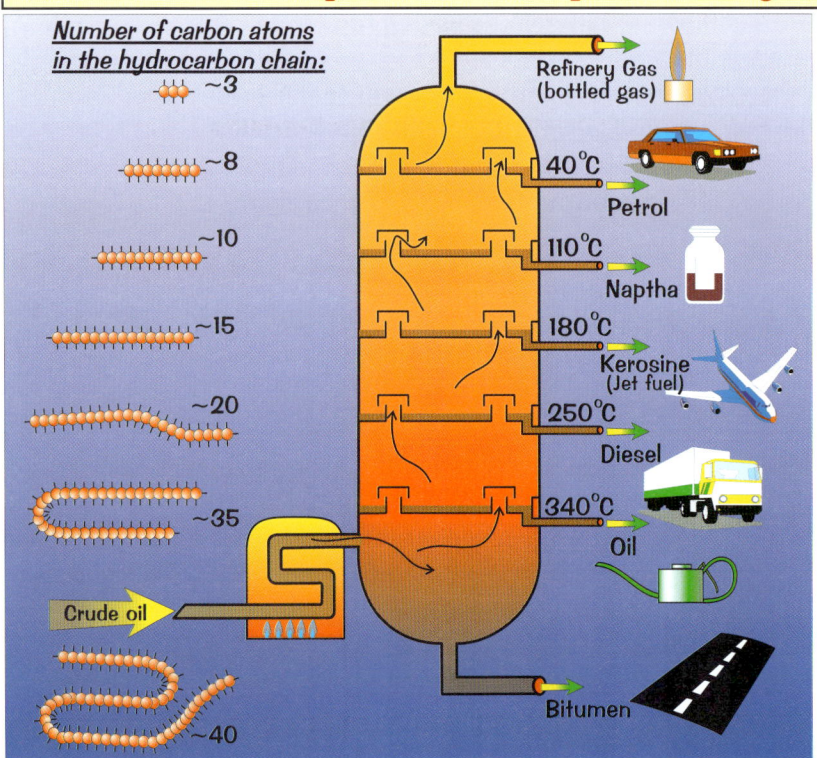

Number of carbon atoms in the hydrocarbon chain:
- ~3
- ~8
- ~10
- ~15
- ~20
- ~35
- ~40

Refinery Gas (bottled gas)
40°C — Petrol
110°C — Naptha
180°C — Kerosine (Jet fuel)
250°C — Diesel
340°C — Oil
Bitumen

Crude oil

1) _Crude oil_ is a mixture of substances, most of which are different sized _hydrocarbon_ molecules.
2) _Hydrocarbons_ are basically _fuels_ such as petrol and diesel.
3) The _bigger_ and _longer_ the molecules, the _less runny_ the hydrocarbon (fuel) is.
4) _Fractional distillation_ splits crude oil up into its separate _fractions_.
5) The _shorter the molecules_, the _lower the temperature_ at which that fraction _condenses_.

The _fractionating column_ works continuously, with heated crude oil piped in _at the bottom_ and the various _fractions_ being constantly tapped off at the different levels where they _condense_.

## Revising for oil — you know the drill...

There are two sections on this page, with a total of 13 important points. You do realise they _won't_ ask you what colour oil is or whether it grows on trees or comes out of the ground, etc. No, they'll ask you about these more technical details, _so make sure you learn them all_.

*SEG Syllabus* — *Module Three — Structure and Changes*

# Using Hydrocarbons

**Useful Products from Oil**

## Hydrocarbons are long chain molecules

Long chain molecules made of carbon and hydrogen, in fact.

As the _SIZE_ of the hydrocarbon molecule _INCREASES_:

1) The _BOILING POINT_ increases

2) It gets _LESS FLAMMABLE_

(doesn't set on fire so easy)

3) It gets _MORE VISCOUS_

(doesn't flow so easy)

4) It gets _LESS VOLATILE_

(i.e. doesn't evaporate so easily)

The _vapours_ of the more _volatile_ hydrocarbons are _very flammable_ and pose a serious _fire risk_. So don't smoke at the petrol station. (In fact, don't smoke at all, it's stupid.)

## Complete combustion of Hydrocarbons is safe

It won't come as any surprise to learn that burning (combustion) gives out heat. Chemists call combustion an _exothermic_ reaction. _EX_- as in _EXit_. Giving out energy. The complete combustion of any hydrocarbon in oxygen will produce only _carbon dioxide_ and _water_ as waste products, which are both quite _clean_ and _non poisonous_.

| hydrocarbon + oxygen → carbon dioxide + water | (+ energy) |

Many _gas room heaters_ release these _waste gases_ into the room, which is perfectly OK. As long as the gas heater is working properly and the room is well ventilated there's no problem. When there's _plenty of oxygen_ the gas burns with a _clean blue flame_.

The downer with this type of combustion is that _carbon dioxide_ is given off. Although this is not poisonous, it does contribute to the _greenhouse effect_. This causes the Earth to _warm up_ slightly, as the carbon dioxide traps the heat from the Sun. The rise in temperature will then cause changes in the climate, and melting of the polar ice caps. Deforestation also contributes to the problem.

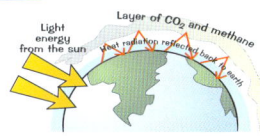

## But Incomplete combustion of Hydrocarbons is NOT safe

If there isn't enough oxygen the combustion will be _INCOMPLETE_. This gives _carbon monoxide_ and _carbon_ as waste products, and produces a _smoky yellow flame_:

| hydrocarbon + oxygen → $CO_2$ + $H_2O$ + carbon monoxide + carbon | (+ energy) |

The _carbon monoxide_ is a _colourless_, _odourless_ and _poisonous_ gas and it's _very dangerous_. Every year people are _killed_ while they sleep due to _faulty_ gas fires and boilers filling the room with _deadly_ carbon monoxide, CO, and nobody realising. The black carbon given off produces sooty marks and is a _clue_ that the fuel is _not_ burning fully.

---

### The one burning question is — have you learnt it all...

Four features of hydrocarbons which change with increasing chain length, and the details for complete and incomplete combustion. The stuff about the _greenhouse effect_ is not to be sniffed at, either. _All worth juicy marks in the Exam_. So learn and enjoy.

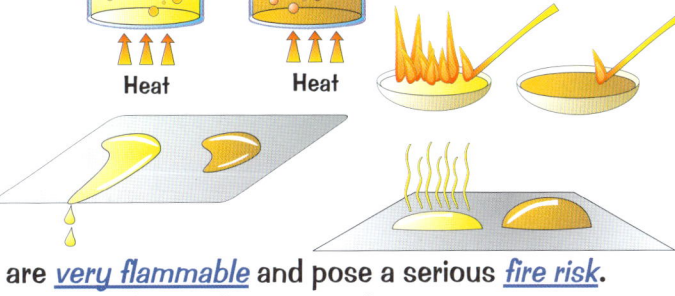

MODULE THREE — STRUCTURE AND CHANGES          SEG SYLLABUS

# Alkanes and Alkenes

*Useful Products from Oil*

Crude oil contains both alkanes and alkenes. They are both hydrocarbons. An example of an alkane is methane (natural gas, $CH_4$), and ethene ($C_2H_4$) is our example of an alkene.

## ALKANES have all C–C SINGLE bonds

1) They're made up of *chains* of carbon atoms with *single* covalent bonds between them.
2) They're called *saturated* hydrocarbons because they have *no* spare bonds left.
3) This is also why they *don't* decolourise *bromine water* — *no* spare bonds.
4) They *won't* form polymers — same reason again, *no* spare bonds.
5) The first four alkanes are *methane* (natural gas), *ethane*, *propane* and *butane*.
6) They burn cleanly producing *carbon dioxide* and *water*.

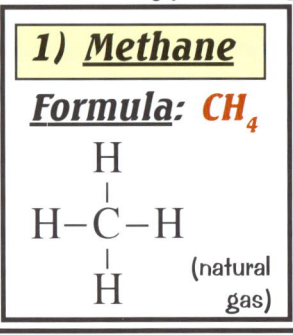

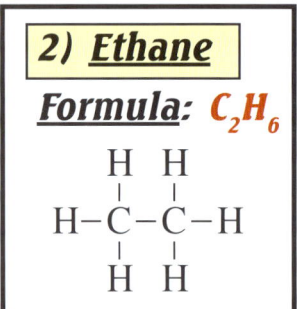

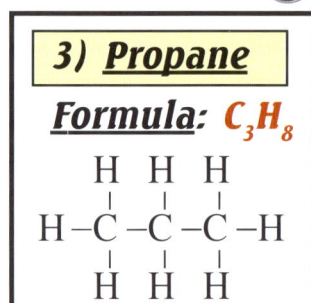

Bromine water + alkane — still brown.

### 1) Methane
Formula: $CH_4$

H
|
H–C–H
|
H
(natural gas)

### 2) Ethane
Formula: $C_2H_6$

H H
| |
H–C–C–H
| |
H H

### 3) Propane
Formula: $C_3H_8$

H H H
| | |
H–C–C–C–H
| | |
H H H

## ALKENES have a C=C DOUBLE bond

1) They're *chains* of carbon atoms with some *double* bonds.
2) They are called *unsaturated* hydrocarbons because they have some *spare* bonds left.
3) This is why they will decolourise *bromine water*. They form *bonds* with bromide ions.
4) They form *polymers* by *opening up* their double bonds to "*hold hands*" in a long chain.
5) The first three alkenes are *ethene*, *propene* and *butene*.
6) They tend to burn with a *smoky flame*, producing *soot* (carbon).

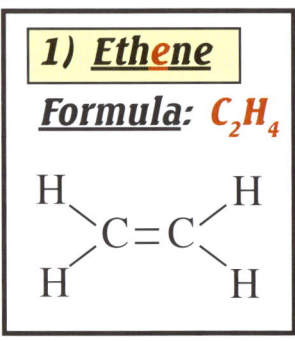

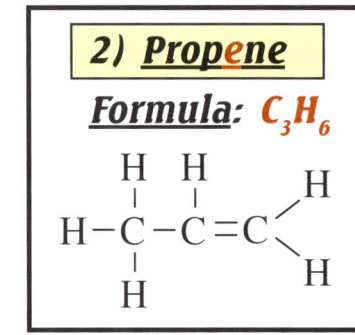

Bromine water + alkene — decolourised

### 1) Ethene
Formula: $C_2H_4$

H        H
 \      /
  C = C
 /      \
H        H

### 2) Propene
Formula: $C_3H_6$

    H H      H
    | |     /
 H–C–C = C
    |      \
    H       H

### 3) Butene
Formula: $C_4H_8$

   H H      H H
   | |      | |
H–C–C = C–C–H
   |      | |
   H      H H

### IMPORTANT POINTS to be noted:

1) *Bromine water* is the *standard* test to distinguish between alkanes and alkenes.
2) *ALKENES* are more *reactive* due to the *double* bond all poised and ready to just pop open.
3) Notice the names: "*Meth-*" means "*one* carbon atom", "*eth-*" means "*two* C atoms", "*prop-*" means "*three* C atoms", "*but-*" means "*four* C atoms", etc. The only difference then between the names of *alkanes* and *alkenes* is just the "*-ane*" or "*-ene*" on the end.
4) *ALL ALKANES* have the formula: $C_nH_{2n+2}$    *ALL ALKENES* have the formula: $C_nH_{2n}$

## Alkane anybody who doesn't learn this lot properly...

Six details and three structural diagrams for alkanes and alkenes, plus four extra points.
It really isn't that difficult to learn the whole page until you can scribble it down from memory.
Try doing it for five minutes: *Learn, cover, scribble, check, relearn, cover, scribble, check, etc.*

*SEG Syllabus*    *Module Three — Structure and Changes*

# Cracking Hydrocarbons

**Useful Products from Oil**

## Cracking — *splitting up* long chain hydrocarbons

1) *LONG CHAIN* hydrocarbons form *thick* gloopy liquids like *tar* which aren't all that useful.
2) The process called *cracking* turns them into *SHORTER* molecules which are *much* more useful.

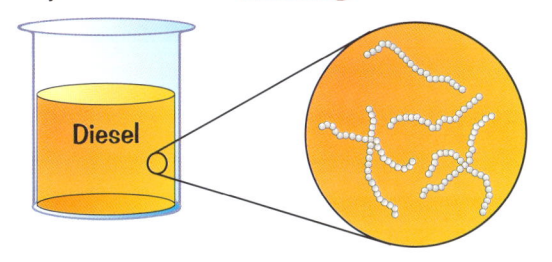

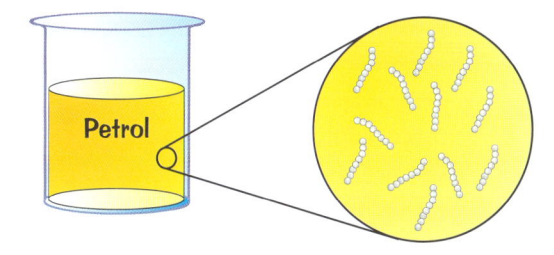

3) *CRACKING* is a form of *thermal decomposition*, which just means *breaking* molecules down into *simpler* molecules by *heating* them.
4) A lot of the longer molecules produced from fractional distillation are *cracked* into smaller ones because there's *more demand* for products like *petrol* and *paraffin* (jet fuel) than for diesel or lubricating oil.
5) More importantly, cracking produces *extra alkenes* which are needed for making *plastics*.

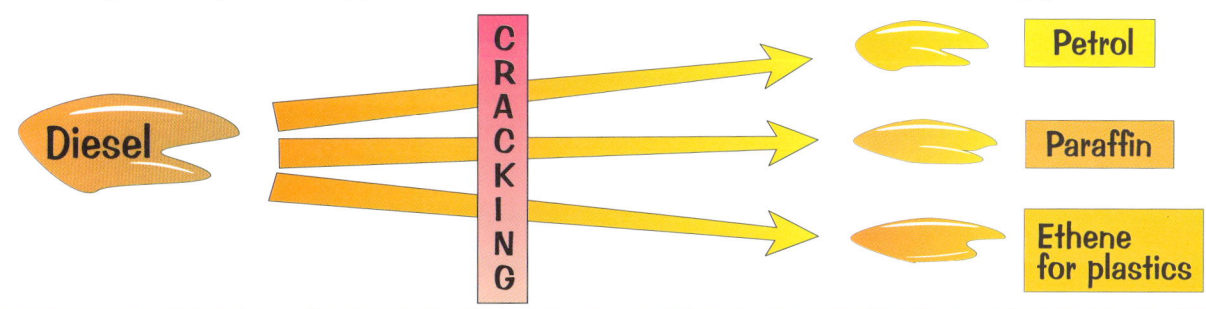

### Industrial Conditions for Cracking: hot, plus a catalyst

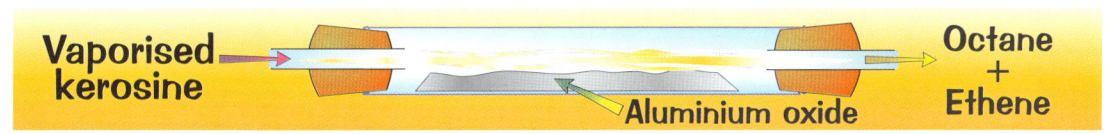

1) <u>Vaporised hydrocarbons</u> are passed over <u>powdered catalyst</u> at about <u>400°C – 700°C</u>.
2) <u>Aluminium oxide</u> is the catalyst used.
   The <u>long chain</u> molecules <u>split apart</u> or "crack" on the <u>surface</u> of the bits of catalyst.

| *Long chain hydrocarbon* molecule | → | *Shorter alkane* molecule | + | *Alkene* |

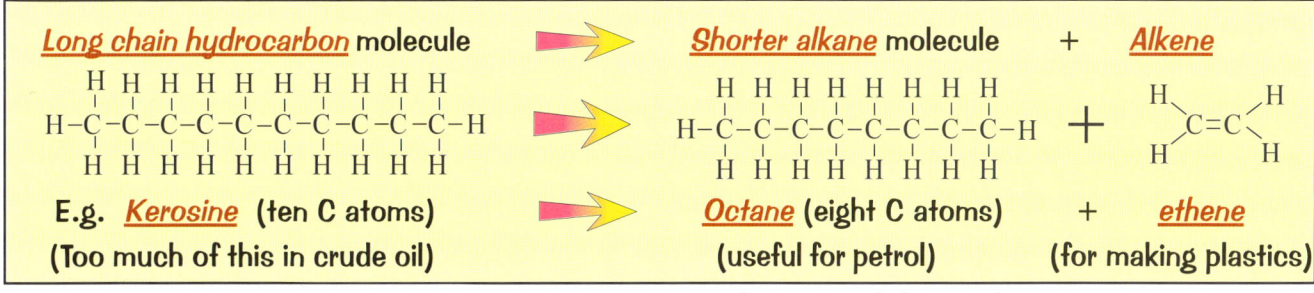

E.g. *Kerosine* (ten C atoms)  →  *Octane* (eight C atoms)  +  *ethene*
(Too much of this in crude oil)    (useful for petrol)    (for making plastics)

You don't need to memorise the exact temperature, or the name of the catalyst. Be aware that a <u>catalyst</u> is used, and it's very <u>hot</u>. Also make sure you know that a long <u>saturated</u> hydrocarbon gives another (not quite so) long saturated hydrocarbon, and a small <u>alkene</u>, like ethene.

## Chemistry — what a cracking subject it is...

Five details about the whys and wherefores, and an example showing typical products: a shorter chain alkane and an alkene. *LEARN IT ALL.*

MODULE THREE — STRUCTURE AND CHANGES     SEG Syllabus

# Polymers

**Useful Products from Oil**

Polymers and plastics were first discovered in about 1933. By 1970 it was all too late. Those halcyon days when they made *proper* motor cars with leather seats and lovely wooden dashboards were over. Sigh.

## Polymers are lots of small molecules joined together

1) 'Poly-' just means 'lots of-'. So polymer means 'lots of mers'. I've no idea what a 'mer' is, but a polymer is a long molecule made by joining lots of smaller molecules (called monomers) together in a long chains.
2) Ethene ($C_2H_4$) makes polyethene (written $C_nH_{2n}$), which you just might have heard of as polythene. It's very useful for making carrier bags and pop bottles and other such essentials.

## Alkenes open their double bonds to form Polymers

Under a bit of pressure and with a bit of a catalyst to help it along, many small alkenes will open up their double bonds and "join hands" to form polymers.

If no other products are formed during the polymerisation reaction, the process is called addition polymerisation.

Ethene becoming polyethene or "polythene" is the easiest example of polymerisation:

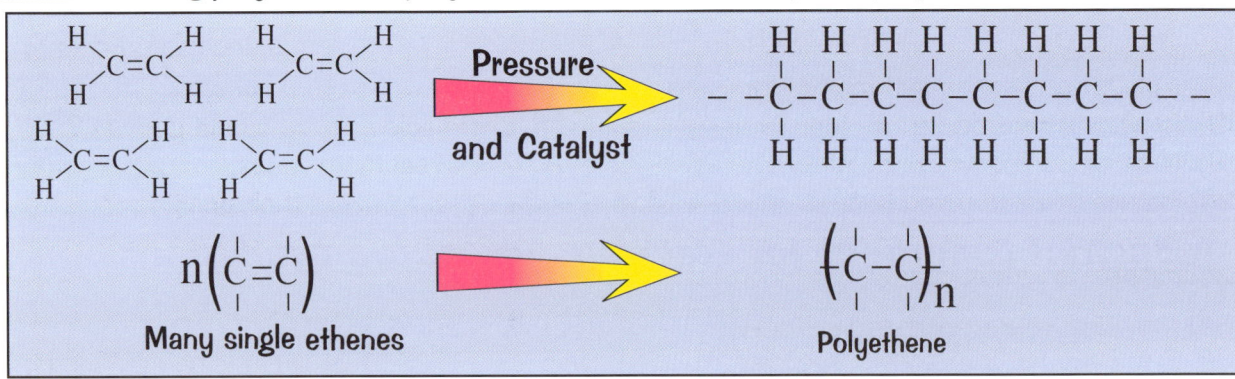

$$n\left(\begin{matrix} | & | \\ C=C \\ | & | \end{matrix}\right) \longrightarrow \left(\begin{matrix} | & | \\ C-C \\ | & | \end{matrix}\right)_n$$

Many single ethenes → Polyethene

...but you also need to know that propene makes (you guessed it) polypropene. Polypropene is useful for making crates and ropes.

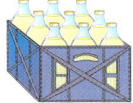

## Raw Materials

1) Polythene is made from ethene, and ethene comes from crude oil, so crude oil is the raw material we make polythene bags from.
2) Unfortunately, we are using crude oil at a huge rate, and need to keep finding new deposits in the ground — which are often more difficult and more expensive to extract.
3) Also, people sometimes object to having their nice beautiful landscape views turned into horrible oil wells.

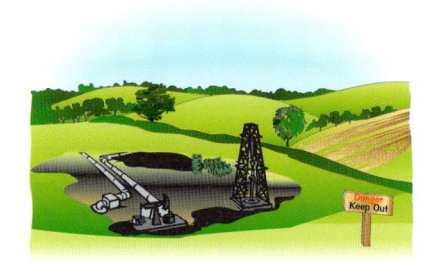

## Revision — it's all about stringing lots of facts together...

Learn what polymerisation is and practise the set of diagrams for ethene. Also learn all the examples given for the different types of plastics. *Then cover the page and scribble it all down.*

SEG SYLLABUS — MODULE THREE — STRUCTURE AND CHANGES

# Revision Summary for Module Three

*These certainly aren't the easiest questions you're going to come across. That's because they test what you know without giving you any clues. At first you might think they're impossibly difficult. Eventually you'll realise that they simply test whether you've learnt the stuff or not.*
*If you're struggling to answer these then you need to do some serious learning.*

1) Sketch an atom. Give five details about the nucleus and five details about the electrons.
2) What do the mass number and proton number represent?
3) Calculate the electron configuration for each of the following elements: $^{4}_{2}He$, $^{12}_{6}C$, $^{31}_{15}P$, $^{39}_{19}K$.
4) What feature of atoms determines the order of the modern periodic table?
5) What are the periods and groups? Explain their significance in terms of electrons.
6) Draw diagrams to show the electron arrangements for the first twenty elements.
7) What are the electron arrangements of the noble gases? Name three properties of them?
8) Give two uses each for helium, neon and argon.
9) Which group is the alkali metals? What is their outer shell like?
10) List three physical properties, and two chemical properties of the alkali metals.
11) Give details of the reactions of the alkali metals with water and chlorine, and of burning in air.
12) What are the trends of the alkali metals as you go down a group?
13) What do alkali metal compounds look like?
14) Describe the trends in appearance and reactivity of the halogens as you go down the Group.
15) List four properties common to all the halogens.
16) Give details, with equations, of the reaction of the halogens with metals, including silver.
17) Explain the reason for the difference in reactivity between the different halogens.
18) To what extent do Cu, Al, Mg, Fe and Zn react with dilute acid? What would you see?
19) Write down the twelve common metals in the order of the reactivity series.
20) Where do carbon and hydrogen fit in and what is the significance of their positions?
21) Describe the reaction of all twelve metals a) when heated in air, b) with water (or steam).
22) What does pH measure?
23) Describe fully the colour of universal indicator for pH 1, pH 7 and pH 14.
24) What type of ions are always present in a) acids and b) alkalis? What is neutralisation, in terms of ions?
25) Give three real life examples of neutralisation.
26) What is the equation for reacting acid with metal? Which metal(s) don't react with acid?
27) What type of salts do hydrochloric acid and sulphuric acid produce?
28) Explain how each of the four factors that increase the rate of a reaction increase the *number of collisions* between particles.
29) What are the three different ways of measuring the speed of a reaction?
30) What is the definition of a catalyst? What does a catalyst do to the activation energy?
31) Describe how fossil fuels were formed. What length of time did it take?
32) What does crude oil consist of?
33) Draw the full diagram of fractional distillation of crude oil.
34) What are hydrocarbons? Describe four properties and how they vary with the molecule size.
35) Give the equations for complete and incomplete combustion of hydrocarbons.
36) Which type is dangerous and why? What is the difference between the flames for each type?
37) What are alkanes and alkenes? What is the basic difference between them?
38) List four differences in the chemical properties of alkanes and alkenes.
39) What is "cracking"? Why is it done?
40) What are polymers? What kind of substances can form polymers?
41) Name two types of plastic, give their physical properties and say what they're used for.

**MODULE THREE — STRUCTURE AND CHANGES**                **SEG SYLLABUS**

# Force and Transfers

## Circuits

**Electrical Circuits & Mains Electricity**

### Current Is Just the Flow of Charges

1) <u>CURRENT (I)</u> is the <u>flow of charges</u> round a circuit. The charges are normally <u>electrons</u>, but could be dissolved <u>ions</u> if the current is flowing through a <u>solution</u> (like in <u>electrolysis</u>).
2) <u>VOLTAGE (V)</u> is the <u>driving force</u> that pushes the current round — kind of like "<u>electrical pressure</u>". The <u>proper</u> name for <u>voltage</u> is "<u>potential difference</u>" or "<u>P.D.</u>".
3) <u>RESISTANCE (R)</u> is anything in the circuit that <u>slows the flow down</u>.
4) <u>THERE'S A BALANCE</u>: the <u>voltage</u> is trying to <u>push</u> the current round the circuit, but the <u>resistance</u> is <u>opposing</u> it — together they decide <u>how big</u> the current will be:

> If you *increase the VOLTAGE* — then *MORE CURRENT* will flow.
> If you *increase the RESISTANCE* — then *LESS CURRENT* will flow
> (or *MORE VOLTAGE* will be needed to keep the *SAME CURRENT* flowing).

### Energy Is Transferred from Cells and Other Sources

Anything that <u>supplies electricity</u> is also supplying <u>energy</u>. So cells, batteries, generators etc. all <u>transfer energy</u> to components in the circuit. <u>Learn these as examples</u>:

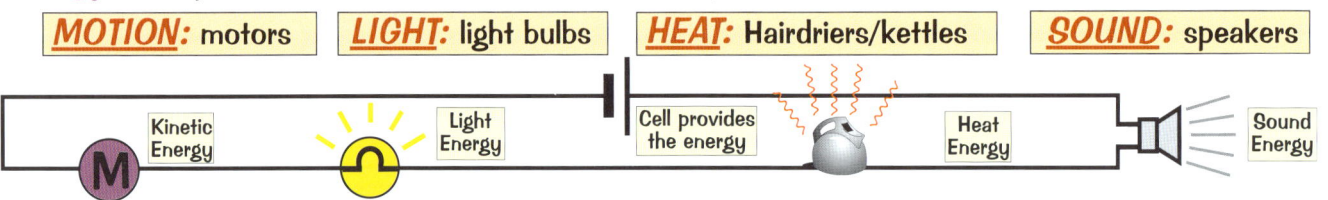

**MOTION:** motors  **LIGHT:** light bulbs  **HEAT:** Hairdriers/kettles  **SOUND:** speakers

### All Resistors Produce Heat When Current Flows Through Them

This is important. Whenever a <u>current</u> flows through anything with <u>electrical resistance</u> (which is pretty well <u>everything</u>), then <u>electrical energy</u> is converted into <u>heat energy</u>. The amount of heat produced (in <u>joules</u>) will be the same as the amount of <u>electrical energy</u> lost by the circuit.

### And This Heat Can Be Useful...

1) A resistor heats the <u>air</u> in a <u>hairdrier</u>.
2) A resistor heats the <u>water</u> in an <u>immersion heater</u>.
3) The <u>filament</u> of a <u>light bulb</u> is a resistor made from <u>tungsten</u>. It gets so hot that it <u>glows</u> — bright enough to light the room.

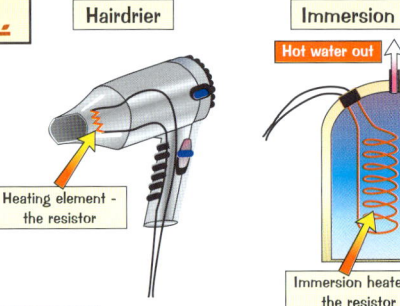

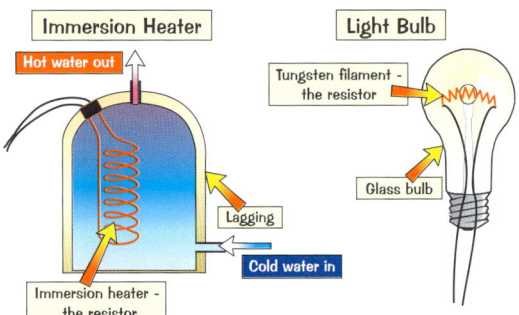

### Circuit Calculations: V=IR

<u>Voltage</u> is measured in <u>VOLTS</u> (V), <u>current</u> in <u>AMPS</u> (A), and resistance in <u>OHMS</u> ($\Omega$). They're related by the formula voltage = current × resistance, or V=IR, as shown in the formula triangle:

So if you wanted the formula for resistance, you'd just cover the 'R' in the triangle to give:

$$\text{Resistance} = \frac{\text{Voltage (P.D.)}}{\text{Current}}$$

**EXAMPLE:** If the potential difference across a component is <u>3V</u>, and the current flowing through it is <u>0.5A</u>, then its resistance must be <u>R=3/0.5 = 6$\Omega$</u>.

### In the end, you'll have to learn this — resistance is futile...

There are quite a lot of important details on this page and you need to <u>learn all of them</u>. The only way to make sure you really know it is to <u>cover up the page</u> and see how much of it you can <u>scribble down</u> from <u>memory</u>. Sure, it's not that easy — but it's the only way. Enjoy.

*SEG Syllabus*  *Module Four — Force and Transfers*

# Circuits

**Electrical Circuits & Mains Electricity**

## The Diode

Also known as a "_semiconductor diode_", this is a special device that lets current flow freely through it in _one direction_, but _not_ in the other (i.e. there's a very high resistance in the _reverse_ direction). This turns out to be real useful in various _electronic circuits_.

## Circuit Symbols You Should Know:

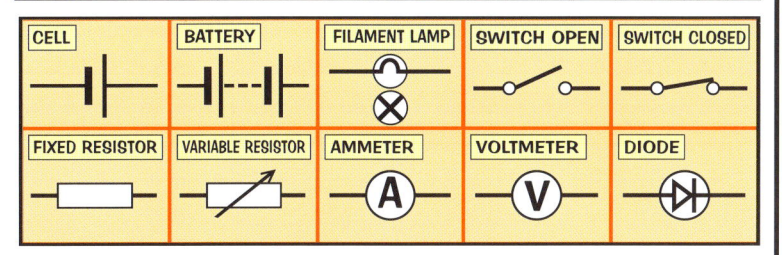

| CELL | BATTERY | FILAMENT LAMP | SWITCH OPEN | SWITCH CLOSED |
| FIXED RESISTOR | VARIABLE RESISTOR | AMMETER | VOLTMETER | DIODE |

## Four Hideously Important Voltage-Current Graphs

V-I graphs show how the current varies as you change the voltage. Learn these four real well:

### Resistor
The current through a **RESISTOR** (at constant temperature) is _proportional to voltage_.

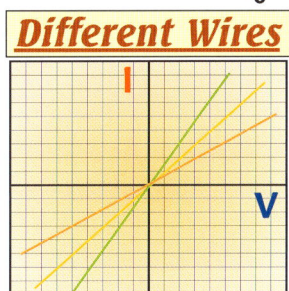

### Different Wires
_Different wires_ have different _resistances_, hence the different _slopes_.

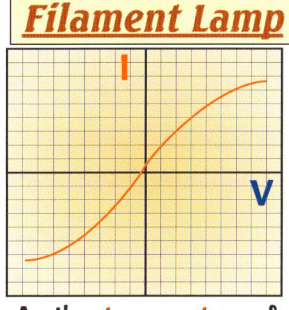

### Filament Lamp
As the _temperature_ of the filament _increases_, the _resistance increases_, hence the _curve_.

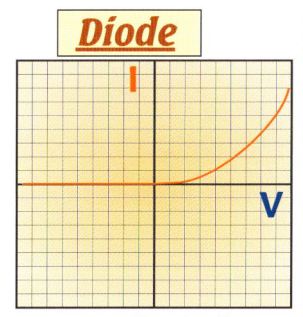

### Diode
Current will only flow through a diode _in one direction_, as shown.

For the _straight-line graphs_ the resistance of the component is _steady_, and the _STEEPER_ the graph, the _LOWER_ the resistance. If the graph _curves_, it means the resistance is _changing_. In that case R can be found for any point by taking the _pair of values_ (V,I) from the graph and sticking them in the formula _R = V/I_. Easy.

## Light Dependent Resistor or "LDR" to You

1) In _bright light_, the resistance _falls_.
2) In _darkness_, the resistance is _highest_.
3) This makes it a useful device for various _electronic circuits_ e.g. _automatic night lights_; _burglar detectors_.
4) At a given _light intensity_, the _voltage-current graph_ will be a _straight line_, as with a _normal resistor_.

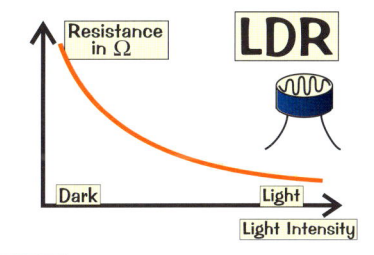

## Thermistor (Temperature-Dependent Resistor)

1) In _hot_ conditions, the resistance _drops_.
2) In _cool_ conditions, the resistance goes _up_.
3) Thermistors make useful _temperature detectors_, e.g. _car engine_ temperature sensors and electronic _thermostats_.
4) At a given _temperature_, the _voltage-current graph_ will be a _straight line_, as with a _normal resistor_. However, because _current_ produces a _heating effect_, in practice the greater the current, the less the resistance, so the _voltage-current graph_ will _curve upwards_. So be careful.

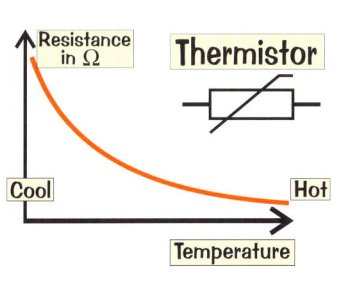

## "Diode" — wasn't that a film starring Bruce Willis...

Another page of basic but important details about electrical circuits. You need to know all those circuit symbols as well as the extra details for the special devices below them. When you think you know it all try _covering the page_ and _scribbling it all down_. See how you did, _then try again_.

MODULE FOUR — FORCE AND TRANSFERS          SEG SYLLABUS

# Series Circuits

*Electrical Circuits & Mains Electricity*

You need to be able to tell the difference between series and parallel circuits *just by looking at them*. You also need to know the *rules* about what happens with both types. Read on.

## Series Circuits — All or Nothing

1) In *series circuits*, the different components are connected *in a line*, *end to end*, between the +ve and –ve of the power supply (except for *voltmeters*, which are always connected *in parallel*, but they don't count as part of the circuit).
2) If you remove or disconnect *one* component, the circuit is *broken* and they all *stop*.
3) This is generally *not very handy*, and in practice, *very few things* are connected in series.

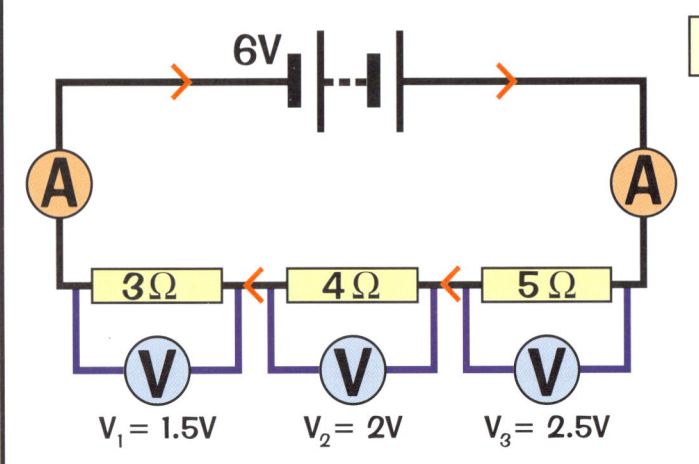

### In Series Circuits:

1) The *total resistance* is just the *sum* of all the resistances.
2) The *same current* flows through *all parts* of the circuit.
3) The *size of the current* is determined by the *total P.D. of the cells* and the *total resistance* of the circuit: i.e. I = V/R
4) The *total P.D.* of the *supply* is *shared* between the various *components*, so the *voltages* round a series circuit *always add up* to equal the *source voltage*.
5) The *bigger* the *resistance* of a component, the bigger its *share* of the *total Pd*.

V₁ = 1.5V   V₂ = 2V   V₃ = 2.5V

*Voltages* add to equal the *supply*: 1.5+2+2.5=6V
Total resistance = 3+4+5 = 12 Ohms
Current = V/R = 6/12 = 0.5A

## Connection of Voltmeters and Ammeters

1) *Voltmeters* (for measuring *voltage*) are always connected *in parallel* around components. In a *series circuit*, you can put voltmeters *around each component*. The readings from all the components will *add up* to equal the reading from the *voltage source*. Simple, so learn it.
2) *Ammeters* (for measuring *current*) can be put *anywhere* in a *series circuit* and will ALL GIVE THE SAME READING.

## Christmas Fairy Lights Are Wired in Series

*Christmas fairy lights* are about the *only real-life example* of things connected in *series*, and we all know what a *pain* they are when the *whole lot go out* just because *one* of the bulbs is slightly dicky.

The only *advantage* is that the bulbs can be *very small* because the total 230V is *shared out between them*, so *each bulb* only has a *small voltage* across it.

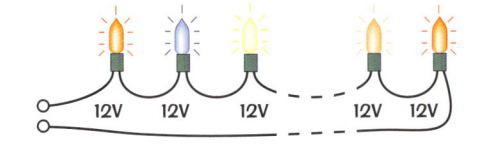

*By contrast* a string of lights as used on say a *building site* are connected in *parallel* so that each bulb receives the *full 230V*. If *one* is removed, *the rest stay lit* which is most *convenient*.

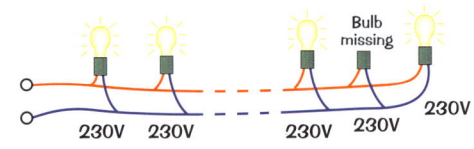

Make sure you know the *difference* between these two wiring diagrams.

### Series circuits — phew, it's just one thing after another...

They really do want you to know the difference between series and parallel circuits. It's not that tricky but you do have to make a real effort to *learn all the details*. That's what this page is for. Learn all those details, then *cover the page* and *scribble them all down*. Then try again...

*SEG Syllabus* — *Module Four — Force and Transfers*

# Parallel Circuits

**Electrical Circuits & Mains Electricity**

*Parallel circuits* are much more *sensible* than series circuits and so they're *much more common* in *real life*.

## Parallel Circuits — Independence and Isolation

1) In *parallel circuits*, each component is *separately connected* to the +ve and −ve of the *supply*.
2) If you remove or disconnect *one* of them, it will *hardly affect the others at all*.
3) This is *obviously* how *most things* must be connected, for example in *cars* and in *household electrics*. You have to be able to switch everything on and off *separately*.

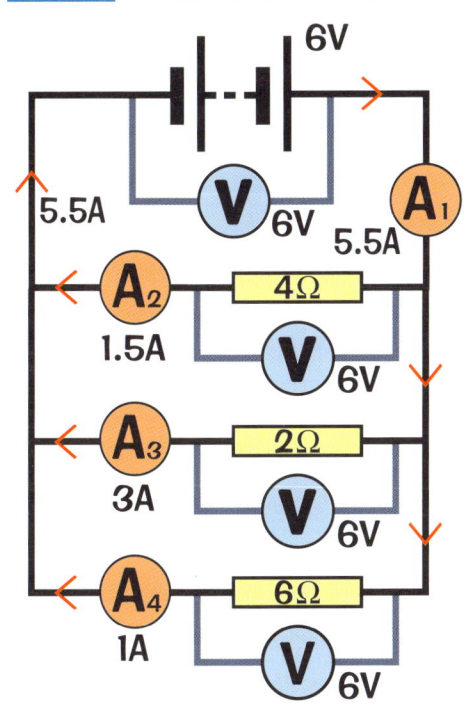

### In Parallel Circuits:

1) *All components* get the *full source P.D.*, so the voltage is the *same* across all components.
2) The *current* through each component *depends on its resistance*.
   The *lower* the resistance, the *bigger* the current that'll flow through it.
3) The *total current* flowing around the circuit is equal to the *total* of all the currents in the *separate branches*.
4) In a parallel circuit, there are *junctions* where the current either *splits* or *rejoins*. The total current going *into* a junction *always equals* the total currents *leaving* — fairly obviously.
5) The *total resistance* of the circuit is *tricky to work out*, but it's *always LESS* than the branch with the *smallest resistance*.

*Voltages* all equal to *supply voltage*: =6V
*Total R* is *less than* the *smallest*, i.e. *less than* 2Ω
*Total Current* ($A_1$) = *sum* of all branches = $A_2 + A_3 + A_4$

## Connection of Voltmeters and Ammeters

1) Once again the *voltmeters* are always connected *in parallel* around components.
2) *Ammeters* can be placed *in each branch* to measure the *different currents* flowing through each branch, as well as *one near the supply* to measure the *total current* flowing out of it.

## Everything Electrical in a Car Is Connected in Parallel

*Parallel connection* is *essential* in a car to give these *two features*:

1) Everything can be *turned on and off separately*.
2) Everything always gets the *full voltage* from the battery.

The only *slight effect* is that when you turn *lots of things on* the lights may go *dim* because the battery can't provide *full voltage* under *heavy load*. This is normally a *very slight* effect. You can spot the same thing at home when you turn a kettle on, if you watch very carefully.

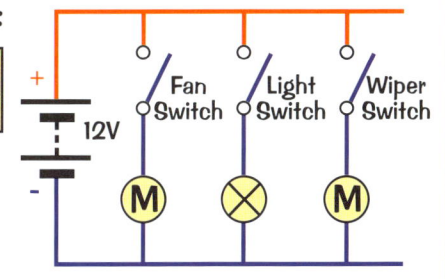

## Electric circuits — unparalleled dreariness...

Make sure you can scribble down a parallel circuit and know what the advantages are. Learn the five numbered points and the details for connecting ammeters and voltmeters, and also what two features make parallel connection essential in a car. Then *cover the page* and *scribble it*...

*MODULE FOUR — FORCE AND TRANSFERS*   *SEG SYLLABUS*

# Electricity in the Home

**Electrical Circuits & Mains Electricity**

Now then, did you know... electricity is dangerous. It can kill you. Well just watch out for it, that's all.

## Plugs and Cables — Learn the Safety Features

### Get the Wiring Right:

1) The _right coloured wire_ to each pin, and _firmly screwed_ in.
2) _No bare wires_ showing inside the plug.
3) _Cable grip_ tightly fastened over the cable _outer layer_.

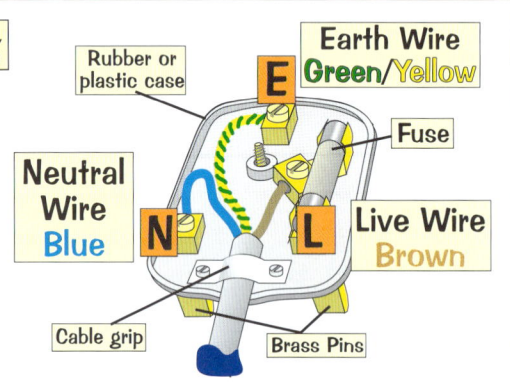

*Rubber or plastic case*
*Earth Wire — Green/Yellow*
*Fuse*
*Neutral Wire — Blue*
*Live Wire — Brown*
*Cable grip*
*Brass Pins*

### Plug Features:

1) The _metal parts_ are made of copper or brass because these are _very good conductors_.
2) The case, cable grip and cable insulation are all made of _plastic_ because this is a really good _insulator_ and is _flexible_ too.
3) This all keeps the electricity flowing _where it should_.

## Earthing and Fuses Prevent Fires and Shocks

The LIVE WIRE alternates between a HIGH +VE AND −VE VOLTAGE, with an average of about 230V. The NEUTRAL WIRE is always at 0V. Electricity normally flows in and out through the live and neutral wires only. The EARTH WIRE and _fuse_ (or circuit breaker) are just for _safety_ and _work together_ like this:

1) If a _fault_ develops in which the _live_ somehow touches the _metal case_, then because the case is _earthed_, a _big current_ flows in through the _live_, through the _case_ and out down the _earth wire_.
2) This _surge_ in current _blows the fuse_, which _cuts off_ the _live supply_.
3) This _isolates_ the _whole appliance_, making it _impossible_ to get an electric _shock_ from the case. It also prevents the risk of _fire_ caused by the heating effect of a large current.
4) _Fuses_ should be _rated_ as near as possible to, but _just higher_ than, the _normal operating current_ (see the next page).

*TOASTER — heater coil*
*Fault — Allows live to touch metal case*
*Big current now flows out through earth*
*Big current surges to earth*
*Big surge in current blows fuse......*
*...which isolates the appliance from the live*
*Safe*

All appliances with _metal cases_ must be "_earthed_" to avoid the danger of _electric shock_. "Earthing" just means the metal case must be _attached to the earth wire_ in the cable.
If the appliance has a _plastic casing_ and no metal parts _showing_ then it's said to be DOUBLE INSULATED. Anything with _double insulation_ like that _doesn't need an earth wire_, just a live and neutral.

## Circuit Breakers Act as Resettable Fuses

1) The _current_ flowing in the _live_ and _neutral_ wires should normally be _the same_.
2) But if a _fault_ develops, some current might _flow to earth_ — possibly through someone.
3) Then there'll be _less current_ flowing in the _neutral_ wire than in the _live_ wire.
4) A RESIDUAL CIRCUIT BREAKER compares the currents in these two wires, and _shuts off_ the supply _(breaks the circuit)_ if there's a _difference_.

Circuit breakers have _two main advantages_ over _fuses_:
1) If the circuit is broken, you _don't have to replace a fuse_ — merely reset the circuit breaker.
2) They switch the current off _much faster_ than a fuse, so they're safer. They're commonly used with _high risk appliances_ like _lawnmowers_ for this reason.

## Some people are so careless with electricity — it's shocking...

A few too many words on this page I think. Just so much to learn. Make sure you know all the details for wiring a plug. Trickiest of all, make sure you understand how earthing and fuses act together to make things safe. Learnt it all? Good-O. _Cover the page_ and _scribble it down_.

*SEG Syllabus*  *Module Four — Force and Transfers*

# Electricity in the Home

**Electrical Circuits & Mains Electricity**

## Electrical Power and Fuse Ratings

1) *Electrical Power* is defined as the *rate of transfer of electrical energy*. It is measured in *watts* (W), which is just *joules per second* (J/s).
2) The standard formula for *electrical power* is:      P=VI
3) If you *combine* it with $V=I \times R$ by replacing the "V" with "I×R", you get:      $P=I^2R$
4) If instead you use V=I×R and replace the "I" with "V/R", you get:      $P=V^2/R$
5) You *choose* which *one* of these formulae to use, purely and simply by seeing which one contains the *three quantities* that are *involved* in the problem you're looking at.

## Calculating Fuse Ratings — Always Use the Formula: "P=VI"

Most electrical goods indicate their *power rating* and *voltage rating*. To work out the *FUSE* needed, you need to work out the *current* that the item will normally use. That means using "P=VI", or rather, "I=P/V".

**EXAMPLE:** A hairdrier is rated at 240V, 1.1kW. Find the fuse needed.

**ANSWER:** I = P/V = 1100/240 = 4.6A. Normally, the fuse should be rated just a little higher than the normal current, so a 5 amp fuse is ideal for this one.

## Reading Your Electricity Meter and Working Out the Bill

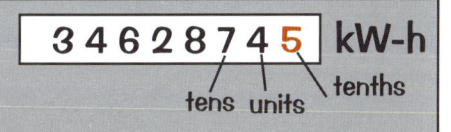

**3 4 6 2 8 7 4 5** kW-h
              tens units tenths

The reading on your meter shows the *total number of units* (kW-h) used since the meter was fitted. Each bill is worked out from the *INCREASE* in the meter reading since it was *last read* for the previous bill.

## Kilowatt-Hours (kW-h) Are "UNITS" of Energy

1) Your electricity meter counts the number of "*UNITS*" used.
2) A "*UNIT*" is otherwise known as a *kilowatt-hour*, or *kW-h*.
3) A "*kW-h*" might sound like a unit of power, but it's not — it's an *amount of energy*.

> A *KILOWATT-HOUR* is the amount of electrical energy used by a *1 KW APPLIANCE* left on for *1 HOUR*.

4) Make sure you can turn *1 kW-h* into *3,600,000 joules* like this:
"E=P×t" = 1kW × 1 hour = 1,000W × 3,600 secs = *3,600,000 J*    ( =3.6 MJ)
(The formula is "Energy = Power×time", and the units must be converted to *watts* and *seconds* first).

## The Two Easy Formulae for Calculating the Cost of Electricity

These must surely be the two most *trivial and obvious* formulae you'll ever see:

| No. of *UNITS* (kW-h) used = *POWER* (in kW) × *TIME* (in hours) | Units = kW × hours |
|---|---|
| *COST* = No. of *UNITS* × *PRICE* per UNIT | Cost = Units × Price |

**EXAMPLE:** Find the cost of leaving a 60W light bulb on for a) 30 minutes b) one year.

**ANSWER:** a) No. of UNITS = kW × hours = 0.06kW × ½hr = 0.03 units.
            Cost = UNITS × price per UNIT (6.3p) = 0.03 × 6.3p = *0.189p* for 30 mins.

       b) No. of UNITS = kW × hours = 0.06kW × (24×365)hr = 525.6 units.
            Cost = UNITS × price per UNIT (6.3p) = 525.6 × 6.3p = *£33.11* for one year.

**N.B.** Always turn the *power* into *kW* (not watts) and the *time* into *hours* (not minutes).

## Kilowa Towers — the best lit hotel in Hawaii...

This page has five sections and you need to learn the stuff in all of them. Start by memorising the headings, then learn the details under each heading. Then *cover the page* and *scribble down* what you know. Check back and see what you missed, and then *try again*. And keep trying.

*MODULE FOUR — FORCE AND TRANSFERS*      *SEG SYLLABUS*

# Electromagnetic Induction

Sounds terrifying, but it really isn't that complicated. For some reason though they use the word *"induction"* rather than *"creation"*, but it amounts to the *same thing*. I reckon they're just trying to confuse you.

**ELECTROMAGNETIC INDUCTION:** The creation of a *VOLTAGE* (and/or current) in a wire that is in a *CHANGING MAGNETIC FIELD*.

1) Of course if the *field didn't change*, but the *wire* moved *through* it, then from the *wire's point of view* it would still look like the *field was changing*.
2) So *this also generates a voltage in the wire*.

This means there's *two* different situations in which you get *EM induction*. You need to know about *both* of them:

a) The *conductor* moves across a *magnetic field* and *"cuts"* through the field lines (as in the diagram to the right — a coil is moved between the poles of a magnet).

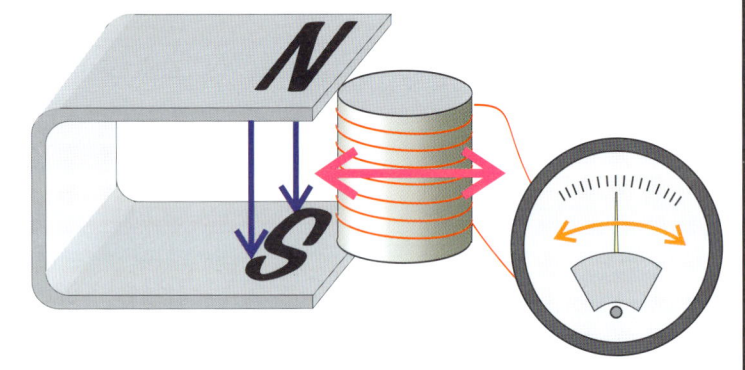

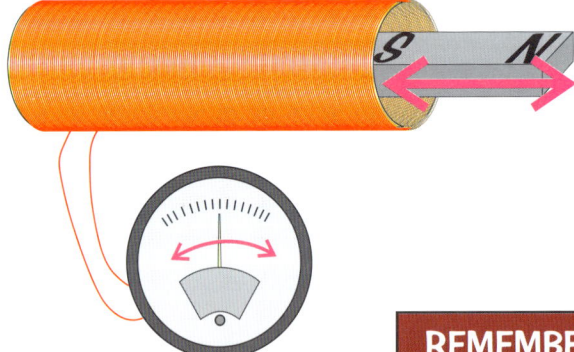

b) The *magnetic field* through a closed coil *CHANGES*, i.e. gets *bigger* or *smaller* or *reverses* (as in the diagram to the left — a magnet is moved into or out of a stationary coil).

**REMEMBER THESE POINTS:**

1) If the direction of *movement* is *reversed*, then the *voltage/current* will be *reversed* too.
2) The current will also be reversed if the *opposite pole* of the magnet is shoved into the coil.

## The Dynamo Principle

A voltage and/or current will be produced in a coil when there is relative movement between it and a magnetic field.

This is a pretty handy effect, as it's used in *generators* to produce our *mains electricity*. It's called the *DYNAMO PRINCIPLE*.

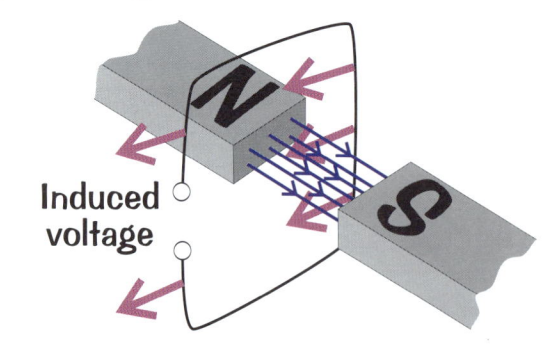

Induced voltage

## Four Factors Affect the Size of the Induced Voltage:

1) The *STRENGTH* of the *MAGNET*
2) The *SPEED* of movement
3) The *number of TURNS* on the *COIL*
4) The *AREA* of the *COIL*

### Electromagnetic induction — pretty tricky stuff...

Electromagnetic induction gets my vote for "Definitely Most Tricky Topic in GCSE Science". If it wasn't so important maybe you wouldn't have to bother learning it. The trouble is this is how all our electricity is generated. So it's pretty important. *Learn and scribble*...

# Electromagnetic Induction

## Generators

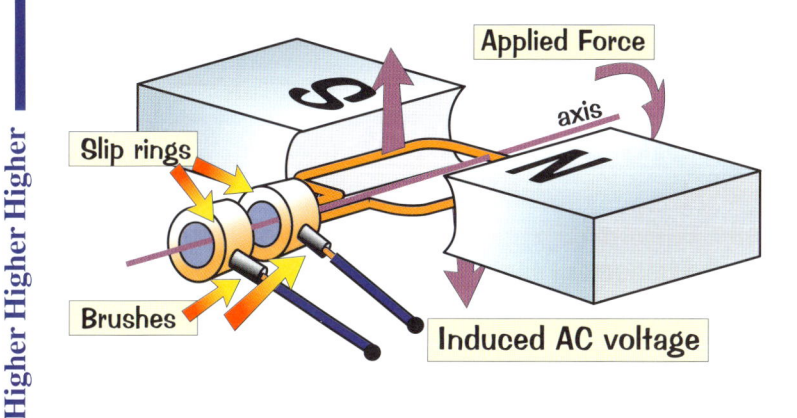

1) Generators *rotate* a coil in a *magnetic field* to generate electricity by the *dynamo principle* (see the previous page).
2) Their *construction* is pretty much like a *motor* (see Module 8 if you're doing it).
3) The *difference* is the *slip rings*, which are in *constant contact* with the brushes so the contacts *don't swap* every ½ turn.
4) This means they produce *AC voltage*.
5) Note that *faster* revs produce not only *more* peaks, but *higher* overall voltage too.

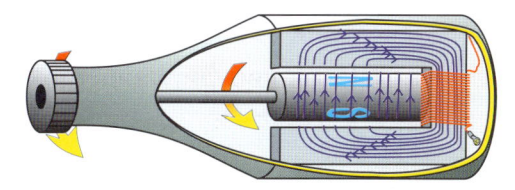

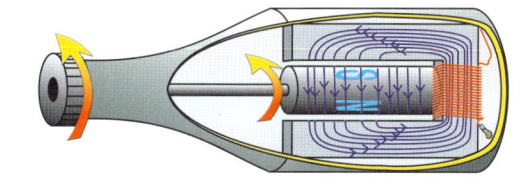

## Dynamos

*Dynamos* are slightly different from *generators* because they rotate the *magnet* instead of the coil. The *coil* now *surrounds* the magnet and *doesn't move*. This still causes the *field through the coil* to *swap* every half turn, so the output is *just the same* — an *alternating current* (*AC*).

## The Two Types of Current

### Direct Current (DC)

1) The *current* from a *battery* stays *constant* if the circuit doesn't change.
2) It flows in just *one direction* — from the *positive to the negative* terminal.
3) Since it has only one direction, it is called *direct current* (*DC*).

Direct Current at 2V in one direction

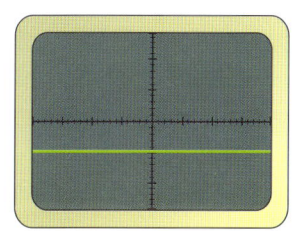

Direct Current at 1V in the other direction

### Alternating Current (AC)

1) *Mains electricity* on the other hand is *alternating current* (*AC*).
2) This means that the *direction* of the current *changes continually*.
3) The *frequency* of the supply tells you *how many times it changes* from one direction to the other and *back again* each *second*.

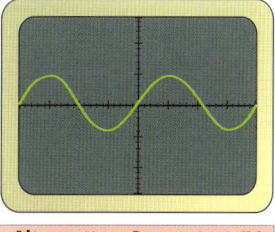

Alternating Current at 1V at one frequency

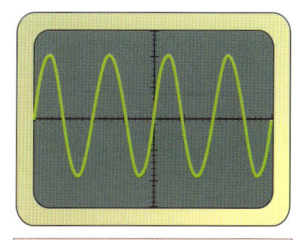

Alternating Current at 2V at twice the frequency

## This page could generate a bit of a headache...

Well, at least there's only *two* types of current for you to learn about. You'd better make sure you know the cathode ray oscilloscope stuff though — they like to throw that sort of thing into Exams. And of course you know the best way to *learn* it — *cover and scribble*...

MODULE FOUR — FORCE AND TRANSFERS                     SEG SYLLABUS

# Speed and Velocity

## Speed and Velocity Are Both Just: HOW FAST YOU'RE GOING

Speed and velocity are both measured in m/s (or km/h or mph). They both simply say how fast you're going, but there's a subtle difference between them that you need to know:

**SPEED** is just HOW FAST you're going (e.g. 30mph or 20m/s) with no regard to the direction.
**VELOCITY** however must ALSO have the DIRECTION specified, e.g. 30mph *north* or 20m/s, 060°

Seems kinda fussy I know, but they expect you to remember that distinction, so there you go.

## Speed, Distance and Time — the Formula:

$$\text{Speed} = \frac{\text{Distance}}{\text{Time}}$$

You really ought to get pretty slick with this very easy formula.
As usual the formula triangle version makes it all a bit of a breeze.
You just need to try and think up some interesting word for remembering the order of the letters in the triangle, s$^d$t. Errm... sedit, perhaps... well, you think up your own.

**EXAMPLE:** A cat skulks 20m in 35s. Find  a) its speed  b) how long it takes to skulk 75m.
**ANSWER:** Using the formula triangle:  a) s = d/t = 20/35 = **0.57m/s**
                                         b) t = d/s = 75/0.57 = 131s = **2 min 11 sec**

A lot of the time we tend to use the words "speed" and "velocity" interchangeably.
For example to calculate velocity you'd just use the above formula for speed.

## Distance-Time Graphs

## Very Important Notes:

1) **GRADIENT = SPEED**.
2) *Flat* sections are where it's *stopped*.
3) The *steeper* the graph, the *faster* it's going.
4) *Downhill* sections mean it's *coming back* toward its starting point.
5) *Curves* represent *acceleration* or deceleration.
6) A *steepening* curve means it's *speeding up* (increasing gradient).
7) A *levelling off* curve means it's *slowing down* (decreasing gradient).

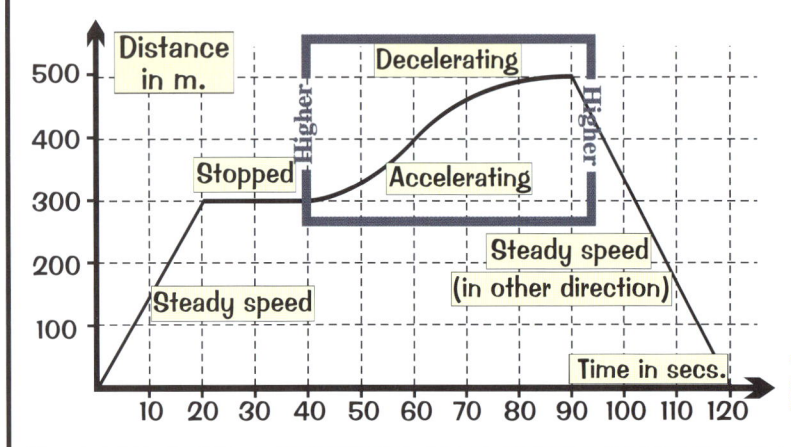

## Calculating Speed from a Distance-Time Graph — It's Just the Gradient

For example the speed of the return section of the graph is:

Speed = gradient = $\frac{\text{vertical}}{\text{horizontal}} = \frac{500}{30} =$ **16.7 m/s**

Don't forget that you have to use the scales of the axes to work out the gradient. *Don't* measure in *cm*!

## Understanding speed — it can be an uphill struggle...

Make sure you know the difference between speed and velocity — it's a favourite way to catch you out in Exams. And as for those distance-time graphs, they can be real tricky — unless you make a real effort to *learn all the numbered points*. So what are you waiting for... *Enjoy*.

# Mass, Weight and Gravity

**Force & Motion**

## Gravity Is the Force of Attraction Between All Masses

Gravity attracts all masses, but you only notice it when one of the masses is really really big, e.g. a planet. Anything near a planet or star is attracted to it very strongly. This has three important effects:

1) It makes all things accelerate towards the ground (all with the same acceleration, g, which = $10m/s^2$ on Earth).
2) It gives everything a weight.
3) It keeps planets, moons and satellites in their orbits. The orbit is a balance between the forward motion of the object and the force of gravity pulling it inwards.

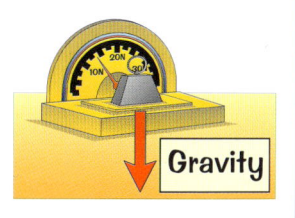

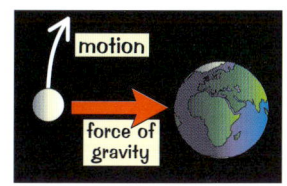

## Weight and Mass Are Not the Same

To understand this you must learn all these facts about mass and weight:

1) MASS is the AMOUNT OF MATTER in an object.
   For any given object this will have the same value ANYWHERE in the Universe.
2) WEIGHT is caused by the pull of gravity. In most questions the weight of an object is just the force of gravity pulling it towards the centre of the Earth.
3) An object has the same mass whether it's on Earth or on the Moon — but its weight will be different. A 1 kg mass will weigh LESS on the Moon (1.6N) than it does on Earth (10N), simply because the force of gravity pulling on it is less.
4) Weight is a force measured in newtons. It must be measured using a spring balance or newton meter.
   MASS is NOT a force. It's measured in kilograms with a mass balance (never a spring balance).
5) One very fancy definition of a newton:

**ONE NEWTON is the force needed to give a MASS OF 1 kg an ACCELERATION OF $1m/s^2$**

## The Very Important Formula Relating Mass, Weight and Gravity

$$W = m \times g$$

(Weight = mass × g)

1) Remember, weight and mass are NOT the same. Mass is in kg, weight is in newtons.

2) The letter "g" represents the strength of the gravity and its value is different for different planets.
   On Earth g = 10 N/kg. On the Moon, where the gravity is weaker, g is just 1.6 N/kg.

3) This formula is hideously easy to use:

EXAMPLE: What is the weight, in newtons, of a 5kg mass, both on Earth and on the Moon?

Answer: "W = m × g". On Earth: W = 5 × 10 = 50N (The weight of the 5kg mass is 50N).
On the Moon: W = 5 × 1.6 = 8N (The weight of the 5kg mass is 8N).

See what I mean. Hideously easy — as long as you've learnt what all the letters mean.

## Learn about gravity NOW — no point in "weighting" around...

Very often, the only way to "understand" something is to learn all the facts about it. That's certainly true here. "Understanding" the difference between mass and weight is no more than learning all those facts about them. When you've learnt all those facts, you'll understand it...

MODULE FOUR — FORCE AND TRANSFERS    SEG SYLLABUS

# Terminal Velocity

**Force & Motion**

## Balanced and Unbalanced Forces

*TAKE NOTE!* To move with a *steady speed* the forces must be in *BALANCE*. If there is an *unbalanced force* then you get *ACCELERATION*, not steady speed. That's *rrrreal important*, so don't forget it.

1) You only get *acceleration* with an overall *resultant* (unbalanced) *force*.
2) The *bigger* the *unbalanced force*, the *greater* the *acceleration*.

### 1) Steady Velocity — All Forces in Balance!

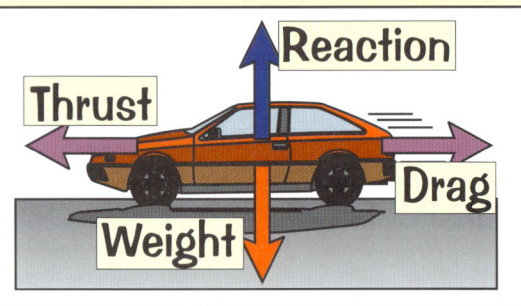

(Diagram: car with Thrust, Reaction, Drag, Weight)

### 2) Acceleration — Unbalanced Forces

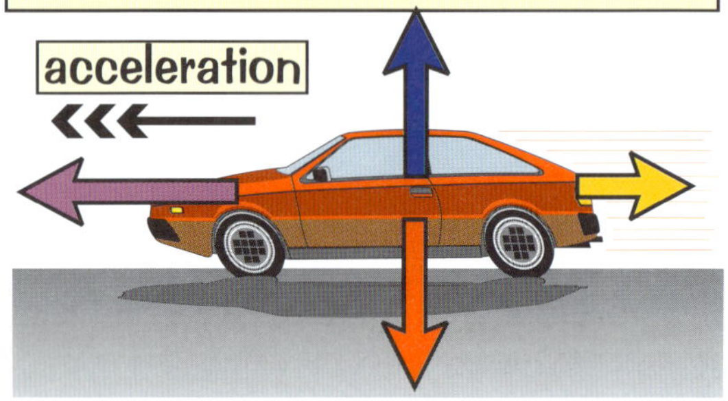

(Diagram: car with acceleration arrows)

## Cars and Free-Fallers All Reach a Terminal Velocity

When cars and free-falling objects first *set off* they have *much more* force *accelerating* them than *resistance* slowing them down. As the *speed* increases the resistance *builds up*. This gradually *reduces* the *acceleration* until eventually the *resistance force* is *equal* to the *accelerating force* and then it won't be able to accelerate any more. It will have reached its maximum speed or *TERMINAL VELOCITY*.

(Graph: Velocity vs Time showing curve approaching "Maximum speed, or 'terminal velocity'")

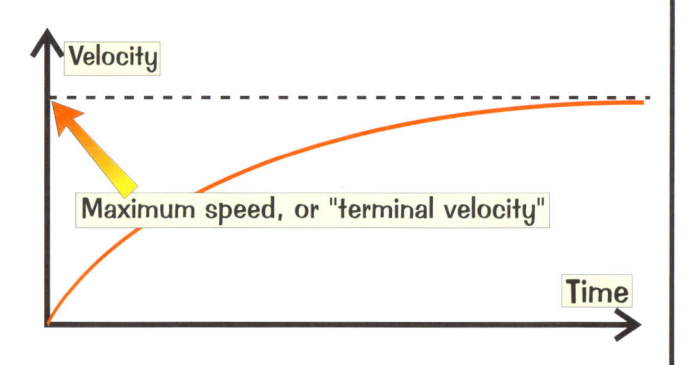

## The Terminal Velocity of Falling Objects Depends on Their Shape and Area

The *accelerating force* acting on *all* falling objects is *GRAVITY*, and it would make them all fall at the *same* rate if it wasn't for *air resistance*. To prove this, on the Moon, where there's *no air*, hamsters and feathers dropped simultaneously will hit the ground *together*.
However, on Earth, *air resistance* causes things to fall at *different* speeds, and the *terminal velocity* of any object is determined by its *drag* in *comparison* to its *weight*. The drag depends on its *shape and area*.

The most important example is the human *skydiver*. Without his parachute open he has quite a *small* area and a force of "$W=mg$" pulling him down. He reaches a *terminal velocity* of about *120mph*.
But with the parachute *open*, there's much more *air resistance* (at any given speed) and still only the same force "$W=mg$" pulling him down. This means his *terminal velocity* comes right down to about *15mph*, which is a *safe speed* to hit the ground at.

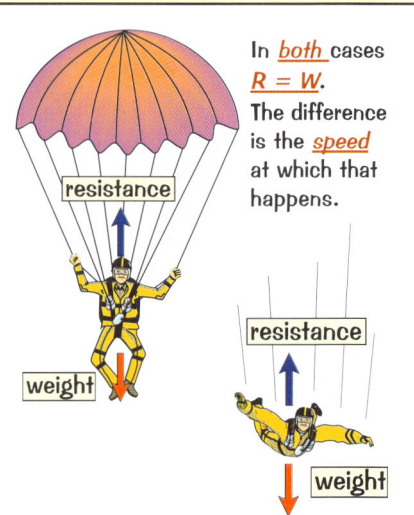

In *both* cases $R = W$. The difference is the *speed* at which that happens.

## This really is terminally dreary stuff...

...But you've still got to know it. Make sure you can draw that graph for terminal velocity, and — more importantly — make sure you can explain it. And the same goes for balanced and unbalanced forces. It's pretty simple so long as you make the effort to *learn it*. So *scribble*...

*SEG SYLLABUS* — *MODULE FOUR — FORCE AND TRANSFERS*

# Turning Forces

**Force & Motion**

## A "Moment" Is a Turning Force

When a force acts on something that has a *pivot*, it creates a *turning force* called a *"moment"*. MOMENTS are *calculated* using this formula:

**MOMENT = FORCE × PERPENDICULAR DISTANCE**

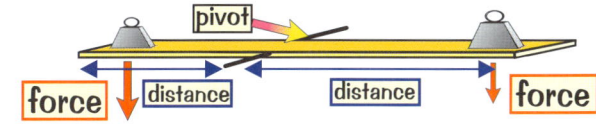

*Also*, for the system to be in *equilibrium*, (i.e. all *nicely balanced* and *not moving*) then *this must be true* too:

**TOTAL CLOCKWISE MOMENT = TOTAL ANTICLOCKWISE MOMENT**

### Example:

Q: Bob just manages to move a boulder by pulling down with a force of *1,000N* on a *lever*, as shown in the diagram. What is the *force exerted on the boulder*?

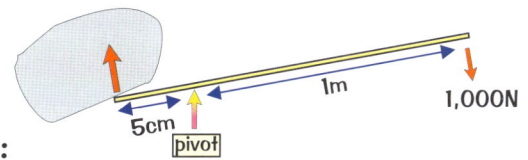

A: From the diagram, Bob's force is *1m from the pivot*, so:
TOTAL CLOCKWISE MOMENT = 1m × 1,000N = *1,000Nm*
This must *balance* the anticlockwise moment, so:
TOTAL ANTICLOCKWISE MOMENT = 1,000Nm = 0.05m × F
(Remember to *convert 5cm to m*!) So the force exerted on the boulder is:
F = 1,000Nm / 0.05m = *20,000 N*.
That's a pretty big force, I'd say. Now you know why levers are so handy...

## Stretching, Compressing, Bending, Twisting, Shearing...

When a *combination of forces* are applied to a *solid object*, they can cause a *variety of effects*. You need to learn the diagrams below well enough to be able to put in all the details for each:

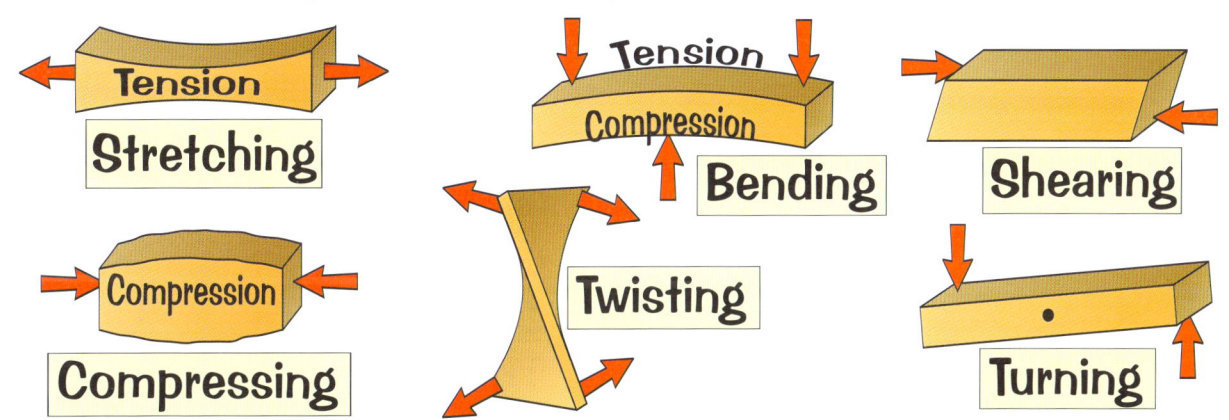

**Stretching** — Tension
**Bending** — Tension / Compression
**Shearing**
**Compressing** — Compression
**Twisting**
**Turning**

Make sure you can put in *all the forces* in all the *right places* and also identify in each case the places where the solid is under *tension* or *compression*. Note that sometimes an object does *not return* to its *original shape* when the forces are removed. This is known as *INELASTIC BEHAVIOUR*. (*Hooke's Law* applies to stretched objects — see the next page).

## What's a turning force called? Just a moment...

I would never have thought there were so many different forces. Well, you learn something new every day, and today it just happens to be turning forces. Make sure you can do those calculations — they can be a bit tricky I know, but the only way to get better is to *practise*...

*MODULE FOUR — FORCE AND TRANSFERS*            *SEG SYLLABUS*

# Hooke's Law

**Force & Motion**

## Stretching Springs — Extension Is Proportional to Load

This is *seriously easy*. It just means:

> If you **STRETCH** something with a **STEADILY INCREASING FORCE**, then the **LENGTH** will **INCREASE STEADILY** too.

The important thing to measure in a stretching experiment is not so much the total length as the **EXTENSION**;

> **EXTENSION** is the **INCREASE IN LENGTH** compared to the original length with *no force applied*.

For most materials, you'll find that *THE EXTENSION IS PROPORTIONAL TO THE LOAD*, which just means that if you *double* the load, the *extension will double too*.

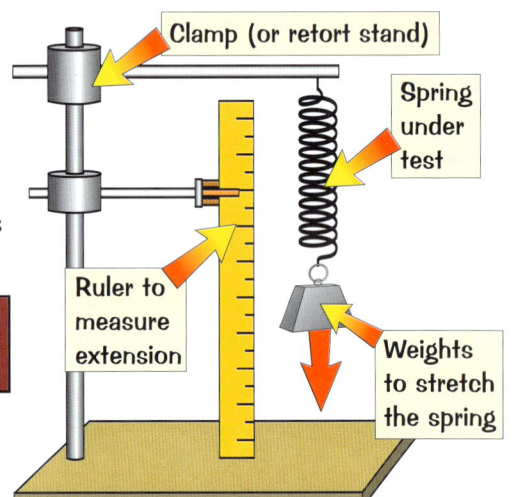

*Diagram labels: Clamp (or retort stand); Spring under test; Ruler to measure extension; Weights to stretch the spring*

## The Behaviour of the Spring Changes at the Elastic Limit:

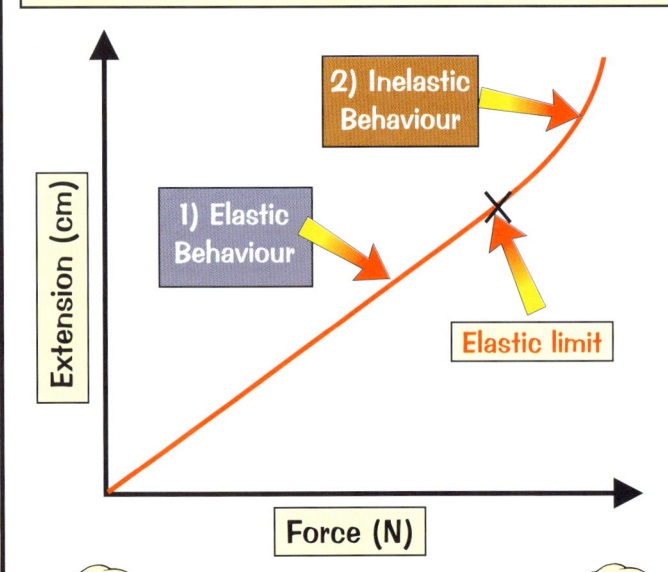

*Graph: Extension (cm) vs Force (N), showing 1) Elastic Behaviour, 2) Inelastic Behaviour, and the Elastic limit point.*

### Region 1 — Elastic behaviour

1) In this region, when the load is *doubled* the extension *doubles too*.
2) The spring will *always return* to its original *size and shape* when the load is removed.

### The Elastic Limit

1) The *elastic limit*. This is the point at which the behaviour of the spring suddenly changes.
2) *Below* this point the spring *keeps* its original *size and shape*.
3) *Above* this point the spring behaves *inelastically*.

### Region 2 — Inelastic behaviour

1) In this region the spring *doesn't return* to its original *size and shape* when the load is *removed*.
2) The extension no longer doubles when the load is doubled.

If you put *too much* load on the spring then it will be *permanently damaged*.

You should **LEARN** that *elastic behaviour* always gives *A STRAIGHT LINE GRAPH THROUGH THE ORIGIN*.

## Stretching springs — always loads of fun...

This is pretty standard stuff, so make sure you know all the little details, including the graph. You'd better be able to describe what happens in each region, and say exactly what the elastic limit is. Once you think you know it all, you know what to do: *cover, scribble, check, etc*.

SEG SYLLABUS — MODULE FOUR — FORCE AND TRANSFERS

# Waves — Basic Principles

**Waves & the EM Spectrum**

*Waves are different* from anything else. They have various features which *only waves have*:

## Amplitude, Wavelength and Frequency

Too many people get these *wrong*. Take careful note:
1) The *AMPLITUDE* goes from the *middle* line to the *peak*, NOT from a trough to a peak.
2) The *WAVELENGTH* covers a *full cycle* of the wave, e.g. from *peak to peak*, not just from "two bits that are sort of separated a bit".
3) *FREQUENCY* is how many *complete waves* there are *per second* (passing a certain point).

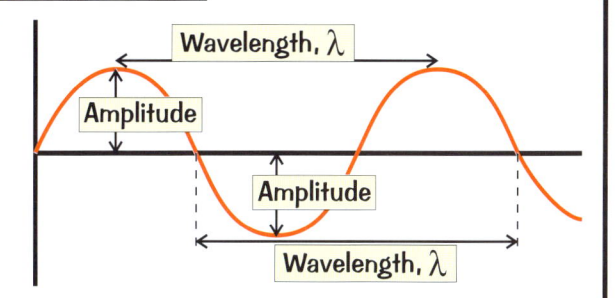

## The Electromagnetic Spectrum

Light is what's known as an electromagnetic wave — but it's not the only one. We split electromagnetic waves (EM waves) into *seven* basic types, as shown below.

| RADIO WAVES | MICRO-WAVES | INFRA-RED | VISIBLE LIGHT | ULTRA-VIOLET | X-RAYS | GAMMA RAYS |
|---|---|---|---|---|---|---|
| 1m–$10^4$m | $10^{-2}$m (3cm) | $10^{-5}$m (0.01mm) | $10^{-7}$m | $10^{-8}$m | $10^{-10}$m | $10^{-12}$m |

These EM waves form a *continuous spectrum* — the different regions *merge* into each other. There's nothing special about light — it's just that our *eyes* have only evolved to detect this *very narrow range* of EM waves. All EM waves travel at *exactly* the same *speed* in a *vacuum* — oddly enough, it's called the speed of light. They travel a bit slower in *other media* though, like glass and water. The colours disperse when white light is shone through a prism, due to fractional differences in the speed of the different colours through glass. You need to *learn this diagram* and know that violet light *bends* more than red.

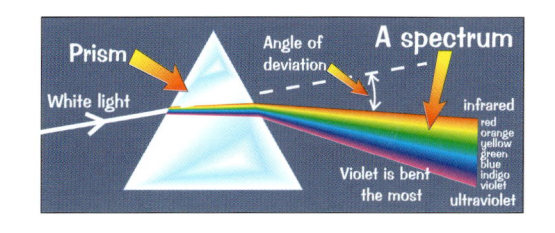

## As the Wavelength Changes, So Do the Properties

1) As the *wavelength* of EM radiation changes, its *interaction* with matter changes — particularly the way it is *absorbed*, *reflected* or *transmitted* by a given substance.
2) As a rule the EM waves at *each end* of the spectrum tend to be able to *pass through* material, whilst those *nearer the middle* are *absorbed*.
3) Also, the ones at the *top end* (high frequency, short wavelength) tend to be the most *dangerous*, whilst those lower down are generally *harmless*.
4) When *any* EM radiation is *absorbed* it can have *two effects*:
    a) *Heating*    b) Creation of a *tiny alternating current* with the *same* frequency as the radiation.
5) You need to know all the details on the next two pages on the different parts of the EM spectrum.

### Waves Can Be REFLECTED and REFRACTED

1) They might test whether or not you realise these are *properties* of waves, so *learn them*.
2) The two words are *confusingly similar*, but you MUST learn the *differences* between them.
3) Light and sound are *reflected* and *refracted*, and this shows that they travel as waves.

## Learn about waves — just get into the vibes, man...

This is all very basic stuff on waves. Four sections with some tasty titbits in each. *Learn* the headings, then the details. Then *cover the page* and see what you can *scribble down*. Then try again until you can remember the whole lot. It's all just *easy marks to be won... or lost*.

*MODULE FOUR — FORCE AND TRANSFERS*  *SEG SYLLABUS*

# Microwaves and Infrared

*Waves & the EM Spectrum*

## Radio Waves Are Used Mainly for Communications

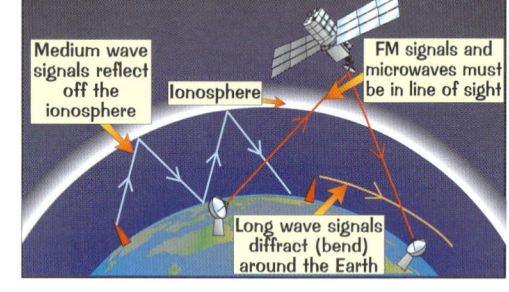

1) **Radio Waves** are used mainly for *communication* — e.g. *TV and FM Radio* use *short wavelength* radio waves of about *1m wavelength*.
2) To receive these wavelengths you need to be more or less in *direct sight* of the transmitter, because they will *not* bend (diffract) over hills or travel very far *through* buildings.
3) The *longer wavelengths* can travel further because they are *reflected* from an *electrically charged layer* in the Earth's upper atmosphere (the ionosphere). This means they can be sent further around the Earth.

## Microwaves Are Used for Cooking and Satellite Signals

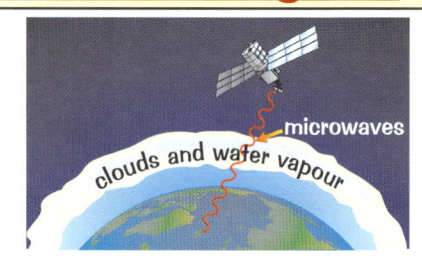

1) *Microwaves* have *two* main uses: *cooking* food and *satellite* transmissions.
2) These two applications use two *different frequencies* of microwaves.
3) Satellite transmissions use a frequency that *passes easily* through the *Earth's atmosphere* — including *clouds*. 
4) The frequency used for *cooking*, on the other hand, is one that's readily *absorbed* by *water molecules*. This is how a microwave oven works. The microwaves pass easily *into the food* and are then *absorbed* by the *water molecules*, heating the food from the *inside*.
5) Microwaves can therefore be *dangerous*, as they can be absorbed by *living tissue* and the heat will *damage or kill* the cells, causing a sort of "*cold burn*".

## Infrared Radiation — Night Vision and Remote Controls

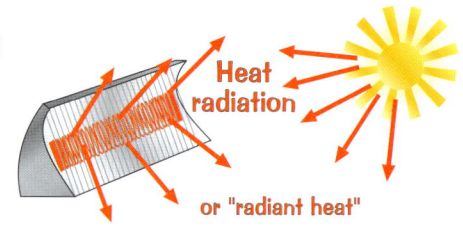

1) *Infrared* (or IR) is otherwise known as *heat radiation*. This is given out by all *hot objects* and you *feel it* on your *skin* as *radiant heat*. Infrared is readily *absorbed* by *all* materials and *causes heating*.
2) *Radiant heaters* (i.e. those that *glow red*, like *toasters* and *grills*) use infrared radiation.
3) Infrared is also used for all the *remote controls* of *TVs and videos*. It's ideal for sending *harmless* signals over *short distances* without *interfering* with radio frequencies (like the TV channels).
4) Infrared is also used for *night-vision equipment*. The *police* use this to spot miscreants *running away*, like you've seen on TV.

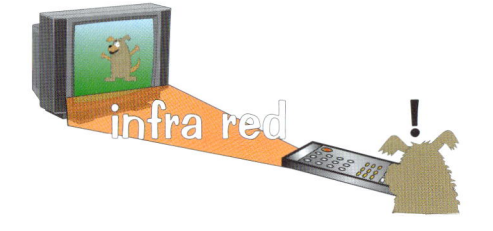

## Microwaves — I thought you got those on calm beaches...

Each part of the EM spectrum is different, and you definitely need to know all the details about each type of radiation. These are just the kind of things they'll test in your Exams. Do *mini-essays* for microwaves and IR. Then *check* to see how you did. Then *try again... and again...*

*SEG Syllabus*  MODULE FOUR — FORCE AND TRANSFERS

# Visible, UV, X-rays, γ-Rays

*Waves & the EM Spectrum*

## Visible Light Is Used to See with and in Optical Fibres

Visible light is pretty useful. We use it for seeing with for one thing. You could say that a use of it is in an _endoscope_ for seeing inside a patient's body, but let's face it — where do you draw the line? — it's also used in _microscopes_, _telescopes_, _kaleidoscopes_, pretend telescopes made of old toilet rolls, it's used for seeing in the dark (torch, lights, etc.) and for saying "hi" to people without speaking. Seriously though, it is also used in _optical fibre digital communications_, which is the best one by far for your answer _in the Exam_ (see Module 9 if you're doing it).

## Ultraviolet Light Causes Skin Cancer

1) This is what causes _sunburn_ and _skin cancer_ if you spend _too much time_ in the _sun_.
2) It also causes your skin to _tan_. _Sunbeds_ give out UV rays, but _less harmful ones_ than many of the Sun's.
3) _Darker skin_ protects against UV rays by _preventing_ them from reaching more vulnerable _skin tissues_ deeper down.
4) There are special _coatings_ that _absorb_ UV light and then _give out visible light_ instead. These are used to coat the insides of _fluorescent tubes_ and lamps.
5) Ultraviolet is also useful for hidden _security marks_, which are written in special ink that can only be seen with an ultraviolet light.

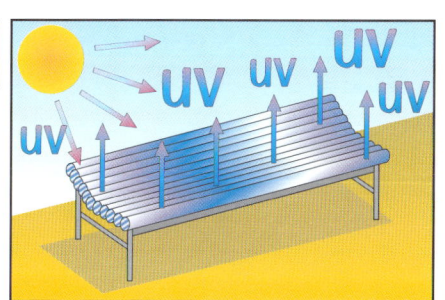

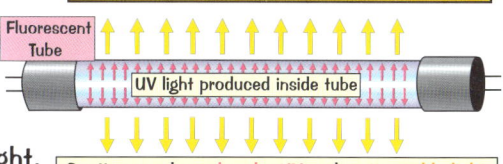

## X-Rays Are Used in Hospitals, but Are Pretty Dangerous

1) These are used in _hospitals_ to take _X-ray photographs_ of people, e.g. to see if they have any _broken bones_.
2) X-rays pass easily through _flesh_, but not through _denser materials_ like _bone_ or _metal_.
3) X-rays can cause _cancer_, so _radiographers_, who take X-ray pictures _all day long_, wear _lead aprons_ and stand behind a _lead screen_ to keep their _exposure_ to X-rays to a _minimum_.
4) X-rays can also be used in _scientific research_ to examine the _structure_ of crystals and other materials.

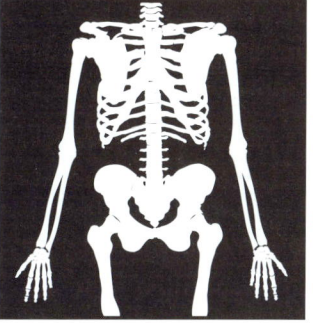

The _brighter bits_ are where _fewer X-rays_ get through. This is a _negative image_. The plate starts off _all white_.

## Gamma Rays Cause Cancer, but Are Used to Treat It Too

1) Gamma rays are used to kill _harmful bacteria_ in food to keep it _fresher for longer_.
2) They are also used to _sterilise medical instruments_, again by _killing the bacteria_.
3) They can also be used in the _treatment of cancer_ because they _kill cancer cells_.
4) Gamma rays tend to _pass through_ soft tissue, but _some_ are _absorbed_ by the cells.
5) In _high doses_, Gamma rays (along with X-rays and UV rays) can _kill normal cells_.
6) In _lower doses_ all these three types of EM Waves can cause normal cells to become _cancerous_.

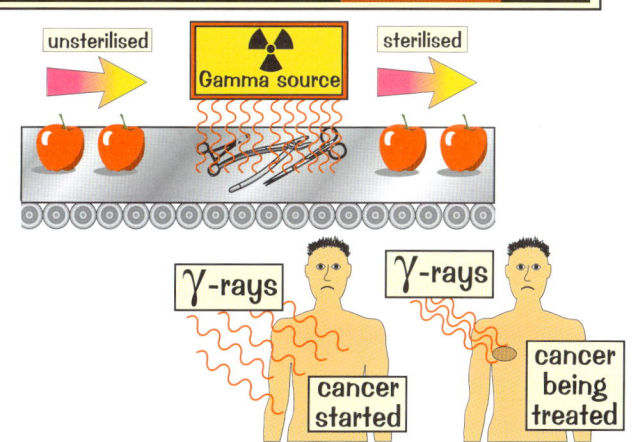

### Radiographers are like teachers — they can see right through you...

Here are the other four parts of the EM spectrum for you to learn. Ace, isn't it. At least there's some groovy diagrams to help relieve the tedium. On this page there are four sections. Do a _mini-essay_ for each section, then _check_, _re-learn_, _re-scribble_, _re-check_, etc. etc.

MODULE FOUR — FORCE AND TRANSFERS          SEG SYLLABUS

# Reflection

*Light*

## The Ripple Tank Is Really Good for Displaying Waves

Learn all these diagrams showing _reflection of waves_. They could ask you to complete _any one of them_ in the Exam. It can be quite a bit _trickier_ than you think unless you've _practised_ them real well _beforehand_.

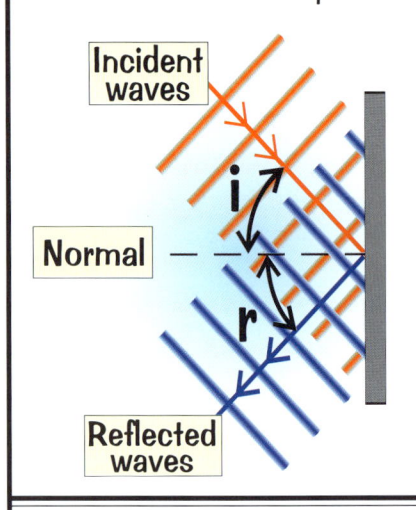

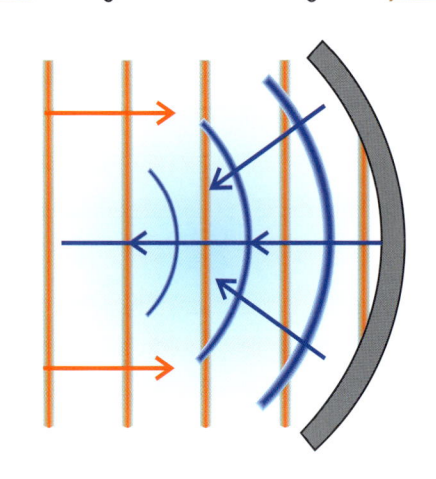

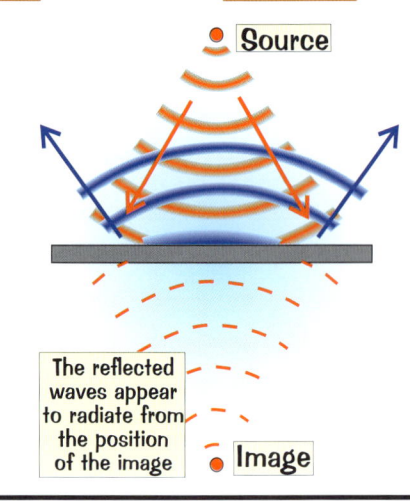

*Incident waves / Normal / i / r / Reflected waves*

*Source / The reflected waves appear to radiate from the position of the image / Image*

## Reflection of Light

_Reflection of light_ is what allows us to _SEE_ objects.
When light reflects from an _even_ surface (_smooth and shiny_ like a _mirror_) then it's all reflected at the _same angle_ and you get a _clear reflection_.
Sound also reflects off _hard surfaces_ in the form of _echoes_.
Reflection of light and of sound gives evidence that light and sound travel as waves.
And don't forget, THE LAW OF REFLECTION applies to _every reflected ray_:

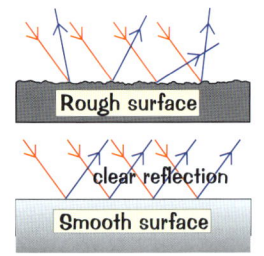

### Angle of INCIDENCE = Angle of REFLECTION

*Rough surface / clear reflection / Smooth surface*

## Reflection in a Plane Mirror — How to Locate the Image

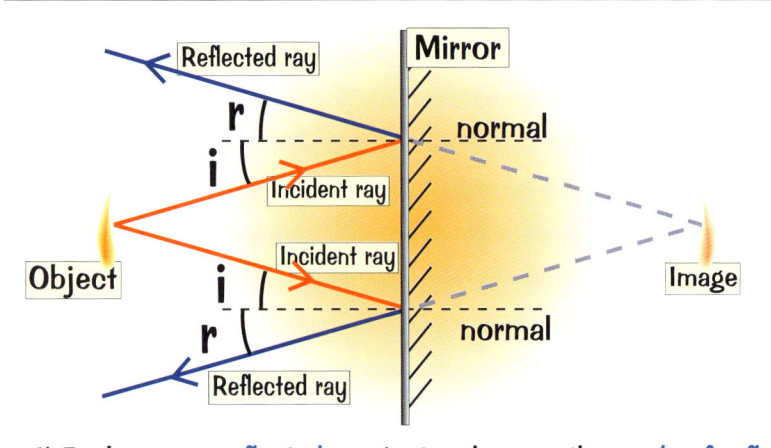

*Reflected ray / Mirror / normal / Incident ray / Object / Incident ray / Image / normal / Reflected ray*

You need to be able to _reproduce_ this entire diagram of _how an image is formed_ in a PLANE MIRROR.
Learn these _two_ important points:

1) The _image_ is the _SAME SIZE_ as the _object_.
2) It is _AS FAR BEHIND_ the mirror as the object is _in front_.

1) To draw _any reflected ray_, just make sure the _angle of reflection_, r, equals the _angle of incidence_, i.
2) Note that these two angles are _ALWAYS_ defined between the ray itself and the dotted _NORMAL_.
3) _Don't ever_ label them as the angle between the ray and the _surface_. Definitely uncool.

### Learn reflection thoroughly — try to look at it from all sides...

First make sure you can draw all those diagrams from memory. Then make sure you've learnt the rest well enough to answer typical meany Exam questions like these: "_Explain why you can see a piece of paper_" "_Why is the image in a plane mirror virtual?_"

*SEG Syllabus* — *MODULE FOUR — FORCE AND TRANSFERS*

… 85

# Refraction — *Light*

*Refraction* is when waves change *direction* as they enter a *different medium*.

## 1) Refraction of Light — the Good Old Glass Block Demo

You can't fail to remember the old "*ray of light through a rectangular glass block*" trick. Make sure you can draw this diagram *from memory*, with every detail *perfect*.

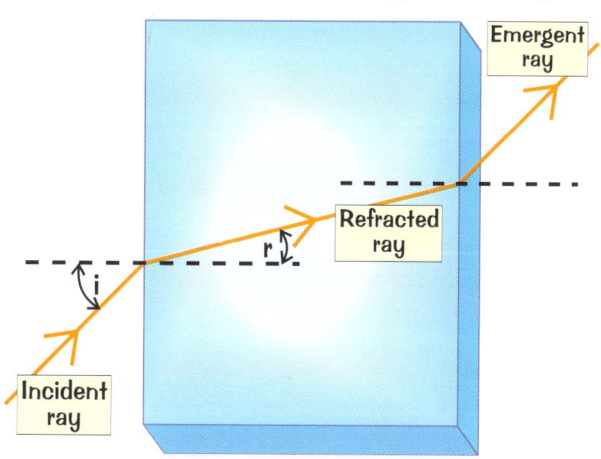

1) *Take careful note* of the positions of the *normals* and the *exact positions* of the angles of *incidence* and *refraction* (and note it's the angle of *refraction* — not *reflection*).
2) Most important of all remember *which way* the ray *bends*.
3) The ray bends *towards* the normal as it enters the *denser medium*, and *away* from the normal as it *emerges* into the *less dense* medium.
4) Try to *visualise* the shape of the *wiggle* in the diagram — that can be easier than remembering the rule in words.

## 2) Sound Also Refracts, but It's Hard to Spot

*Sound* will also refract (change direction) as it enters *different media*. However, since sound is always *spreading out so much*, the change in direction is *hard to spot* under normal circumstances. But just remember, *sound does refract*, OK? The fact that sound and light are both refracted gives *further evidence* that they travel as *waves*.

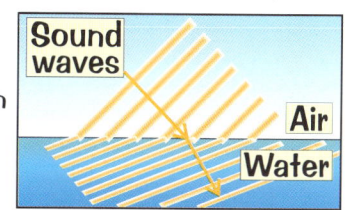

## 3) Refraction Is Always Caused by the Waves Changing Speed

1) When waves *slow down* they bend *towards* the normal.
2) When *light* enters *glass* it *slows down* to about *2/3* of its normal speed (in air) i.e. it slows down to about $2 \times 10^8 \, m/s$ rather than $3 \times 10^8 \, m/s$.
3) When waves hit the boundary *along a normal*, i.e. at *exactly 90°*, then there will be *no change* in direction. That's pretty important to remember, because they often *sneak* it into a question somewhere. There'll still be a change in *speed* and *wavelength*, though.
4) *Some* light is also *reflected* when light hits a *different medium* such as glass.

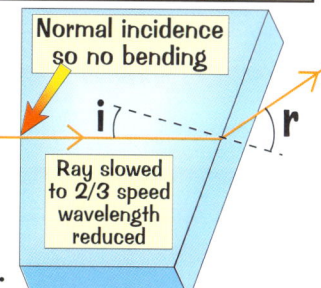

## 4) Refraction Is Shown by Waves in a Ripple Tank Slowing Down

1) The waves travel *slower* in *shallower water*, causing *refraction* as shown.
2) There's a change in *direction* and a change in *wavelength*, but *NO change* in *frequency*.

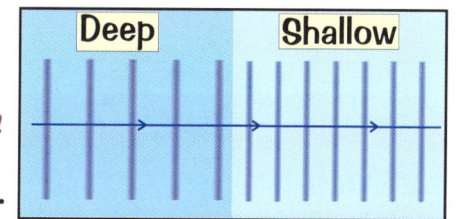

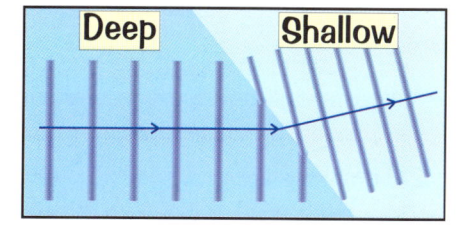

## Revise refraction — but don't let it slow you down...

The first thing you've gotta do is make sure you can spot the difference between the words *refraction* and *reflection*. After that you need to *learn all this stuff about refraction* — so you know exactly what it is. Make sure you know all those *diagrams* inside out. *Cover and scribble*.

MODULE FOUR — FORCE AND TRANSFERS          SEG SYLLABUS

# Revision Summary for Module Four

*Forces and transfers. What fun. This is definitely Physics at its most grisly. The big problem with Physics in general is that usually there's nothing to "see". You're told that there's a current flowing or a force acting, but there's nothing you can actually see with your eyes. That's what makes it so difficult. To get to grips with Physics you have to get used to learning about things that you can't see. Try these questions and see how well you're doing:*

1) Describe what current, voltage and resistance are. What carries current in metals?
2) What are the four types of energy that electricity is commonly converted into?
3) Sketch the four standard V-I graphs and explain their shapes.
4) Scribble down the 10 circuit symbols that you know, with their names.
5) Write down two facts about the:   a) diode   b) LDR   c) thermistor.
6) Sketch a typical series circuit and say why it is a series circuit, not a parallel one.
7) State five rules about the current, voltage and resistance in a series circuit.
8) Give examples of lights wired in series and wired in parallel and explain the main differences.
9) Sketch a typical parallel circuit, showing voltmeter and ammeter positions.
10) State five rules about the current, voltage and resistance in a parallel circuit.
11) Sketch a properly wired plug. Explain how fuses work.
12) Explain fully how earthing works. How does a residual circuit breaker work?
13) Define electrical power, and state its formula.
14) Explain how you would decide what fuse to use for a given electrical appliance.
15) What's a kilowatt-hour? What are the two easy formulae for finding the cost of electricity?
16) Define electromagnetic induction. Sketch three cases in which it occurs.
17) List the four factors that affect the size of an induced voltage. State the Dynamo Principle.
18) Sketch a generator with all the details. Describe how it works, and how a dynamo works.
19) State the two different types of current. List the basic properties of each.
20) Draw what happens to an oscilloscope trace when the voltage is doubled for each type of current.
21) What's the difference between speed and velocity? Give an example of each.
22) Sketch a typical distance-time graph and point out all the important parts of it.
23) Write down four important points (seven for higher level) relating to this graph.
24) Explain how to calculate velocity from a distance-time graph.
25) Explain the difference between mass and weight. What units are they measured in?
26) What's the formula for weight? Illustrate it with a worked example of your own.
27) What is "terminal velocity"? Is it the same thing as maximum speed?
28) What are the two main factors affecting the terminal velocity of a falling object?
29) What is the name given to a turning force? Give its formula.
33) What condition must be met for turning forces to be in equilibrium?
31) List the six different kinds of force. Sketch diagrams to illustrate them all.
32) What is Hooke's Law? Sketch the usual apparatus. Explain what you must measure.
33) Explain the differences between "elastic" and "inelastic" behaviour.
34) With the help of a diagram, define the frequency, amplitude and wavelength of a wave.
35) What aspect of EM waves determines their differing properties?
36) Sketch the EM spectrum with all its details. What happens when EM waves are absorbed?
37) Give full details of the uses of radio waves.
38) Give full details of the two main uses of microwaves, and the three main uses of infrared.
39) Give a sensible example of the use of visible light. What is its main use?
40) Detail three uses of UV light, two uses of X-rays and three uses of gamma rays.
41) What harm will UV, X-rays and gamma rays do in *high* doses? What about in *low* doses?
42) Sketch the patterns when plane ripples reflect at   a) a plane surface, b) a curved surface.
43) Sketch the reflection of curved ripples at a plane surface.
44) What is the law of reflection? Are sound *and* light reflected?
45) Draw a neat ray diagram to show how to locate the position of the image in a plane mirror.
46) What is refraction? What causes it? How does it affect wavelength and frequency?
47) Sketch a ray of light going through a rectangular glass block, showing the angles i and r.

*SEG Syllabus*            *Module Four — Force and Transfers*

# ENERGY SOURCES

## Sources of Power

*Energy Resources*

There are *eleven* different types of *energy resource* that you need to know about. They fit into *two broad types*: RENEWABLE and NON-RENEWABLE.

### Non-Renewable Energy Resources Will Run Out One Day

The non-renewables are NUCLEAR FUELS (uranium and plutonium) and the THREE FOSSIL FUELS: COAL, OIL, and NATURAL GAS.

a) They will ALL RUN OUT one day.
b) They all do DAMAGE to the environment.
c) But they provide MOST OF OUR ENERGY.

### Renewable Energy Resources Will Never Run Out

The renewables include:
1) WIND POWER
2) WAVE POWER
3) TIDAL POWER
4) HYDROELECTRIC
5) SOLAR POWER
6) FOOD SUPPLIES
7) BIOMASS (ESPECIALLY WOOD)

a) These will NEVER RUN OUT.
b) They DO LITTLE DAMAGE TO THE ENVIRONMENT (except visually).
c) The trouble is they DON'T PROVIDE MUCH ENERGY and many of them are UNRELIABLE because they depend on the WEATHER.

### The Sun Is the Ultimate Source for Nine of the Energy Resources

A useful way to show how energy is transferred from one medium to another is to draw an *energy transfer chain*. For most of our energy resources, these will start with the *Sun*:

1) Sun ➡ light energy ➡ photosynthesis ➡ dead plants/animals ➡ FOSSIL FUELS.
2) Sun ➡ heats atmosphere ➡ creates WINDS ➡ and therefore WAVES too.
3) Sun ➡ light energy ➡ SOLAR POWER.

### The Sun Generates Its Energy by Nuclear Fusion Reactions

1) Hydrogen nuclei near the Sun's centre fuse together to form helium nuclei.
2) This process releases energy — it is the ultimate source of the Sun's heat.
3) Some of this energy reaches the Earth in the form of EM waves (mainly as light and heat radiation).

### Most of Our Energy Is Generated from Non-Renewables

LEARN the basic features of the typical power station shown here:

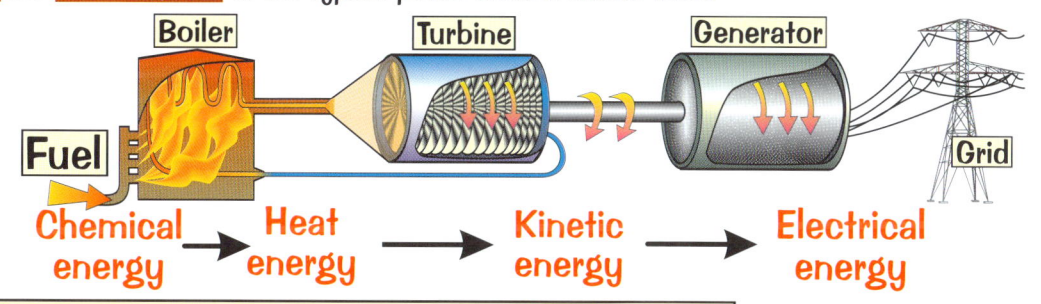

Boiler — Turbine — Generator — Grid
Fuel

Chemical energy → Heat energy → Kinetic energy → Electrical energy

### Nuclear Reactors Are Just Fancy Boilers

1) A nuclear power station is mostly the same as the one shown above, where heat is produced in a boiler to make steam to drive the turbines, etc.
2) The only difference is in the boiler, which is just a tadge more complicated, as shown here:

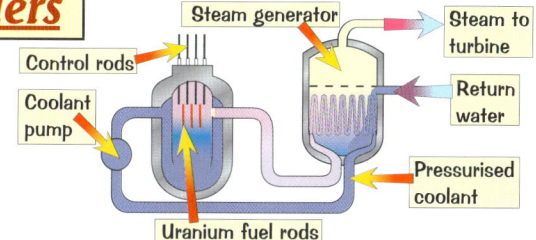

Steam generator, Control rods, Coolant pump, Uranium fuel rods, Steam to turbine, Return water, Pressurised coolant

### Stop fuelling around and learn this stuff properly...

There's a lot of details here on sources of energy — an awful lot of details. Trouble is, in the Exam they could test you on any of them, so I guess you just gotta learn 'em.

*Module Five — Energy Sources*  *SEG Syllabus*

# Power from Renewables

## Wind Power — Lots of Little Wind Turbines

This involves putting lots of windmills (wind turbines) up in exposed places, like on moors or round coasts. Each turbine has a generator inside it, so the electricity is generated directly from the wind turning the blades. The main problems are that they can be a bit of an eyesore, and they're dependent on the weather — there's no power when the wind stops.

## Solar Panels Use the Sun's Energy Directly

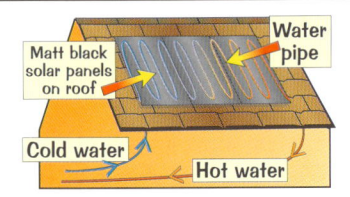

SOLAR PANELS are much less sophisticated than solar cells (like those on some calculators). They simply contain water pipes under a black surface. Heat radiation from the Sun is absorbed by the black surface to heat the water in the pipes. The hot water can then be used for a number of purposes, such as heating a home.

## Pumped Storage Gives Extra Supply Just When It's Needed

Most large power stations have huge boilers that must be kept running all night, even though demand is very low. Pumped storage is a good way of storing this "spare" night-time electricity. It is used to pump water up to a higher reservoir. This can then be released quickly during periods of peak demand, such as at tea time each evening, to supplement the steady delivery from the big power stations. Remember, pumped storage ISN'T a way of generating power — but simply a way of storing energy that's already been generated.

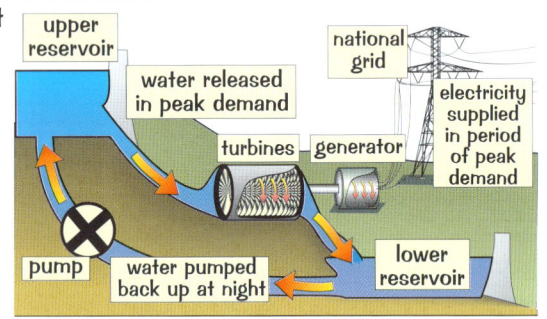

## Wave Power and Tidal Barrages

Don't get these two confused — they're completely different.

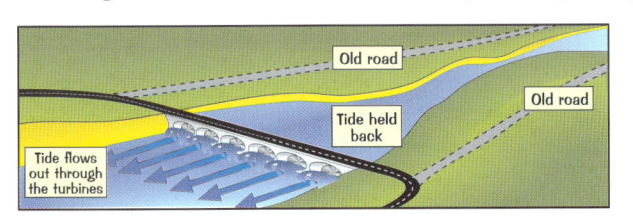

Tidal barrages are big dams with turbines in them, built across places like river estuaries, which fill up to a height of several metres as the tide comes in. The water is then be allowed out through turbines at a controlled speed. It also drives the turbines on the way in.

Wave power uses the motion of waves to generate electricity, by forcing waves through a turbine, as shown right. The up-and-down motion of the waves is used to turn the turbine, which is connected to a generator to produce electricity. You need lots of small wave generators located around the coast.

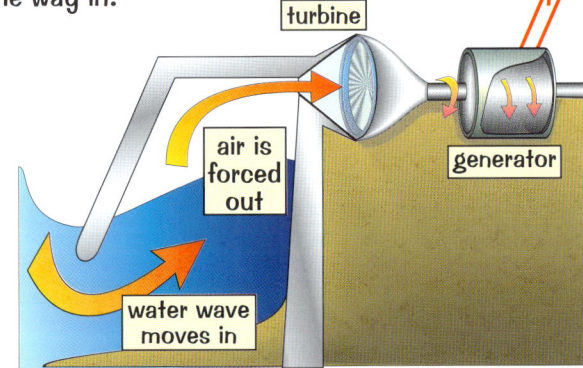

Neither of these methods cause any pollution in their operation. The main problems are spoiling the view and being a hazard or preventing free access to boats.
Wave power is fairly unreliable, since waves tend to die out when the wind drops. Tidal power is more reliable, but the heights of tides still vary, and electricity can't be generated at full tide.

## Learn about wind power — it can blow your mind...

Lots of important details here on all these nice green squeaky clean sources of energy. Perfect mini-essay material, I'd say. Four nice green squeaky clean mini-essays please. Enjoy.

SEG SYLLABUS — MODULE FIVE — ENERGY SOURCES

# Energy Transfer in Reactions

**Energy Transfer in Reactions**

A chemical reaction is a *chemical change* involving a transfer of *energy* to or from the *surroundings*.

## In an Exothermic Reaction, Heat Is GIVEN OUT

An **EXOTHERMIC REACTION** is one which **GIVES OUT ENERGY** to the surroundings, usually in the form of **HEAT** and usually shown by a **RISE IN TEMPERATURE**

1) The best example of an *exothermic* reaction is *burning fuels*.
2) *Neutralisation reactions* (acid + alkali) are also exothermic.

## In an Endothermic Reaction, Heat Is TAKEN IN

An **ENDOTHERMIC REACTION** is one which **TAKES IN ENERGY** from the surroundings, usually in the form of **HEAT** and usually shown by a **FALL IN TEMPERATURE**

Endothermic reactions are *rarer* and harder to spot. So *LEARN* these examples, in case they ask for one:
1) *Photosynthesis* is endothermic — it *takes in energy* from the sun.
2) *Thermal decomposition*, heat must be supplied to cause the compound to *decompose*. The best example is converting *calcium carbonate* into *quicklime* (calcium oxide):

$$CaCO_3 \rightarrow CaO + CO_2$$

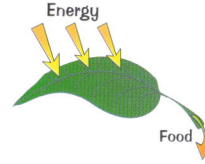

## Energy Must Always Be Supplied to Break Bonds...
## ...and Energy Is Always Released When Bonds Form

1) During a chemical reaction, *old bonds are broken* and *new bonds are formed*.
2) Energy must be *supplied* to break *existing bonds* — so bond breaking is an *endothermic* process.
3) Energy is *released* when new bonds are *formed* — so bond formation is an *exothermic* process.
4) In an *exothermic* reaction, the energy *released* in bond formation is *greater* than the energy used in *breaking* old bonds.
5) In an *endothermic* reaction, the energy *required* to break old bonds is *greater* than the energy *released* when *new bonds* are formed.

## Energy Level Diagrams Show If It's Exo- or Endo-thermic

Basically, it's whether more energy is transferred in the bond *making*, or in the bond *breaking* that decides whether a reaction is exothermic or endothermic. More in breaking and it's *exothermic*. More in making and it's *endothermic*. Simple enough. With energy level diagrams, if it finishes *lower* than it started, it's *exothermic* — it has less energy so must have given some out. If it ends up *higher* than it started, it's *endothermic* — it has more energy than it started with, so must have gained some.

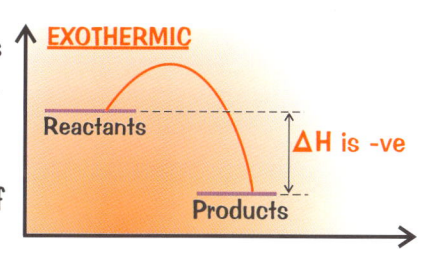

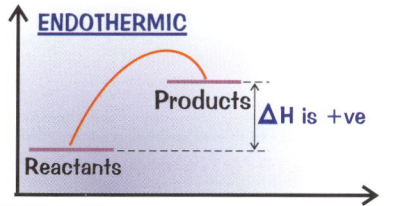

The gap between where the reaction starts and it's highest point on the diagram is the *activation energy*. The bigger this is the more energy it takes to start the reaction off. A *catalyst* is sometimes used to *reduce* it, and make the reaction cheaper. The overall energy change *stays the same*, though.

## Energy transfers and heat — make sure you take it in...

This stuff about exothermic trand endothermic reactions is really quite simple. You've gotta get used to the big words, and make sure you don't get them confused — it's an easy mistake to make. Just remember that an **EX**othermic reaction gives out energy (like an **EX**it of energy) and you'll be fine.

*MODULE FIVE — ENERGY SOURCES*  *SEG SYLLABUS*

# Types of Energy Transfer

**Other Energy Transfers**

## Learn All the Ten Types of Energy

You should know all of these *well enough* to list them *from memory*, including the examples:
1) **ELECTRICAL** ENERGY......................... — whenever a *current* flows.
2) **LIGHT** ENERGY................................... — from the *Sun*, *light bulbs*, etc.
3) **SOUND** ENERGY................................. — from *loudspeakers* or anything *noisy*.
4) **KINETIC** ENERGY, or **MOVEMENT** ENERGY.... — anything that's *moving* has it.
5) **NUCLEAR** ENERGY............................. — released only from *nuclear reactions*.
6) **THERMAL** ENERGY or **HEAT** ENERGY........... — *flows* from *hot objects* to colder ones.
7) **RADIANT HEAT** ENERGY, or **INFRARED** HEAT — given out as *EM radiation* by *hot objects*.
8) **GRAVITATIONAL POTENTIAL** ENERGY........... — possessed by anything that can *fall*.
9) **ELASTIC POTENTIAL** ENERGY.................. — stretched *springs*, *elastic*, *rubber bands*, etc.
10) **CHEMICAL** ENERGY............................ — possessed by *foods*, *fuels*, *batteries*, etc.

### Potential and Chemical Are Forms of Stored Energy

The *last three* above are forms of *stored energy* because the energy is not obviously *doing* anything — it's kind of *waiting to happen*, i.e. waiting to be turned into one of the *other* forms.

## They Like Giving Exam Questions on Energy Transfers

These are *very important examples*. You must *learn them* till you can repeat them all *easily*.

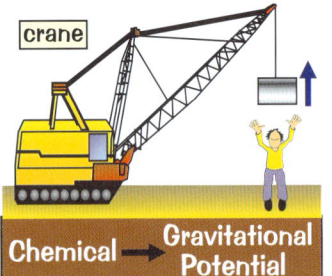

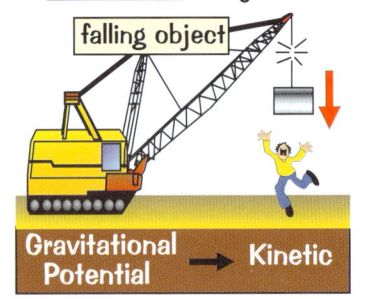

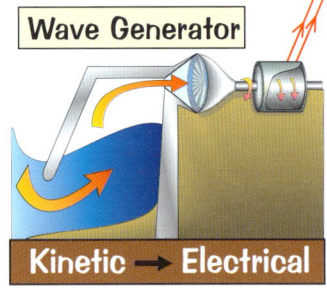

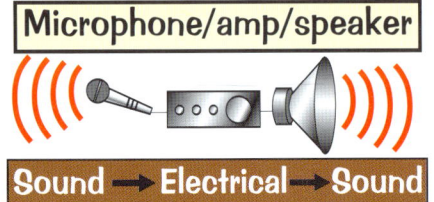

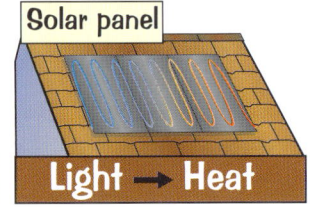

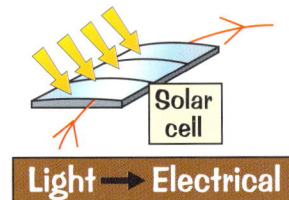

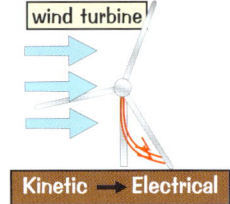

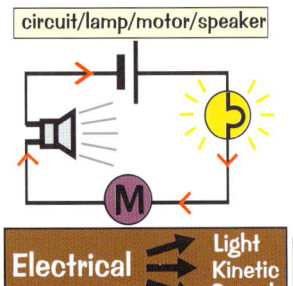

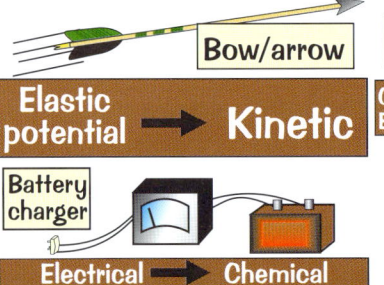

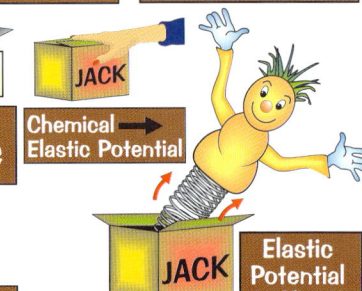

**Eating food / respiration:** Chemical ⇌ Heat / kinetic / chemical

**crane:** Chemical → Gravitational Potential

**falling object:** Gravitational Potential → Kinetic

**Wave Generator:** Kinetic → Electrical

**Microphone/amp/speaker:** Sound → Electrical → Sound

**Solar panel:** Light → Heat

**Solar cell:** Light → Electrical

**wind turbine:** Kinetic → Electrical

**circuit/lamp/motor/speaker:** Electrical → Light / Kinetic / Sound

**Archer/bow:** Chemical → Elastic potential

**Bow/arrow:** Elastic potential → Kinetic

**Battery charger:** Electrical → Chemical

**JACK:** Chemical → Elastic Potential; Elastic Potential → Kinetic

### And DON'T FORGET — ALL types of ENERGY are measured in JOULES

## Learn about energy — and just keep working at it...

They're pretty keen on the different types of energy and also energy transfers. You'll definitely get an Exam question on it, and if you learn all the stuff on this page, you should have it pretty well covered I'd think. *Learn, cover, scribble, check, learn, cover, scribble*, etc. etc.

SEG SYLLABUS — MODULE FIVE — ENERGY SOURCES

# Heat Transfer

**Other Energy Transfers**

## Heat Energy Causes Molecules to Move Faster

Heat energy causes gas and liquid molecules to move around faster, and causes particles in solids to vibrate more rapidly. This shows up as a rise in temperature. The extra kinetic energy of the particles tends to get dissipated to the surroundings. In other words, the heat energy tends to flow away from a hotter object to its cooler surroundings. But then you knew that already. I would hope.

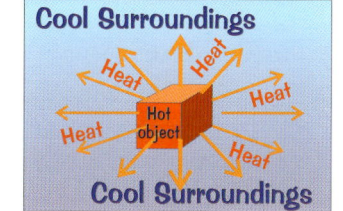

> If there's a **DIFFERENCE IN TEMPERATURE** between two places, then **HEAT WILL FLOW** between them.

## There's Three Types of Heat Transfer

The three distinct methods of heat transfer are: CONDUCTION, CONVECTION and RADIATION. They're covered in more detail on the next two pages, but here's a summary:

1) Conduction occurs mainly in solids, whereas convection occurs only in gases and liquids.
2) Gases and liquids are very poor conductors — convection is usually the dominant process. Where convection can't occur, the heat transfer by conduction is very slow indeed.
3) Radiation travels through anything see-through, including a vacuum.
4) Heat radiation is given out by anything that is warm or hot.
5) The amount of heat radiation which is absorbed or emitted depends on the colour and texture of the surface, but these do not affect convection and conduction.

## Temperature Is Measured in Degrees Celsius (°C)

The Celsius Temperature Scale cunningly defines 0°C to be the melting point of water, and 100°C to be its boiling point, just to make life easier for GCSE Physics students. How thoughtful...

## Evaporation Is Another Way That Heat Can Be Lost

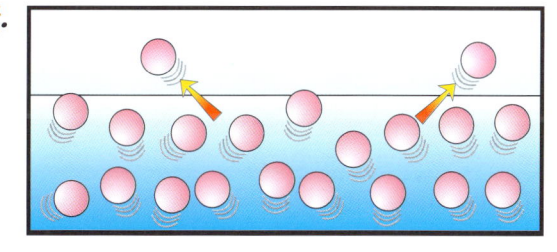

In a liquid the hottest particles are moving the fastest. Fast-moving particles near the liquid surface are likely to break free of the liquid and evaporate. However, only the fastest particles will achieve this, leaving the slower, "cooler" particles behind. This lowers the average energy of the particles left in the liquid and so the liquid as a whole becomes cooler. It therefore takes in heat from its surroundings and thereby cools whatever it's in contact with. This is how sweating helps to cool the body.

You can INCREASE the rate of EVAPORATION from a liquid surface in FOUR different ways:

1) by increasing the SURFACE AREA of the liquid (so more particles are near the surface).
2) by increasing the TEMPERATURE of the liquid (so more particles have enough energy).
3) by DEcreasing the HUMIDITY of the surrounding air (drier air can absorb more water).
4) by increasing the MOVEMENT of the surrounding air (so wet air is rapidly replaced by drier air).

### Don't get hot under the collar — learn about evaporation...

OK, so there's three main sections here, and lots of colourful details to wedge into that brain of yours. Evaporation's particularly tricky — you really do need to know all those points. So what are you waiting for — cover the page and write down those mini-essays.

MODULE FIVE — ENERGY SOURCES  SEG SYLLABUS

# Conduction and Convection

**Other Energy Transfers**

## Conduction of Heat — Occurs Mainly in Solids

**CONDUCTION OF HEAT is the process in which VIBRATING PARTICLES pass on their EXTRA VIBRATIONAL ENERGY to NEIGHBOURING PARTICLES.**

This process continues _throughout the solid_, and gradually the _extra vibrational energy_ (or _heat_) is passed all the way through the solid, causing a _rise in temperature_ at the other side.

HOT — HEAT FLOW — COLD

## Metals Always FEEL Hotter or Colder Because They Conduct So Well

You'll notice if a _spade_ is left out in the _sun_ that the _metal part_ will always _feel_ much _hotter_ than the _wooden_ handle. But _IT ISN'T HOTTER_ — it just _conducts_ the heat into your hand much quicker than the wood, so your hand _heats up_ much quicker.

In _cold weather_, the _metal bits_ of a spade, or anything else, always _feel colder_ because they _take the heat away_ from your hand quicker. But they're _NOT COLDER_... Remember that.

## Non-Metals Are Good Insulators

1) This normal process of _conduction_ (as illustrated above) is always _very slow_.
2) But in most _non-metal solids_ it's the _only_ way that heat can pass through.
3) So _non-metals_ (such as _plastic_, _wood_, _rubber_, etc.) are very good _insulators_.
4) Non-metal _gases and liquids_ are even _worse conductors_, as you will slowly begin to realise if I say it often enough. Metals, on the other hand, are a totally different ball game...

## Convection of Heat — Liquids and Gases Only

**CONVECTION occurs when the more energetic particles MOVE from a _hotter region_ to a _cooler region_ — AND TAKE THEIR HEAT ENERGY WITH THEM.**

Once they have reached the cooler region, the _more energetic_ (i.e. _hotter_) particles _transfer their energy_ by the usual process of _collisions_ — warming up the surroundings. Note that convection simply _can't happen in solids_ because the particles _can't move_.

## Natural Convection Currents Are Caused by Changes in Density

The diagram shows a _typical convection current_. Make sure you _learn_ all the bits about _expansion_ and _density changes_ which _cause_ the convection current. It's all worth _juicy marks_ in the Exam.

Ocean currents are also caused by convection. The ocean near the _Equator_ is heated _most strongly_ by the Sun, causing it to expand, pushing outwards both north and south. It is replaced by colder water _rising up_ from underneath, which is then heated, to continue the cycle. The resulting warm _surface currents_ can travel for _hundreds of miles_. The same thing happens in a beaker, but on a smaller scale.

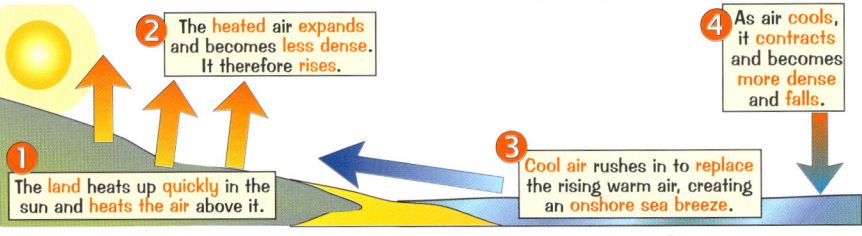

① The land heats up quickly in the sun and heats the air above it.
② The heated air expands and becomes less dense. It therefore rises.
③ Cool air rushes in to replace the rising warm air, creating an onshore sea breeze.
④ As air cools, it contracts and becomes more dense and falls.

## Good conductors are always metals? — what about Henry Wood...

Watch out — it's another pair of Physics words that look so much alike that half of you think they're the same word. Look: CON**VEC**TION. See, it's different from CON**DUC**TION. Tricky that one isn't it. Just like refl**ec**tion and refr**a**ction. Not just a different word though, convection is a _totally different process_ too. Make sure you learn exactly why it isn't like conduction.

SEG Syllabus — Module Five — Energy Sources

# Heat Radiation

**Other Energy Transfers**

*Heat radiation* can also be called *infrared radiation*, and it consists purely of electromagnetic waves. It's just below visible light in the *electromagnetic spectrum*.

## Heat Radiation Can Travel Through a Vacuum

*Heat radiation* is *different* from the other *two methods* of heat transfer in quite a few ways:
1) It travels in *straight lines* at the *speed of light*.
2) It travels through a *vacuum*. This is the *only way* that heat can reach us *from the Sun*.
3) It can be very effectively *reflected* by a *silver* surface.
4) It only travels through *transparent* media, like *air*, *glass* and *water*.
5) Its behaviour is strongly *dependent* on *surface colour and texture*. This *definitely isn't so* for conduction and convection.

## Emission and Absorption of Heat Radiation

1) *All objects* are *continually* emitting and absorbing *heat radiation*.
2) The *hotter* they are, the *more* heat radiation they *emit*.
3) *Cooler objects* around them will *absorb* this heat radiation. You can *feel* this *heat radiation* if you stand near something *hot* like a fire.

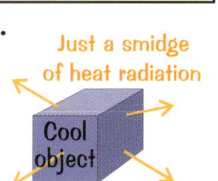

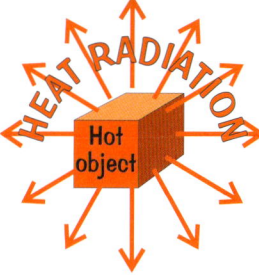

Carbon dioxide ($CO_2$) absorbs *low energy* infrared, but lets *higher energy* infrared *pass through*. This means that the *Sun's radiation* will mostly reach the *Earth's surface*, but *heat emitted* from the Earth tends to be *absorbed* by the atmosphere, from where it is often *re-radiated* back to the surface. So the more $CO_2$ there is in the atmosphere, the *warmer* the Earth gets. This is known as the *GREENHOUSE EFFECT*.

## It Depends an Awful Lot on Surface Colour and Texture

1) *Dark matt* surfaces *ABSORB* heat radiation falling on them much more *strongly* than *bright glossy* surfaces, such as *gloss white* or *silver*. They also *emit* heat radiation *much more* too.
2) *Silvered* surfaces *REFLECT* nearly all heat radiation falling on them.
3) In the lab there are several fairly dull experiments to demonstrate *the effects of surface* on *emission and absorption* of heat radiation. Here are two of the most gripping:

### Leslie's Cube

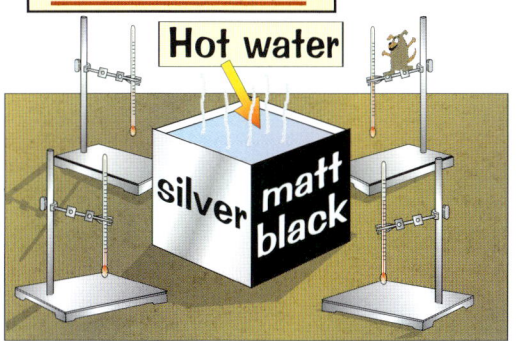

The *matt black* side *EMITS most heat*, so it's that thermometer which gets *hottest*.

The *matt black* surface *ABSORBS most heat*, so its wax *melts* first and the ball bearing *drops*.

### The Melting Wax Trick

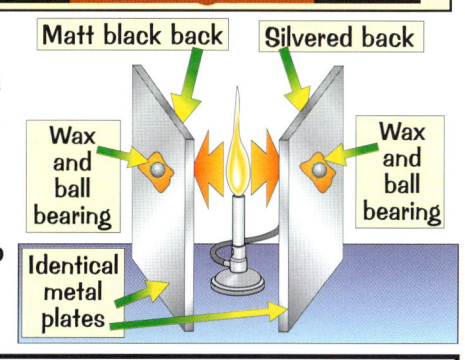

## Revise heat radiation — absorb as much as you can...

The main thing to learn here is that heat radiation is strongly affected by the colour and texture of surfaces. Don't forget that the other two types of heat transfer, conduction and convection, are not affected by surface colour and texture *at all*. Heat radiation is totally different from conduction and convection. *Learn* all the details on this page, then *cover it up* and *scribble*.

*MODULE FIVE — ENERGY SOURCES* — *SEG SYLLABUS*

# Applications of Heat Transfer

**Other Energy Transfers**

The _best_ insulators are ones that trap _pockets of air_. If the air _can't move_, it _can't_ transfer heat by _convection_, and so the heat has to _conduct_ very slowly through the _pockets of air_, as well as the material in between. This really slows it down _big style_.

This is how _clothes_ and _blankets_ and _loft insulation_ and _cavity wall insulation_ and _polystyrene cups_ and _pretty woollen mittens_ and _little furry animals_ and _fluffy yellow ducklings_ work.

## Insulation Should Also Take Account of Heat Radiation

1) _Silvered finishes_ are highly effective _insulation_ against heat transfer by _radiation_.
2) This can work _both ways_, either keeping heat radiation _out_ or keeping heat _in_.

| KEEPING HEAT RADIATION OUT: | KEEPING HEAT IN: |
|---|---|
| Spacesuits | Shiny metal kettles |
| Cooking foil on the turkey | Survival blankets |
| Vacuum flasks | Vacuum flasks (again) |

3) _Matt black_ is rarely used for its thermal properties of _absorbing_ and _emitting_ heat radiation.
4) It's only _useful_ where you want to _get rid of heat_, e.g. the _cooling fins_ or _radiator_ on an engine.

## Insulation in the Home

1) **CAVITY WALL INSULATION** — foam squirted into the gap between the bricks reduces _convection_ and _radiation_ across the gap.
2) **LOFT INSULATION** — a thick layer of fibreglass wool laid out across the whole loft floor reduces _conduction_ and _radiation_ into the roof space.
3) **DRAUGHT-PROOFING** — strips of foam and plastic around doors and windows stop draughts of cold air blowing in, i.e. they reduce heat loss due to _convection_.
4) **DOUBLE GLAZING** — two layers of glass with an air gap reduce _conduction_ and _radiation_.
5) **THERMOSTATS ON RADIATOR VALVES** — these simply prevent the house being _over-warmed_.
6) **HOT WATER TANK JACKET** — lagging such as fibreglass wool reduces _conduction_ and _radiation_ from the hot water tank.
7) **THICK CURTAINS** — big bits of cloth you pull across the window to stop people looking in at you — but also to reduce heat loss by _conduction_ and _radiation_.

## The Vacuum Flask — the Ultimate in Insulation

1) The glass bottle is _double-walled_, with a _thin vacuum_ between the two walls. This stops _all conduction_ and _convection_ through the _sides_.
2) The walls either side of the vacuum are _silvered_ to keep heat loss by _radiation_ to a _minimum_.
3) The bottle is supported with _insulating foam_. This minimises heat _conduction_ to or from the _outer_ glass bottle.
4) The _stopper_ is made from _plastic_ and filled with _cork_ or _foam_ to reduce any _heat conduction_ through it.

In _Exam questions_ you must _always_ say which form of heat transfer is involved at any point — either _conduction_, _convection_ or _radiation_.

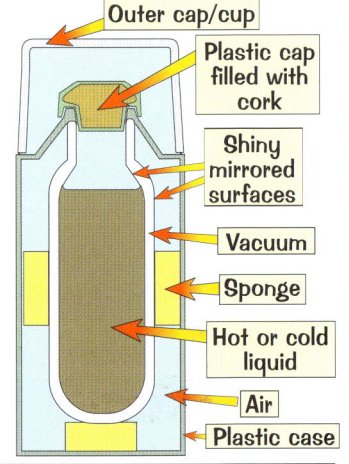

## Heat transfer and insulation — keep taking it all in...

There's a lot more to insulation than you first realise. That's because there are _three ways_ that heat can be transferred, and so effective heat insulation has to deal with _all three_, of course. The venerable vacuum flask is the classic example of all-in-one-full-blown insulation. _Learn it_.

SEG Syllabus — Module Five — Energy Sources

# Efficiency of Machines

**Other Energy Transfers**

**REMEMBER:** Energy is *ONLY USEFUL* when it's *CONVERTED* from one form to another.

1) *Useful devices* are only *useful* because they *convert* energy from *one form* to *another*.
2) In doing so, some useful *input energy* is always *lost or wasted* as *heat*.
3) The *less energy* that's *wasted*, the *more efficient* the device is said to be.
4) The energy flow diagram is pretty much the same for *all devices*. You *MUST* learn this *BASIC ENERGY FLOW DIAGRAM*:

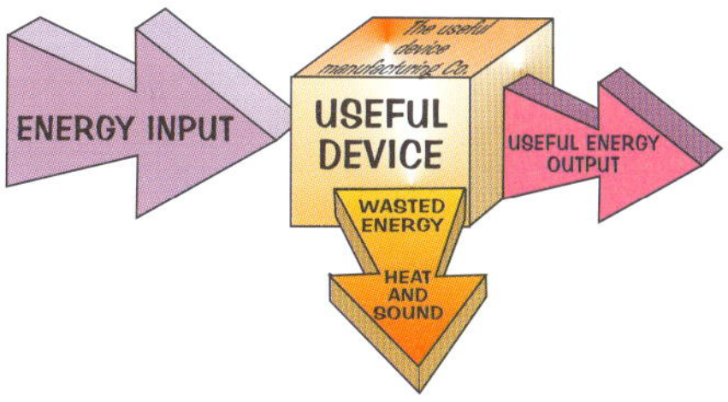

For any *specific example* you can give more detail about the *types of energy* being *input* and *output*, but REMEMBER THIS:

*NO* device is 100% efficient — *WASTED ENERGY* is always *dissipated* as *HEAT* and *SOUND*.

A *machine* is a device which turns *one type of energy* into *another*. The *efficiency* of any device is defined as:

$$\text{Efficiency} = \frac{\text{USEFUL Energy OUTPUT}}{\text{TOTAL Energy INPUT}}$$

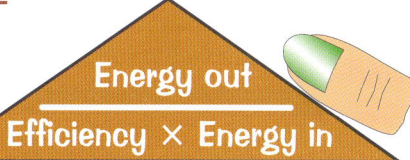

$$\frac{\text{Energy out}}{\text{Efficiency} \times \text{Energy in}}$$

You can give efficiency as a *fraction*, *decimal* or *percentage*, i.e. ¾ or 0.75 or 75%

## Come On! — Efficiency Is Really Simple...

1) You find how much energy is *supplied* to a machine. (The Total Energy *INPUT*).
2) You find how much *useful energy* the machine *delivers* (The Useful Energy *OUTPUT*). They either tell you this directly or they tell you how much it *wastes* as heat/sound.
3) Either way, you get those *two important numbers* and then just *divide* the *smaller one* by the *bigger one* to get a value for *efficiency* somewhere between *0 and 1* (or *0 and 100%*). Easy.
4) The other way they might ask it is to tell you the *efficiency* and the *input energy* and ask for the *energy output*. The best way to tackle that is to *learn* this *other version* of the formula:

**USEFUL ENERGY OUTPUT = Efficiency × TOTAL Energy INPUT**

## Three Important Examples on Efficiency for You to Learn

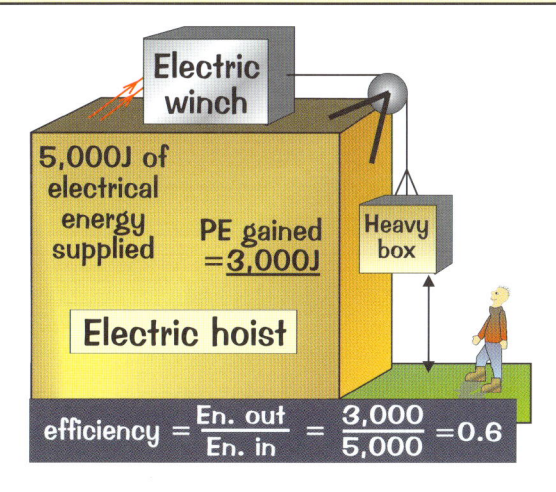

**Electric winch / Electric hoist**
5,000J of electrical energy supplied
PE gained = 3,000J
Heavy box

$$\text{efficiency} = \frac{\text{En. out}}{\text{En. in}} = \frac{3,000}{5,000} = 0.6$$

**Ordinary light bulb** 
1,000J of light energy given out
5,200J of electrical energy supplied

$$\text{efficiency} = \frac{\text{En. out}}{\text{En. in}} = \frac{1,000}{5,200} = 0.19$$

**Electric kettle**
180,000J of electrical energy supplied 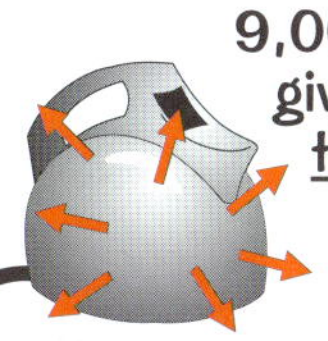
9,000J of heat given out to the room
Think about it!

$$\text{efficiency} = \frac{\text{En. out}}{\text{En. in}} = \frac{171,000}{180,000} = 0.95$$

## Learn about energy transfer — but do it efficiently...

Efficiency is another hideously simple concept. It's a big funny-looking word I grant you, but that doesn't mean it's tricky. Let's face it, efficiency's a blummin' doddle — divide $E_{out}$ by $E_{in}$ and there it is, done. Geesh. *Learn the page*, then *cover it up* and *scribble down* what you know.

*MODULE FIVE — ENERGY SOURCES*    *SEG SYLLABUS*

# Energy Conservation

**Other Energy Transfers**

## Non-Renewables Are Finite Resources

1) We don't have *unlimited supplies* of the *non-renewable* energy sources — especially *fossil fuels*. These fuels are therefore called "*finite*" resources (as opposed to "*infinite*").
2) If we keep using them at the *present rate*, they'll soon *run out*. Well, soonish anyway.
3) Current known reserves for *oil* will only last us around *30 years*, while the known *gas* and *coal* reserves will last maybe *100* and *300* years respectively, if used at their *current rate*.
4) Of course more reserves will be found, but as we have already used the more convenient reserves, they're likely to be in *remote areas* or *deep underground*.
5) The increased difficulty in obtaining the fuels means that they will become *increasingly expensive* as the *supplies dwindle*.
6) Sooner or later we'll have to *stop using fossil fuels* — so the sooner we *develop the alternatives*, the better.

## Environmental Problems with the Use of Non-Renewables

1) The burning of *all three fossil fuels* (coal, oil and gas) releases *carbon dioxide* ($CO_2$), which is increasing the *Greenhouse Effect* (see P. 93). This is almost certain to lead to *climate change* — and there's good evidence that it's *already started*.
2) The burning of *coal* and *oil* also causes *acid rain*. This is now being reduced by cleaning up the *emissions* — for example by the use of *electrostatic smoke precipitators* (see Module 8 if you're doing it).
3) *Coal mining* makes a *mess* of the *landscape*, especially "*open-cast mining*".
4) *Oil spillages* cause serious *environmental problems*. We try to avoid it, but it'll *always happen*.
5) *Nuclear power* is clean but the *nuclear waste* is very *dangerous* and difficult to *dispose of*.
6) Nuclear *fuel* (e.g. uranium) is *cheap* but the *overall cost* of nuclear power is *high* due to the cost of the *power plant* and final *decommissioning*.
7) *Nuclear power* always carries the risk of a *major catastrophe* like the *Chernobyl disaster*.

## The Non-Renewables Need to Be Conserved

1) When the *fossil fuels* eventually RUN OUT we will *have* to use *other forms* of energy.
2) More importantly though is the question of whether we can *afford* to use all the fossil fuels, given their *effects on the environment*. It might be better to stop BEFORE they run out, and not leave it to *future generations* to clean up *our* mess.
3) There is a *general principle* of conservation that *all* people, both now and in the future, should have a *fair and appropriate share* of the *Earth's resources*.
4) It's mainly *first world countries* like *Britain* and the *US* that are using all the *fossil fuels*, so it's up to us to start using less of them. The US in particular emits about a *quarter* of the world's $CO_2$, yet it has just *4% of the population*.
5) To stop the fossil fuels *running out so quickly*, there are *two things* we can do:

### 1) Use Less Energy by Being More Efficient with It:

(i) Better *insulation* of buildings,
(ii) Turning *lights and other things OFF* when not needed,
(iii) Making everyone drive *spiddly little cars* with dippy little engines.

### 2) Use More of the Renewable Sources of Energy

There's loads of *renewable energy resources* just *screaming out* to be used and *further developed*. See P. 88 for details.

---

### It's all doom and gloom — and that's just the weather...

This page is a bit wordy, I have to say. But all this stuff's in the syllabus, so you'd better learn it real good. There's four main sections here, which just happen to be perfect mini-essay material. So *learn the points, cover them up, scribble them down* — surely you know the drill by now...

*SEG Syllabus*  
*Module Five — Energy Sources*

# Radioactivity

## Radioactivity Is a Totally Random Process

Unstable nuclei will decay and in the process give out radiation. This process is entirely random. So if you have 1,000 unstable nuclei, you can't say when any one of them will decay, and neither can you do anything to make a decay happen. Each nucleus will just decay quite spontaneously in its own good time. It's completely unaffected by physical conditions like temperature, or by any chemical bonding, etc. When the nucleus does decay spits out one or more of the three types of radiation, alpha, beta or gamma, and in the process the nucleus will often change into a new element. Alpha and beta are particles, but gamma radiation is part of the electromagnetic spectrum — like light, but with much more energy.

## Alpha Particles Are Helium Nuclei

They are relatively big and heavy and slow moving, and therefore don't penetrate into materials, but are stopped quickly. Because of their size they are strongly ionising, which just means they bash into a lot of atoms and knock electrons off them before they slow down, which creates lots of ions — hence the term "ionising". An α-particle is simply a helium nucleus with a mass of 4 and a charge of +2, made up of 2 protons and 2 neutrons ($^{4}_{2}$He). A typical alpha emission:

$^{226}_{88}$Ra → $^{222}_{86}$Rn + $^{4}_{2}$He
Unstable isotope → New isotope + Alpha particle

## Beta Particles Are Electrons

These are in between alpha and gamma in terms of their properties. They move quite fast and they are quite small (they're electrons). They penetrate moderately before colliding and are moderately ionising too. For every β particle emitted, a neutron turns to a proton in the nucleus. A β particle is simply an electron, with virtually no mass and a charge of -1 ($^{0}_{-1}$e). Every time a beta particle is emitted from the nucleus, a neutron in the nucleus is converted to a proton. A typical beta emission:

$^{14}_{6}$C → $^{14}_{7}$N + $^{0}_{-1}$e
Unstable isotope → New isotope + Beta particle

## Gamma Rays Are Very Short Wavelength EM Waves

They are the opposite of alpha particles in a way. They penetrate a long way into materials without being stopped. This means they are weakly ionising because they tend to pass through rather than colliding with atoms. Eventually they hit something and do damage. A γ-ray is an electromagnetic wave with no mass or charge, but with a very high frequency. After an alpha or beta emission the nucleus sometimes has extra energy to get rid of. It does this by emitting a gamma ray. Gamma emission never changes the proton or mass numbers of the nucleus. A typical α and γ emission:

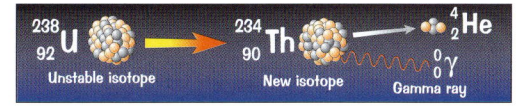

$^{238}_{92}$U → $^{234}_{90}$Th + $^{4}_{2}$He + $^{0}_{0}$γ
Unstable isotope → New isotope + Gamma ray

## Remember What Blocks Each Type of Radiation...

As radiation passes through materials some of the radiation is absorbed. The greater the thickness of material, the more absorption.

They really like this for Exam questions, so make sure you know what it takes to block each of the three:

ALPHA particles are blocked by paper.
BETA particles are blocked by thin aluminium.
GAMMA rays are blocked by thick lead.

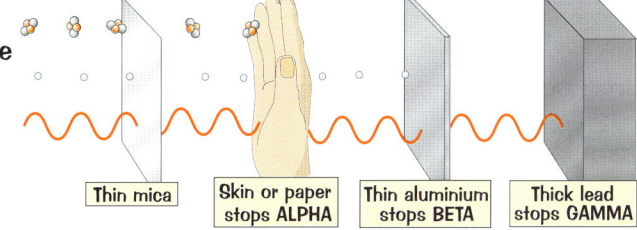

Thin mica | Skin or paper stops ALPHA | Thin aluminium stops BETA | Thick lead stops GAMMA

Of course anything equivalent will also block them, e.g. skin will stop alpha, but not the others; a thin sheet of any metal will stop beta; and very thick concrete will stop gamma just like lead does.

## Alpha give the odd mistake — just don't beta lazy to learn it...

Alpha, beta and gamma. You do realise those are just the first three letters of the Greek alphabet don't you: α, β, γ — just like a, b, c. They might sound like complex names to you but they were just easy labels at the time. Anyway, learn all the facts about them — and scribble.

*MODULE FIVE — ENERGY SOURCES*                              SEG SYLLABUS

# Half-life

*Radioactivity*

## The Radioactivity of a Sample Always Decreases over Time

This is *pretty obvious* when you think about it — after an unstable nucleus has decayed, there'll be one less unstable nucleus left. *How quickly* the activity *drops off* varies a lot from one radioisotope to another. For *some* it can take *just a few hours* before nearly all the unstable nuclei have *decayed*, whilst others can last for *millions of years*. We use the idea of HALF-LIFE to measure how quickly the activity *drops off*:

> HALF-LIFE is the TIME TAKEN for THE NUMBER OF PARENT atoms in a sample to HALVE.

## Measuring the Half-Life of a Sample Using a Graph

*Several readings* are taken of *count rate* and the results can then be *plotted* as a *graph*, which will *always* be shaped like the one below. The *half-life* is found from the graph by finding the *time interval* on the *bottom axis* corresponding to a *halving* of the *activity* on the *vertical axis*. Easy peasy.

*One trick* you really do need to know about is the business of the *background radiation*, which also adds to the count and gives *false readings*. You have to measure the background count *first* and then *subtract it* from *every* reading you get, before plotting the results on the *graph*.

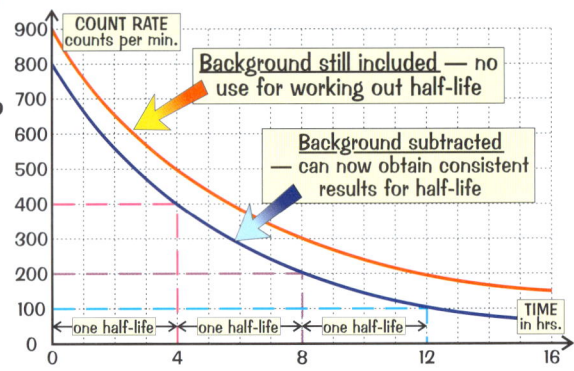

[Graph: COUNT RATE (counts per min.) vs TIME in hrs. Orange curve labelled "Background still included — no use for working out half-life". Blue curve labelled "Background subtracted — can now obtain consistent results for half-life". X-axis marked 0, 4, 8, 12, 16 with "one half-life" intervals.]

The basic idea of half-life is maybe a little confusing, but Exam calculations are *pretty straightforward*, so long as you do them slowly, STEP BY STEP, like this one:

A VERY SIMPLE EXAMPLE: The activity of a radioisotope is 640cpm (counts per minute). Two hours later it has fallen to 40 counts per minute. Find the half-life of the sample.

ANSWER: You must go through it in SHORT SIMPLE STEPS like this:

| INITIAL count: | | after ONE half-life: | | after TWO half-lives: | | after THREE half-lives: | | after FOUR half-lives: |
|---|---|---|---|---|---|---|---|---|
| 640 | (÷2)→ | 320 | (÷2)→ | 160 | (÷2)→ | 80 | (÷2)→ | 40 |

Notice the careful *step-by-step method*, which tells us that it takes *four half-lives* for the activity to fall from 640 to 40. Hence *two hours* represents four half-lives so *the half-life is 30 minutes*.

## Carbon-14 Calculations — or Radiocarbon Dating

*Carbon-14* makes up about 1/10,000,000 (one *ten-millionth*) of the carbon in the *air*. This level stays fairly *constant* in the *atmosphere*. The same proportion of C-14 is also found in *living things*. However, when they *die*, the C-14 is trapped *inside* the wood or wool or whatever, and it gradually *decays* with a *half-life* of *5,600 years*. By simply measuring the *proportion* of C-14 found in some old *axe handle*, *burial shroud*, etc., you can easily calculate *how long ago* the item was living material.

EXAMPLE: An axe handle was found to contain 1 part in 40,000,000 carbon-14. Calculate the age of the axe.

ANSWER: The C-14 was originally *1 part in 10,000,000*. After *one half-life* it would be down to *1 part in 20,000,000*. After *two half-lives* it would be down to *1 part in 40,000,000*. Hence the axe handle is *two C-14 half-lives* old, i.e. 2 × 5,600 = *11,200 YEARS OLD*.

Note the same old *step-wise method*, going down one half-life at a time.

## Definition of half-life — a freshly woken teenager...

People can get really confused by the idea of half-life. Remember — a radioactive sample will never completely decay away because the amount left just keeps halving. So the only way to measure how long it "lasts", is to time how long it takes to drop by half. That's all it is. Peasy

*SEG Syllabus* — *Module Five — Energy Sources*

# Background Radiation

**Radioactivity**

*Background radiation* comes from:
1) Radioactivity of naturally occurring substances *all around us* — in the *air*, in *food*, in *building materials*, and in the *rocks* under our feet.
2) Radiation from *space*, which is known as *cosmic rays*. These come mostly from the *Sun*.
3) Radiation due to *human activity*, e.g. *fallout* from *nuclear explosions* or *dumped nuclear waste*. This represents a *tiny* proportion of the total background radiation.

**Where the Radiation *Entering Our Bodies* Typically Comes From:**

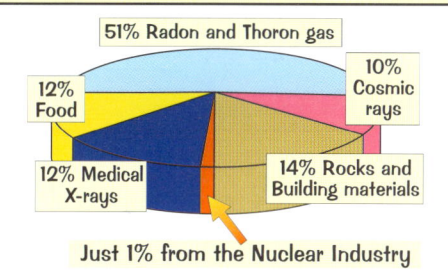

- 51% Radon and Thoron gas
- 10% Cosmic rays
- 12% Food
- 12% Medical X-rays
- 14% Rocks and Building materials
- Just 1% from the Nuclear Industry

## Detecting Radiation — the Geiger-Müller Tube and Counter

This is the most *familiar type* of *radiation detector*. You see them on TV documentaries going *click-click-clickety-click*, whilst the grim-faced reporter delivers his sombre message of impending doom and the terrible state of the planet. It's also the type used for *experiments in the lab*, as the counter allows you to record the number of *counts per minute*.

When an *alpha*, *beta* or *gamma* enters the *G-M tube*, it causes a small pulse of electricity which is sent to the electronic *counter*. It can also be amplified and fed to a loudspeaker to give that characteristic *clicking sound*.

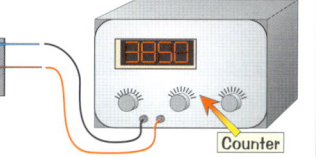

## Photographic Film Also Detects Radiation

1) Radiation was first *discovered by accident* when *Henri Becquerel* left some *uranium* on some *photographic plates*, which became "*fogged*" by it.
2) These days *photographic film* is a useful way of detecting radiation.
3) Workers in the *nuclear industry* or those using *X-ray equipment* such as *dentists* and *radiographers* wear *little blue badges* that have a bit of *photographic film* in them.
4) The film is checked *every now and then* to see if it's got fogged *too quickly*, which would mean that the person was getting *too great an exposure* to radiation.

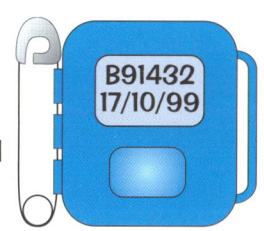

## Radiation Harms Living Cells

*Alpha*, *beta* and *gamma* radiation will cheerfully enter living cells and *collide* with molecules, causing *ionisation*, which *damages* or *destroys* the molecules. *Lower* doses tend to cause *minor* damage without *killing* the cell, but this can give rise to *mutant* cells, which divide *uncontrollably*. This is *cancer*. *Higher* doses tend to *kill cells* completely, which causes *radiation sickness* if a lot of your body cells *all get blatted at once*. The *extent* of the harmful effects depends on *two things*: a) How much *exposure* you have to the radiation. b) The *energy* and *penetration* of the radiation emitted.

### Outside the Body, β and γ Sources Are the Most Dangerous

This is because *beta and gamma* can get *inside* to the delicate *organs*, whereas alpha is much less dangerous because it *can't penetrate* the skin.

### Inside the Body, an α Source Is the Most Dangerous

*Inside the body* alpha sources do all their damage in a *very localised area*. Beta and gamma sources on the other hand are *less dangerous* inside the body because they mostly *pass straight out* without doing much damage.

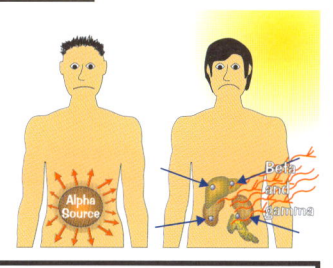

## Background radiation — it's no good burying your head in the sand...

Make sure you remember those two ways of measuring radiation: G-M tube and photographic film. And don't forget that you need a counter as well as the G-M tube — it's not much cop without one. This page is ideal for the good old mini-essay method I reckon, just to make sure you've taken all the important points on board. So *learn and scribble*.

MODULE FIVE — ENERGY SOURCES          SEG SYLLABUS

# Uses of Radioactive Materials

**Radioactivity**

## 1) Radiotherapy — the Treatment of Cancer Using γ-Rays

1) Since high doses of gamma rays will _kill all living cells_, they can be used to _treat cancers_.
2) The gamma rays have to be _directed carefully_ and at just the right _dosage_, so as to kill the _cancer cells_ without damaging too many _normal cells_.

## 2) Tracers in Medicine — Always Short Half-Life γ-Emitters

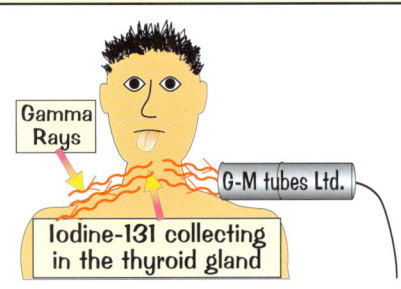

1) Certain _radioactive isotopes_ can be _injected_ into people (or they can just _swallow_ them) and their progress _around the body_ can be followed with a _detector_. A computer is used to convert the reading to a _TV display_, showing where the _strongest_ reading is coming from. A well-known example is the use of _iodine-131_, which is absorbed by the _thyroid gland_, just like normal iodine-127. The iodine-131 gives out _radiation_ that can be _detected_ to indicate whether or not the thyroid gland is _taking in the iodine_ as it should.

2) _All isotopes_ taken _into the body_ must be _GAMMA sources_ (never alpha or beta), so that the radiation _passes out_ of the body. They must also have a _short_ half-life of just _a few hours_, so that the radioactivity inside the patient _quickly_ disappears.

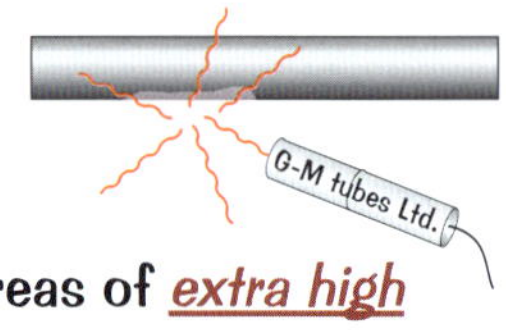

## 3) Tracers in Industry — for Finding Leaks

This is _much the same technique_ as the medical tracers.
You just _squirt your radioisotope in_, and then use a detector _outside_ the pipe to find areas of _extra high_ radioactivity, which indicate that stuff is _leaking out_. This is real useful for _underground_ pipes, to save you digging up half the road trying to find the leak. The isotope used _must_ be a _gamma emitter_, so that the radiation can be _detected_ even through _metal or earth_, which may be _surrounding_ the pipe. It should also have a _short half-life_, so as not to cause a _hazard_ if it collects somewhere.

## 4) Thickness Control in Industry and Manufacturing

This is a classic application and is _pretty popular in Exams_. It's really very simple. You have a _radioactive source_ and you direct it _through_ the stuff being made — usually a continuous sheet of _paper_ or _cardboard_ or _metal_, etc. The _detector_ on the _other side_ is connected to a _control unit_.

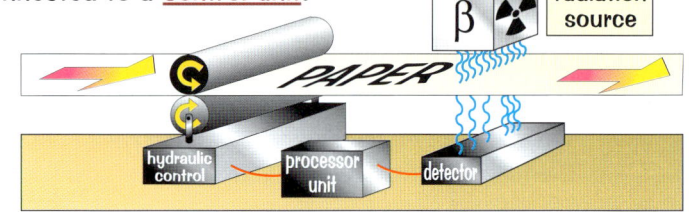

When the amount of radiation detected _goes down_, it means the stuff is coming out _too thick_, so the control unit _pinches the rollers up_ a bit to make it _thinner_ again. If the reading _goes up_, it means it's _too thin_, so the control unit _opens the rollers out_ a bit. Simple. The source must have a nice _long half-life_ (of several _years_ at least!), otherwise the strength would gradually _decline_ and the silly control unit would keep _pinching up_ the rollers trying to _compensate_. It must also be a _BETA source_ for _paper and cardboard_, or a _GAMMA source_ for _metal sheets_. This is because the stuff being made must _PARTLY_ block the radiation.

## Radioactive Materials Can Be a Bit of a Nightmare

These _handy uses_ of radiation are all _well and good_, but don't forget that the _increased use_ of radioactive materials can lead to _social_, _economic_ and _environmental_ problems. These include:
1) The risk of _leaks_ of radioactive material, which can be _dangerous_ and _very expensive_ to clean up.
2) The _pollution_ and other _environmental problems_ caused by the _mining_ of the radioactive isotopes.
3) The _expense_ of and _pollution_ caused by _disposal_ of the radioactive materials after they've been used.
4) The _dangers_ to _workers_ who use the radioactive materials from day to day.

## Radiation sickness — well yes, it does all get a bit tedious...

Quite a few picky details here. It's easy to kid yourself that you don't really need to know all this stuff. Well take it from me, you _do_ need to know it all and there's only one sure-fire way to find out whether you do or not. _Mini-essays_ please, with all the picky details in. Enjoy.

SEG SYLLABUS — MODULE FIVE — ENERGY SOURCES

# The Solar System

*The Solar System & the Unvierse*

The *order* of the planets can be remembered with this little jollyism:

| Mercury, | Venus, | Earth, | Mars, | Jupiter, | Saturn, | Uranus, | Neptune, | Pluto |
|---|---|---|---|---|---|---|---|---|
| (My | Very | Energetic | Mum | Just | Swam | Under | North | Pier) |

**MERCURY**, **VENUS**, **EARTH** and **MARS** are known as the **INNER PLANETS**.
**JUPITER**, **SATURN**, **URANUS**, **NEPTUNE** and **PLUTO** are much further away and are the **OUTER PLANETS**.

## The Planets Don't Give Out Light, They Just Reflect the Sun's

1) You can *see* some of the nearer planets with the *naked eye* at night, e.g. Mars and Venus.
2) They look just like *stars*, but they are of course *totally different*.
3) Stars are *huge* and *very far away* and *give out* lots of light.
   The planets are *smaller and nearer* and they just *reflect the sunlight* falling on them.
4) Planets always *orbit around stars*. In our Solar System the planets orbit the *Sun* of course.
5) All the planets in our Solar System orbit in the *same plane*, except Pluto (as shown).
6) The orbits of the planets are *slightly elliptical* (elongated circles).

## The Sun Is a Star, Giving Out All Types of EM Radiation

The Sun, like other stars, produces *heat* from *nuclear fusion reactions* that turn *hydrogen into helium*. This makes it really hot. It gives out the *full spectrum* of *electromagnetic radiation*.

## Gravity Is the Force That Keeps Everything in Orbit

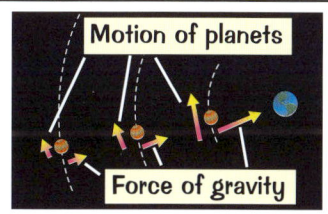

1) *Gravity* is a force of *attraction* that acts between *all* masses.
2) With *very large* masses like *stars* and *planets*, the force is *very big* and acts *a long way out*.
3) So the *closer* a planet gets to the Sun, the *stronger* the *force of attraction*.
4) To *counteract* this stronger gravity, the planet (or moon, comet, space station, etc.) must move *faster* and cover its orbit *quicker*.

## The Inverse Square Law

The size of the force of gravity follows the fairly famous *"inverse square"* relationship. The main effect of that is that the force *decreases very quickly* with increasing *distance*. The *formula* is $F \propto 1/d^2$, but I reckon it's *easier* just to remember the basic idea *in words*:

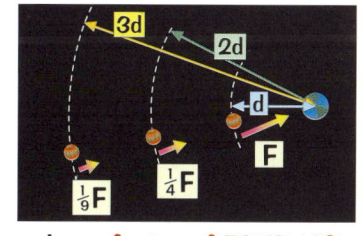

a) If you **DOUBLE the distance** from a planet, the size of the *force* will *decrease* by a *factor of FOUR* ($2^2$).
b) If you **TREBLE the distance**, the *force* of gravity will *decrease* by a *factor of NINE* ($3^2$), and so on.
c) On the other hand, if you get **TWICE as close** the gravity becomes *FOUR times stronger*.

## Learn the planets — they can be quite illuminating...

Planets are ace aren't they. And it's all down to gravity. The best bit is you can usually see one or two of them in the night sky, just by lifting your eyes to the heavens. *Learn* all the little bits on this page, then *cover and scribble*. And keep going till you know it all. *Enjoy*.

*MODULE FIVE — ENERGY SOURCES*     *SEG SYLLABUS*

# Orbiting Bodies

**The Solar System & the Universe**

## Moons Are Sometimes Called Natural Satellites

Most of the planets have natural satellites (moons). The Earth only has <u>one moon</u> of course, but some of the <u>other planets</u> have <u>quite a few</u>. We can only <u>see</u> the Moon because it <u>reflects sunlight</u>. The <u>phase of the Moon</u> depends on where the moon is in its orbit. The position of the Moon determines <u>how much</u> of its <u>illuminated side</u> we can <u>see</u>.

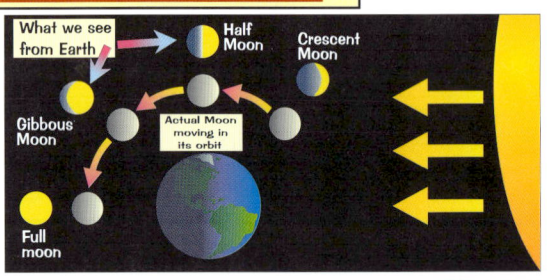

## Asteroids Are Rocks Orbiting in a Belt Between Mars and Jupiter

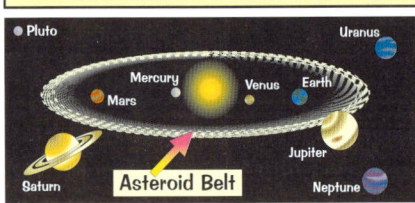

There are <u>several thousand</u> lumps of <u>rock</u> orbiting the Sun in a <u>belt</u> between the orbits of <u>Mars</u> and <u>Jupiter</u>. They can be anything up to <u>1,000 km</u> across. These <u>asteroids</u> usually <u>stay in their orbits</u>, but if they <u>collide</u> and get <u>knocked out</u> of their orbits, they could become <u>meteorites</u>...

## Comets Orbit the Sun, but Have Very Eccentric (Elongated) Orbits

1) The orbits of <u>comets</u> take them <u>very far from the Sun</u>. It can take anything from a <u>few years</u> to <u>several thousand years</u> for them to return.
2) The Sun is <u>not at the centre</u> of the orbit but <u>near to one end</u>, as shown.
3) <u>Comet orbits</u> can be in <u>different planes</u> from the orbits of the planets.
4) Comets are made of <u>ice and rock</u>. As they approach the Sun the <u>ice melts</u>, leaving a <u>bright tail</u> of debris that can be <u>millions of km long</u>.
5) The comet travels <u>much faster</u> when it's <u>nearer the Sun</u> than when it's futher out. This is because the <u>pull</u> of gravity makes it <u>speed up</u> as it gets <u>closer</u>, and then <u>slows it down</u> as it gets <u>further away</u> from the Sun.

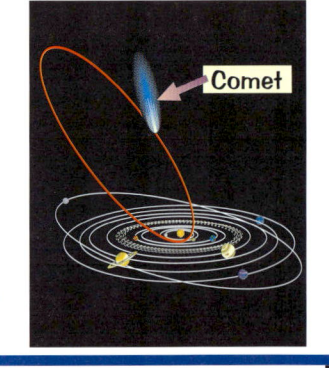

## Planets in the Night Sky Seem to Move Across the Constellations

1) The stars in the sky form <u>fixed patterns</u> called <u>constellations</u>.
2) These all stay <u>fixed</u> in <u>relation to each other</u> and simply "<u>rotate</u>" as the Earth spins.
3) The <u>planets</u> look <u>just like stars</u>, except that they <u>wander</u> across the constellations over periods of <u>days or weeks</u> — or even <u>years</u> for the really <u>way-out</u> ones like Pluto.
4) Their position and movement depends on where they are <u>in their orbit</u>, compared to us.
5) Many early astronomers thought that the Earth remained stationary, and all the stars and planets rotated around it. However the <u>peculiar movement</u> of the planets made astronomers like Copernicus realise that the Earth <u>wasn't the centre of the Universe</u> after all, but was in fact just <u>the third rock from the Sun</u>. It's <u>very strong evidence</u> for the <u>Sun-centred</u> model of the Solar System.
6) Alas, the boys at the <u>Spanish Inquisition</u> were less than keen on such heresy, and poor old <u>Copernicus</u> had a pretty hard time of it for a while. In the end though, "<u>the truth will out</u>".

There's been many other theories about the Earth's structure and the organisation of the Solar System. Their acceptance or rejection often depended more on their social and historical context (like what the Church thought at that time) than on science.

## Learn this page — but keep shtum to the boys in the red robes...

Lots more cosmic bits and bobs for you to know about. There's more to the Solar System than just planets you know. Make sure you learn all the details about these different lumps of rock. It's all in the syllabus, so they could ask you about any of it. <u>Mini-essays</u> please. Now.

SEG Syllabus

MODULE FIVE — ENERGY SOURCES

# Days and Seasons

*The Solar System & the Universe*

## The Rotation of the Earth Causes Day and Night

1) As the Earth slowly <u>rotates</u> any point on the Earth's surface moves from the <u>bright side</u> in the <u>sunlight</u> round into the <u>darkness</u>. As the Earth keeps rotating it eventually comes back into the sunshine again.
   This sequence describes <u>day-dusk-night-dawn</u>.

2) A <u>full rotation</u> takes <u>24 hours</u> of course — a full day. Next time you watch the <u>Sun set</u>, try to <u>imagine yourself</u> helpless on that <u>big rotating ball</u> as you move silently across the <u>twilight zone</u> and into the <u>shadows</u>.

3) Also notice that because of the <u>tilt</u> of the axis, places in the <u>northern hemisphere</u> are spending <u>much longer</u> in the <u>sunshine</u> than in the <u>shade</u> (night time), whereas places in the <u>southern hemisphere</u> are spending more time in the <u>dark</u>. This is only because of the <u>time of year</u>. See below.

4) Also notice that the further towards the <u>poles</u> you get, the <u>longer</u> the days are in <u>summer</u> and the longer the <u>nights</u> are in <u>winter</u>. Places *inside* the <u>arctic circle</u> have <u>24 hours a day</u> of sunlight in <u>midsummer</u>, whilst in <u>midwinter</u> the Sun <u>never rises</u> at all.

5) At the <u>equator</u>, by contrast, the length of day <u>never varies</u> from one season to the next. It's always <u>12 hours of day</u> and <u>12 hours of night</u>. The position of the <u>shadows</u> shows all this.

## The Orbit of the Earth Around the Sun Takes 365¼ Days

One <u>full orbit</u> of the Earth around the Sun is <u>approximately 365 days</u> (one year). This is split up into <u>the seasons</u>:

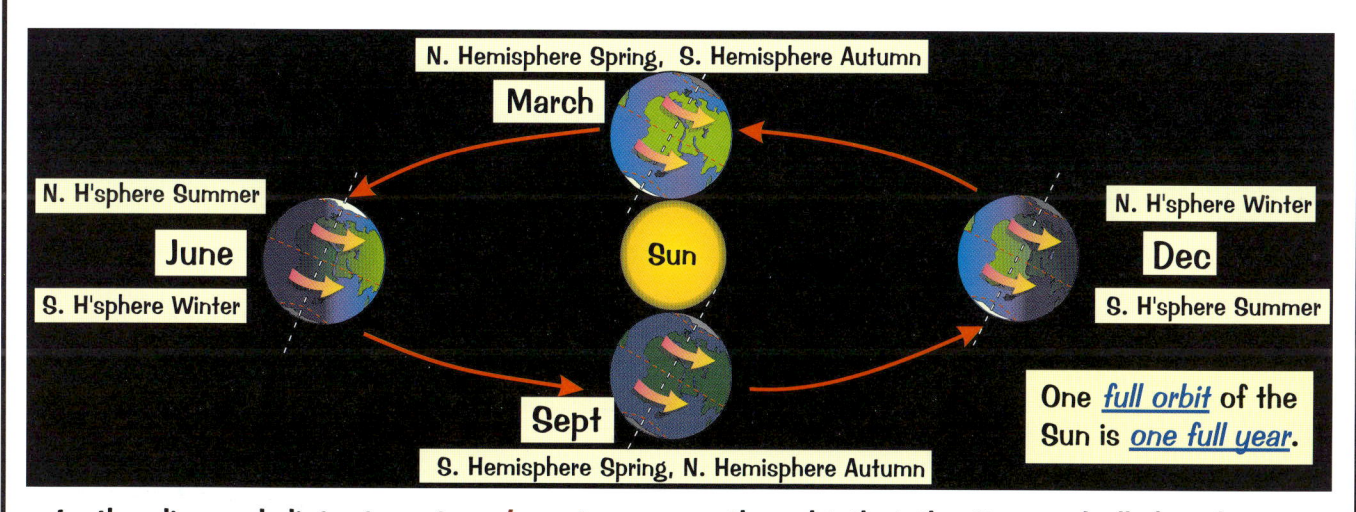

N. Hemisphere Spring, S. Hemisphere Autumn — **March**
N. H'sphere Summer / S. H'sphere Winter — **June**
**Sun**
N. H'sphere Winter / S. H'sphere Summer — **Dec**
S. Hemisphere Spring, N. Hemisphere Autumn — **Sept**

One <u>full orbit</u> of the Sun is <u>one full year</u>.

In the dim and distant past <u>early astronomers</u> thought that the Sun and all the planets <u>orbited the Earth</u>. i.e. that the Earth was the <u>centre of the Universe</u>.
As we all know this was <u>very wrong</u>, but then they also thought the Earth was flat, and that the moon was made of cheese.

## See Norway at Christmas — take a good torch...

This stuff about what causes the Sun to seem to "rise" and "set" and how the seasons are caused is surely irresistible-just-gotta-know-all-about-it kind of information, isn't it? Surely you must be filled with burning curiosity about it every time the dawn breaks — aren't you?

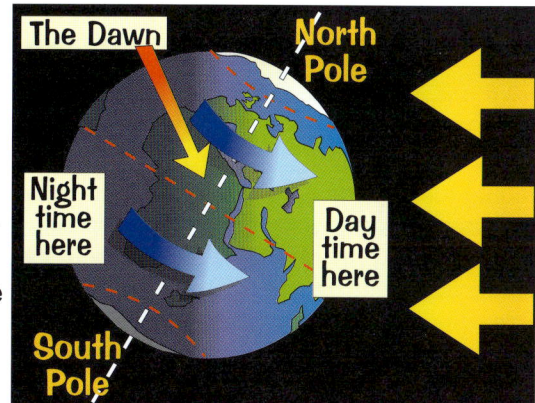

MODULE FIVE — ENERGY SOURCES

# Satellites and the Universe

*The Solar System & the Universe*

## Artificial Satellites Are Very Useful

They're called "artificial" satellites because moons are sometimes called "natural" satellites.

## Low Orbit Satellites Are for Weather and Spying

In a low polar orbit, a satellite will take just a few hours to complete an orbit. As the Earth rotates beneath, the satellite can monitor the whole surface of the Earth each day. These satellites are used for monitoring the weather and/or observing the Earth (which could mean spying, or it could mean looking at things like forests or rock deposits).

## The Hubble Telescope Has No Atmosphere in the Way

The big advantage of having telescopes on satellites is that they can look out into space without the distortion and blurring caused by the Earth's atmosphere. This allows much greater detail to be seen of distant stars and also the planets in the Solar System. Satellites have also been put in orbits around other planets in the Solar System like Venus and Mars — for an even better view of these planets' surfaces.

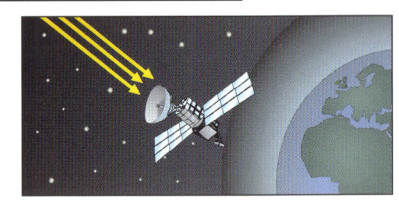

## Geostationary Satellites Are Used for Communications

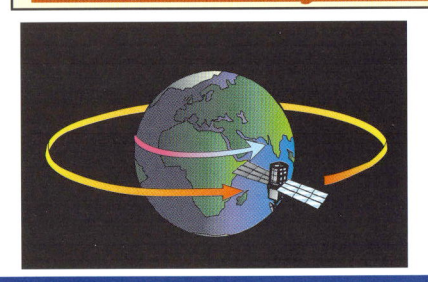

These are also called geosynchronous satellites. They are put in quite a high orbit over the equator that takes exactly 24 hours to complete. This means that they stay above the same point on the Earth's surface because the Earth rotates with them — hence the name geo(Earth)stationary. It makes them ideal for telephone and TV because they're always in the same place and they can transfer signals from one side of the Earth to the other in a fraction of a second.

## Our Sun Is in the Milky Way Galaxy

The Sun's one of billions of stars that form the Milky Way galaxy. The whole thing's held together by gravity and rotates — kinda like a catherine wheel, only much slower. The Sun is in one of the spiral arms of the Milky Way.

## The Universe Is Kinda Big

The Milky Way is 100,000 light years across. But that's nothing. There's billions of galaxies, themselves often millions of times further apart than the stars are within a galaxy. That's millions of light years. So you'll soon begin to realise that the Universe is mostly empty space and is really really big. Ever been to the NEC? Yeah? Well, it's even bigger than that.

## The Light Year Is a Measure of Distance, NOT Time

**A LIGHT YEAR is the DISTANCE that light travels IN ONE YEAR.**

To get this in km you first multiply the speed of light by the number of seconds in a year:
So one light year = 300,000,000 m/s × (60×60×24×365¼) secs = $9.5 \times 10^{15}$ m
So 4.2 light years (the distance of the next nearest star from the Sun) will be 4.2 × ($9.5 \times 10^{15}$) = $4 \times 10^{16}$ m or 40,000,000,000,000 km. (Hmm, best take a few butties, eh?)

## Learn about satellites — and look down on your friends...

More gripping facts about the Universe. It's just so big — look at those numbers: 1 light year is 9½ million million km, our galaxy is 100,000 of those across, and the Universe contains billions of galaxies, many of them separated by millions of light years. Man, that's what I call big.

*SEG Syllabus*  MODULE FIVE — ENERGY SOURCES

# Revision Summary for Module Five

*It's an outrage — just so much stuff you've gotta learn — it's all work, work, work, no time to rest, no time to play. But then that's the grim cruel reality of life in 1990s Britain — just drudgery, hard work and untold weariness... "And then he woke up and it had all been a dream..." Yeah, maybe life's not so bad after all — even for hard-done-to teenagers. Just a few jolly bits and bobs to learn in warm, cosy, comfortable civilisation. Practise these questions over and over again till you can answer them all effortlessly. Smile and enjoy.* ☺

1) List the four non-renewable sources of energy. Sketch a typical power station.
2) Draw three energy chains that start with the Sun. Where does the Sun's energy come from?
3) Explain the pros and cons of wind power and solar panels.
4) What's pumped storage all about. What problem does it solve?
5) Explain the differences between wave and tidal power. What are the pros and cons of each?
6) Say what exothermic and endothermic reactions are. Give an example of each.
7) Explain the difference between exothermic and endothermic reactions in terms of bond energies.
8) List ten different types of energy, and give twelve different examples of energy transfers.
9) What causes heat to flow from one place to another? What do molecules do as they heat up?
10) Explain what evaporation is. Write down the four factors that increase its rate.
11) Give a strict definition of conduction of heat and say which materials are good conductors.
12) What causes natural convection currents? Describe how they produce ocean currents.
13) List five properties of heat radiation. Which kind of objects emit and absorb heat radiation?
14) Describe two experiments to demonstrate the effect of different surfaces on radiant heat.
15) List the seven main ways to reduce energy losses from houses.
16) Which types of heat transfer are insulated against in: a) double glazing; b) draught-proofing.
17) Draw a fully labelled diagram of a vacuum flask, and explain exactly what each bit is for.
18) Draw an energy flow diagram for a "useful device". What forms does the wasted energy take?
19) What's the formula for efficiency? Give three worked examples on efficiency.
20) List seven environmental hazards with non-renewables and four ways that we can use less.
21) List the advantages and disadvantages of using renewable and non-renewable energy sources.
22) What are the three types of radiation, and how do they compare in penetrating power and ionising power? List several things that will block each of the three types.
23) List three places where the level of background radiation is increased, and explain why it is.
24) Name two ways to detect radiation, and explain how the equipment is used in each case.
25) Sketch a typical graph of activity against time. Define half-life, and show how it can be found.
26) Which kinds of source are most dangerous  a) inside the body   b) outside the body?
27) Describe a situation in which the killing of living cells by gamma rays can be helpful.
28) Describe in detail how radioactive isotopes are used in each of the following:
    a) tracers in medicine   b) tracers in industry   c) thickness control.
29) Briefly describe some social, economic and environmental problems with using radiation.
30) List the nine planets of the Solar System, and get them in the right order.
31) How does the Sun produce all its heat?   What does the Sun give out?
32) What is it that keeps the planets in their orbits? What other things are held in orbits?
33) Who had trouble with the boys in the red robes? Why did he have such trouble?
34) What are asteroids? Between which two planets do most of them orbit?
35) What and where are comets? What are they made of? Sketch a diagram of a comet orbit.
36) Sketch a diagram to explain how day and night come about.
37) Sketch a diagram to show how the seasons come about.
38) How long does a full rotation of the Earth take? How long does a full orbit of the Sun take?
39) Explain fully what a low polar orbit satellite does, and state what they're used for.
40) Explain fully what a geostationary satellite does, and state what they're used for.
41) What is the Hubble Telescope and where is it? What's the big idea there then?
42) What is the Milky Way? Sketch it and show the Sun in relation to it.
43) What is a light year? How big is it?

*MODULE FIVE — ENERGY SOURCES*  *SEG SYLLABUS*

# Index

## Numbers
1 in 4 chance 30
3 : 1 ratio 27

## A
a jolly example 9
a nice life 42
a real effort 43
a veritable dream 37
a very harsh world 37
absorbed 10, 81, 82, 88
absorbing 93
AC 75
acceleration 77, 78
ace 45, 46
Acid Appreciation Action Group 58
acid rain 39, 56
acidic soils 56
acids 49, 51, 56, 57, 58, 59
activation energy 60
active uptake 17
adaptation 33
addictive 42
ADH 17, 18
air 3, 49
air resistance 78
airships 47
alcohol 42
alkali metals 48, 49
alkaline 49
alkalis 56, 57
alkane 65
alkenes 65, 66
allele 21, 22, 26
alloys 6
alpha particles/emission 97, 99
alternating current. *See* AC
aluminium 3, 51, 52, 55, 57
aluminium chloride 51
aluminium oxide 55, 65
amino acids 10, 16
ammeters 70, 71
ammonia 58
ammonium chloride 58
ammonium nitrate fertiliser 58
amp 68
amplitude 81
amylase 10
angles of incidence/reflection and refraction 84, 85
animal cells 9
anti-rejection drugs 17
antibiotics 17, 42
antibodies 14
antitoxins 14
anus 10
aqueous 8, 49
arctic circle 103
arctic creatures 34
argon 3, 47
arteries 14
artificial fertilisers 40
artificial selection 29
asexual reproduction 23
atomic number 44, 46
atoms 3, 8, 44, 45
Austrian monk 28

## B
background radiation 31, 98, 99
bacteria 10, 14, 42
balance receptors 13
balanced ecosystem 41
base 56
basic stuff 1
battery 71, 90
bending 79
beta particles/emission 97, 99, 100
big bubbles of gas 2
big fancy words 22, 43
big molecules 10
big rotating ball 103
big surface area 10
bile 10
biological control of pests 41
bitter 13
bitumen 62
block diagram of a reflex arc 12
blood 16, 17, 18
blood plasma 15, 17
blood sugar 19
blood vessels 42
blue budgies 31
blue flame 63
body temperature 19, 34
boiling 2, 4
boiling points 62
bottled gas 62
bouncing 1
brain 13
brass 72
breaking bonds 2
breeding 29
broken bones 83
bromine 49, 50, 51
bromine water 64
bronchitis 42
bronze 6
burglar detectors. 69
burn 49
burning 89
butane 64
butene 64

## C
cables 72
cactus 34
caesium 48
calcium 52
calcium chloride 55
calcium hydroxide 56
camel 34
cancer 31, 83, 99, 100
carbohydrates 15
carbon 52, 62, 64
carbon dioxide 3, 14, 38, 39, 58, 63, 64
carbon monoxide 42
carbon tetrachloride 50
carbonates 58
carcinogens 31
carrier 30
cars 39, 71
cat 32
catalysts 5, 10, 59, 65, 66
cattle rearing 38
cavity wall insulation 94
cell fibres 23
cell membrane 9
cell nucleus 21, 22
cells 9, 68, 70
central nervous system 13
centromere 21, 22
chalk 61
changes of state 2
changing environment 36
characteristic 31
charged particles 44
chat-up lines 5
checkerboard 25
chemical change 5
chemical energy 90
chemical equations 8
chemical stimuli 13
chemicals 12, 31
chip butties 49
chlorine 49, 50, 51
Christmas fairy lights 70
chromatid 21, 22
chromosomes 9, 22, 23, 24, 25, 31
cigarette smoke 31
cilia 42
circuit 70, 71
circuit calculations 68
circular barrier/ripples 84
circulatory system 14
clean blue flame. 63
clot, blood 14
clothes and blankets 94
cloudy precipitate 61
coal 62, 87
coil of wire 75
coke 52
cold! 47
collide 1
collision theory 60
coloured flames 49
combustion 62
common sense 34
communications 82
competition 33
competition reactions 53
component 70
compounds 3
compressed 1
compressing 79
concentration 59, 60, 61
condense 4, 62
conduct electricity 6
conduction, heat 6, 91, 92, 94
confused haze 5
constant internal environment 16
constellations 102
continuous variation 32
control mechanism 18
convection currents 92
convection, heat 91, 92, 94
cooking foil 94
cooking food 82
cooling fins 94
cooling graphs 2
Copernicus 102
copper 3, 6, 52, 54, 57
copper sulphate 54
copper(II) sulphate 54
cornea 12
corrosion 52, 55
cosmic rays 99
cost = units × price 73
covalent bonds 50, 51, 64
crazy acrobatics 27
CRO displays 75
cross-breeding 27
crude oil 62
crystals 4, 49
current 70, 71, 72
curtains 94
cytoplasm 9

## D
dangerous 63, 81, 82, 83, 96, 99
Darwin's theory 37
daughter cells 23
DC 75
DDT 38
dead plants or animals 35
death 42
decay 62
decay, radioactive 97
decolourise 64
definitely uncool 84
deforestation 39
dehydrating 16
delightful name 22
denser 83, 85
density 1, 47, 48, 92
deoxygenated blood 14
desert creatures 34
diabetes 29
dialysis 17
diamond 7
diesel 62, 65
differentiate 23
diffraction 82
diffusion 3
digestion 10, 14
digestive enzymes 10
dilute acid 53
dinky little ears 34
dinosaurs 35
diode 69
diploid 22
dippy little engines 96
direct current 75
discontinuous variation 32
disease 14
disease-resistance 29
displacement 5, 54
dissipated as heat 91
dissolve 3, 49
distance-time graphs 76
distillation 4
DNA 22, 23, 29, 31
dominant 22, 26, 27, 28
doom and gloom 96
dosage of radiation 83
double bonds 64, 66
double circulatory system 14
double glazing 94
double helix 22
double insulation 72
drag 78
draught-proofing 94
driving force 68
drought 38
drugs 29, 42
dust particles 42
dwarf plants 28
dyes 4, 56

## E
Earth 101
earthing and fuses 72
Earth's atmosphere 82, 104
easy marks 3
easy peasy 4, 55
eccentric orbits 102
ecosystem 33, 39, 41
effectors 13
egg cells 15, 22, 24
elastic 90
elastic limit 80
elastic potential energy 90
electrical discharge tubes 47
electrical energy 90
electrical impulses 12, 13
electrical power 73
electrical pressure 68
electrical signal 12
electricity meter 73
electrolysis 52
electromagnetic waves/ radiation/spectrum 93, 101
electron configurations 44
electron shells 45
electrons 6, 44, 45, 46, 48
elements 3
EM spectrum 31
EM waves 87
EM waves/radiation 97, 101
emphysema 42
endocrine glands 15
endoscope 83
endothermic reactions 5, 89
energy 63
energy flow diagram 95
energy input/output 95
energy level diagrams 89
energy levels 45
energy of waves 68
energy transfer 90, 95
environment 40
environmental problems 39
environmental variation 32
enzymes 10, 29
equations 8
equilibrium 79
ethane 64
ethene 64, 65, 66
evaporation 2, 4
every cell in the body 14
evolution 31, 35
excess ions 16
excretion 9
exocrine glands 15
exothermic reactions 5, 89
expansion 1
explosion 59
exposure, radiation 83, 99
extension, Hookes law 80
extinction 35
extra hair 15
eye 12, 13

## F
F1 26, 27
F2 26, 27
faeces 10, 16
fancy words 16, 27
fantastic 42
fateful and magical moment 22
fats 10
fatty acids & glycerol 10
faulty DNA 31
faulty gas fires 63
feedback mechanism 18
feels hotter or colder 92
fertilisation 24, 25
fertilisers 41, 58
fertility treatment 15
fetus 24
fibre glass wool 94
filament lamp 69
filter 16
filter paper 4
fire risk 63
fish 56

*SEG Syllabus*

# Index

fish, trees and statues 39
fizzing 49
flame 49
flammable 62
flat spots 2
flooding 38, 39
fluorescent tubes 83
fluorine 49, 50
flying doughnut 14
focusing 12
fond farewell 10
food 16, 90, 99
food chain 38, 41
force diagrams 78
force of attraction 1, 77, 101
forces 2
formula triangle 76
fossil fuels 39, 87, 96
fossils 35
fractional distillation 4, 62, 65
fractionating column 4, 62
free-fallers, terminal velocity 78
freezing 2
frequency, of waves 81, 82
fuel filling nightmare 72, 90
fuels 5, 62, 89
full shells 46
fume cupboard 50
funnel 4
fuse ratings 73

## G

gall bladder 10
galvanising 55
gametes 22, 24, 25, 27, 30
gamma rays 31
gamma sources/emission
  83, 97, 99, 100
gas room heaters 63
gas syringe 59, 61
gases 1, 2, 3, 8, 47, 50, 62
gene
  21, 22, 26, 28, 29, 31, 32, 37
generating power 88
generators 75
genetic diagram 28
genetic variation 32
genetics 22
genotype 22, 25, 26, 27, 30
germs 16
get your head round it 43
giant ionic lattices 49
giant structure 6
giraffes 37
girl or boy? 25
glands 15
glass block demo 85
gloopy liquids 65
glowing splint test 61
glucose 17, 19
glycogen 10
gobble up 14
gold 52
gradient 76
Grand Canyon 35
graph, for half life 98
graphite 7
gravitational potential energy 90
gravity 77, 78, 101, 102
grazers 33
green, slimy and horrible 41
greenhouse effect 38, 63, 96
gripping facts 104
group O 47

groups 46, 47, 48, 50
growth 9, 23
growth hormones 29
gullet 10

## H

$H^+_{(aq)}$ ions 56
haemoglobin 14
hairs 16
hairy mammoth 35
half-life 98, 100
halogens 50
hamsters 27
haploid 22
haploid gametes 24
happier 45
harmful/harmless 81, 82, 83
harmless insects 38
hazards 88
HCl 50, 51, 56, 58, 61
heart 14
heart attacks and strokes 42
heat loss 19
heat radiation 82, 93, 94
heat transfer 91, 93
heat when a current flows 68
heat/ heat energy 2, 5
heat/heat energy
  90, 91, 92, 95, 101
heating 81
hedges 41
height characteristic 28
helium 47
helium nuclei 97
heterozygous 22, 26, 27
hideously easy 77
hideously important 69
hideously simple 95
high doses 83
high pressure 14
higher doses 99
homeostasis 16
homologous 25
homologous pairs 24
homozygous 22, 26, 27
Hooke's law 80
hormones 15
household electrics 71
human chromosomes 25
hump 34
hydrocarbons 62, 63, 65
hydrochloric acid
  10, 51, 56, 58, 61
hydrogen 49, 52, 53, 57
hydrogen bromide 51
hydrogen chloride 50
hydrogen iodide 51
hydrogen peroxide 61
hydrogencarbonates 58
hydroxides 49, 57
hypothalamus 18

## I

identical twins 32
idle creative genius 32
image, in plane mirror 84
incidence, angle of 84, 85
incomplete combustion 63
indicator 56
induced voltage 74, 75
industrial food factory 41
inelastic behaviour 79
inert gases 47
infinite void 41
infra-red (or IR) 82, 90, 93
inks 4

input energy 95
insulators 92
insulin 10, 19, 29
interbreed 36
internal environment 16
intestine 10
iodine 49, 50, 51
iodine-131 100
ionic 49, 50
ionic compounds 48, 49
ionisation 97, 99
ionising radiation 31
ions 17, 31, 44, 56
iris 12
iron 3, 5, 6, 14, 51,
  52, 54, 55, 57
iron nail 54, 55
iron oxide 5
iron powder 3
iron sulphate 54
iron sulphide 3
iron(III) bromide 51
it makes your head hurt 31
it tastes horrid 4
it's shocking 72

## J

jet fuel 62, 65
joules 73, 90
juicy marks 92
Jupiter 101

## K

kerosine 62, 65
kidney failure 17
kidneys 16, 17
kill cells, radiation 82, 99
kilowatt-hours 73
kinetic energy 90, 91
krypton 47

## L

lakes 40, 41
Lamarck's Theory 37
large chunk 9
large intestine 10
large surface area 34
lasers 47
lattice 1
law of reflection 84
LDR 69
lead 52
learn and enjoy
  7, 44, 51, 53, 63
learn stuff 2
learn the boring facts 50
life processes 9
life's tough 43
light 84
light and dark 12
light bulbs 47
light dependent resistor. See
  LDR
light energy 90
light receptors 13
light sensitive 12
lime 56
limiting factors 33
lipase 10
liquids 1, 4, 8, 50
lithium 48, 49
live wire 72
liver 10
load 80
loft insulation 94
lot of practise 8

loudspeakers 90
low birth weight 42
low polar orbit satellites 104
low pressure 14
lower doses 83, 99
lubricating oil 65
lung cancer 42
lungs 14

## M

magnesium 5, 52, 55, 57
magnesium oxide 8, 55, 56
magnetic field 74
malaria 30
male or female 25
malleable 6
managed ecosystem 41
marble chips 61
Mars 101
mass 44, 77, 79, 101
mass balance 59, 77
mass number 44
matt black, surfaces 94
matter 1
maximum profit 41
maximum speed 78
measure the speed of a reaction 59
media, for waves 81, 85, 93
mega-death 40
meiosis 22, 24
melting 2
melting of the polar ice-caps 38
Mendel 28
mercury (metal) 7
Mercury (planet) 101
metal displacement reactions 54
metal halides 51
metallic crystal structure 6
metals 6, 46, 48, 51, 52
methane 38, 64
microbes 14
microscope 44
microwaves, ovens 82
migration 33
Milky Way galaxy 104
mineral salts 14
missing links 35
mitochondria 9
mitosis 22
mixtures 3, 62
modern farming 29, 40, 41
modern science 28
molecular compounds 50
molecular structure 51
molecules 1, 2, 50, 63, 65
monatomic 47
monohybrid crosses 26, 27
moonshine 4
most grisly 86
mostly empty space 104
motor neurones 13
movement 9
MRS NERG 9
mucous 30
muscles 13
mutagens 31
mutant cells, cancer 99
mutations 31, 36

## N

naptha 62
natural convection 92
natural gas 62, 64, 87

natural habitat 40, 41
natural history record 35
natural satellites 102
natural selection 31, 36, 37
natural timeless beauty 40
negative feedback 18
negatively charged 44
neon 47
Neptune 101
nerve cells/fibres 13
nervous impulses 13
nervous system 13
neurones 12, 13
neutral atom 44
neutral salts 49
neutral wire 72
neutralisation 5, 56, 89
neutrons 44
newton/ newton meter 77
nice green countryside 66
nickel 6
nicotine 42
night-time electricity 88
nitrates 40
nitric acid 58
nitrogen 3, 45
nitrogen oxides 39
no charge 44
noble gases 47
non-metals 7, 50, 92
non-renewables 87, 96
normal, light rays 84, 85
northern hemisphere 103
notorious squeaky pop 49, 57
nuclear energy/fuel 90
nuclear fusion reactions 87
nuclear radiation 31
nuclear waste 99
nucleus 9, 21, 23,
  25, 31, 44, 45
nutrients 10
nutrition 9

## O

octane 65
odourless 63
oesophagus 10
oestrogen 15
offspring 25
OH⁻ ions 49, 56
ohm 68
oil 62, 87
optical fibres 83
orbits 44, 77, 101
organ system 9
organic farming/ fertilisers 41
organic fertilisers 41
organism 9
oscilloscope display 75
otters 38
outer shell 45
ovaries 15, 24
oxides 49, 53, 55, 57
oxygen 3, 61, 63
oxyhaemoglobin 14

## P

P.D. 68, 70, 71
pancreas 10
parachute 78
paraffin 65
parallel circuits 71
particles 44
particularly nasty bug 35
party balloons 47
pea plant 28

107

**SEG SYLLABUS**

# Index

peak demand 88
peculiar movement of the planets 102
penetration, radiation 97
penicillin 36, 42
peppered moth 36
periodic table 46
pesticides 41
pestle and mortar 4
petrol 62, 63, 65
pH indicator 49
pH scale 56
phenotype 22, 25, 26, 27, 30
photographic film 99
photosynthesis 89
physical attributes 22
physical characteristics 26
physical state 8
plane mirror 84
plane waves 84
planets 101, 102
plant adaptations 34
plant cells 9
plasma 14
plastics 65, 66
platelets 14
platinum 52
Pluto 101
pockets of air, insulation 94
poisonous 38, 39, 42, 50, 63
poisons 10
polar bear 34
polar ice-caps 38
pollution 36, 41
polyethene 66
polymers 51, 64, 66
polypropene 66
polythene 66
population 33
positive charge 44
potassium 48, 49, 52
potassium manganate(VII) 3
potato 23
potential difference 68. See also Pd
power stations 39
power supply 70
precipitate 51
precipitation 5, 59
predators 33
pressure 1, 13, 60, 66
pressure and heat 62
pretty serious stuff 43
pretty tricky 16, 74
products 59
propane 64
propene 64
proper motor cars 66
proportional 80
protease 10
proteins 10
protons 44
puberty 15
pulmonary artery 14
pulmonary vein 14
pummels 10
pupil 12
pure water 4

## R
radiant heat 90
radiation 31
radiation, heat 81, 91, 94
radiation sickness 99
radio waves 82
radioactivity, radio-isotopes, etc 97, 98
radiocarbon dating 98
radiographers, X-rays 83
radiotherapy 100
rainfall 39
random motion 1
rates of reaction 59
raw materials 66
raw sewage 40
reabsorption 16, 17
react 45
reactants 5, 59
reaction rates 60
reactive 48, 50
reactivity series 52
real simple 44
recessive 22, 26, 27, 28
rectangular glass block 85
rectum 10
red blood cells 14, 30
reduction 5, 52
reflection 81, 84
reflexes 12, 13
reforestation 41
refraction 85
relative mass 44
remote controls, for tv 82
removal of hedges 41
renewables, fuels 87, 96
reproduce 23, 37
reproduction 9, 23, 24
reproductive success 36
resistance 70, 71
resistance force 78
resistance is futile 68
resistant "strain" of bacteria 31
respiration 9
responses 12
retina 12
reversible reactions 5
rice growing 38
ripple tank 84, 85
rock and ice 102
rock and soil strata 35
rock salt 4
rods and cones 13
roll off the tongue 27
rubber bands 90
rubidium 48
rust 55, 59

## S
sacrificial protection 55
safety features 72
salivary amylase/ gland 10
salts 4, 13, 49, 51, 56, 57, 58
sand 4
satellite transmissions 82
saturated hydrocarbons 64
Saturn 101
scientific research 83
sea water 4
sea-levels 38
secondary sexual characteristics 15
security marks 83
sediment 62
selective breeding 29
sense organ 13
sensitive 13
sensitivity 9
sensory neurones 13
seriously easy 80
severe downward spiral 42
sexual characteristics 15
shallower water 85
shearing 79
sheep 9
shells 44, 45
shocks 72
shroud, dating of 98
sickle cell anaemia 30
sigh 66
silicon 7
silly names 10
silver 52
silver bromide 51
silver chloride 51
silver halide salts 51
silver iodide 51
silver nitrate 51, 54
silvered finishes 94
simple sugars 10
skin 16
skin cancer 39, 83
skydiver 78
sleep 63
slip rings, generator 75
small intestine 10
small particles 10
smaller molecules 10
smell/ smell receptors 13
smile 52
smoke 63
smoky flame 64
smoky yellow flame 63
sodium 16, 48, 49, 52
sodium carbonate 58
sodium thiosulphate 61
soil erosion 40, 41
soil strata 35
solar power 87, 88
Solar System 102, 104
solids 1, 2, 4, 8, 50
solvents 42
soot 63, 64
sound energy 90
sound-receptors 13
sour 13
southern hemisphere 103
Spanish Inquisition 102
spare bonds 64
specialisation 23
species 36
spectrum 81
speed 76
speed of reaction 57
sperm 15, 22, 24
spiddly little cars 96
spinal chord 13
spreading muck on it 40
spring balance 77
springs 90
squeaky pop (notorious) 49, 53, 57
starch 10
stars 102
state symbols 8
states of matter 1
static electricity 69
statues 39
steady speed 78
steel 6
sterilisation 83
sticky liquid 42
stimulus 13
stomach 10
stored energy 90
strawberry 23
stretching 79
strokes 42
stuff on atoms 44
stuff or not 67
stupefyingly easy 35
stupid 63
sugar 10, 15, 17
sulphur 3, 61
sulphur dioxide 39
sulphuric acid 57, 58
Sun 38, 87, 90, 93, 99, 101, 104
sunbeds, UV rays 83
supply 71
surface area 10, 14, 34, 61
surface colour/texture 93
survival 36, 37
survival advantage 36
survival blankets, silvered 94
survival of the fittest 37
sweat/ sweat gland 16
sweating 34, 91
sweet 13
symbol equation 8
symbols 8
symptoms 30

## T
tails cut off 37
take a few butties 104
tar 42, 65
target organs 15
tarnish 52
taste/ taste receptors 13
teeth 10
temperature 2, 16
temperature detectors 69
temperature receptors 13
tension 79
testes 24
testosterone 15
the bill 73
there's no drivel 13
thermal decomposition 5, 65, 89
thermal energy 90
thermometer 4
thermostatic controls 94
thermostats 69
thickness control 100
thyroid gland 100
timeless mysteries 44
tin 6
tiny 44
tiny capillaries 14
tissue types 17
tongue 13
too cold 16
too hot 16
too much of a good thing 40
total resistance 70, 71
touch 13
toxins 14
tracers in medicine 100
traditional farming 41
transduce 13
treatment of cancer 100
trends 48, 50
tricky 8
trivial and obvious 73
turbines 88
turns 74
TV and radio waves 82
twilight zone 103
twins 32
twisting 79
types of energy 90

## U
ultra-violet light 31, 83
units = kW × hours 73
"units" of Energy 73
universal indicator 56
unsaturated hydrocarbons 64
upbringing 32
uranium 99
Uranus 101
urea 16, 17
ureter 17
urine 16, 17

## V
vacuum 81, 93
vacuum flask 94
vapours 50, 63
variation in plants and animals 32
variety 36
vasoconstriction 16
vasodilation 16
vegan 36
veins 14
velocity 76
Venus 101
vibrate 1, 2
vibration energy (heat) 92
vibration energy(heat) 92
villi 10
viscous 62
visible light 83
volatile 62
volt 68
voltage/ voltmeters 70, 71

## W
waste energy, heat 95
wastes 17
water 3, 17, 18, 49, 63, 64
waterproof 16
wavelength 81
waves 81
wee joke 59
weight 77
what poetry 22
white blood cells 14
wind power/turbines 88
winds 87
wires 69
wound 14
wreck your life 42

## X
X and Y Chromosomes 25
X-rays 31, 83

## Y
yield 29, 40, 41
you are here 104

## Z
zinc 52, 54, 55
zinc nitrate 54
zinc oxide 55
zygote 22, 25, 27, 30
zzzzzzzzzzz 76

**SEG SYLLABUS**